Efficient SAP NetWeaver™ BI Implementation and Project Management

PRESS

SAP PRESS is a joint initiative of SAP and Galileo Press. The know-how offered by SAP specialists combined with the expertise of the publishing house Galileo Press offers the reader expert books in the field. SAP PRESS features first-hand information and expert advice, and provides useful skills for professional decision-making.

SAP PRESS offers a variety of books on technical and business related topics for the SAP user. For further information, please visit our website: *www.sap-press.com*.

Luc Galoppin and Siegfried Caems
Managing Organizational Change During SAP Implementations
2007, app. 368 pp.
ISBN 978-1-59229-104-X

Sabine Schöler, Liane Will, and Marc O. Schäfer
CobiT and the Sarbanes-Oxley Act
2007, app. 175 pp.
ISBN 978-1-59229-128-1

Marco Sisfontes-Monge
CPM and Balanced Scorecard with SAP
2007, 408 pp.
ISBN 978-1-59229-085-7

Michael Missbach, Ralf Sosnitzka, Josef Stelzel, and Matthias Wilhelm
SAP System Operations
2007, 350 pp.
ISBN 978-1-59229-025-3

Gary Nolan

Efficient SAP NetWeaver™ BI Implementation and Project Management

Bonn • Boston

ISBN 978-1-59229-105-2

1st edition 2007

Editor Jawahara Saidullah
Copy Editor John Parker, UCG, Inc., Boston, MA
Cover Design Silke Braun
Layout Design Vera Brauner
Production Iris Warkus
Typesetting Typographie & Computer, Krefeld
Printed and bound in Germany

© 2007 by Galileo Press
SAP PRESS is an imprint of Galileo Press,
Boston, MA, USA
Bonn, Germany

All rights reserved. Neither this publication nor any part of it may be copied or reproduced in any form or by any means or translated into another language, without the prior consent of Galileo Press, Rheinwerkallee 4, 53227 Bonn, Germany.

Galileo Press makes no warranties or representations with respect to the content hereof and specifically disclaims any implied warranties of merchantability or fitness for any particular purpose. Galileo Press assumes no responsibility for any errors that may appear in this publication.

All of the screenshots and graphics reproduced in this book are subject to copyright © SAP AG, Dietmar-Hopp-Allee 16, 69190 Walldorf, Germany.

SAP, the SAP logo, mySAP, mySAP.com, mySAP Business Suite, SAP NetWeaver, SAP R/3, SAP R/2, SAP B2B, SAPtronic, SAPscript, SAP BW, SAP CRM, SAP EarlyWatch, SAP ArchiveLink, SAP GUI, SAP Business Workflow, SAP Business Engineer, SAP Business Navigator, SAP Business Framework, SAP Business Information Warehouse, SAP inter-enterprise solutions, SAP APO, AcceleratedSAP, InterSAP, SAPoffice, SAPfind, SAPfile, SAPtime, SAPmail, SAP-access, SAP-EDI, R/3 Retail, Accelerated HR, Accelerated HiTech, Accelerated Consumer Products, ABAP, ABAP/4, ALE/WEB, BAPI, Business Framework, BW Explorer, Enjoy-SAP, mySAP.com e-business platform, mySAP Enterprise Portals, RIVA, SAPPHIRE, TeamSAP, Webflow and SAP PRESS are registered or unregistered trademarks of SAP AG, Walldorf, Germany.

All other products mentioned in this book are registered or unregistered trademarks of their respective companies.

Contents at a Glance

1 The BW Project Lifecycle 25
2 Defining an Implementation Strategy 59
3 Common BW Implementation Mistakes 97
4 Project Planning in BW 147
5 Gathering and Analyzing BW Requirements 187
6 Sound BW Development Strategies 223
7 Preparing for Go-Live and the Go-Live Process 273
8 After BW Go-Live 307
9 Epilogue 327
   Appendix 333

Acknowledgements

The path to complete a book is a long and winding one. Many people have provided me invaluable help in completing this book. I would like to thank each of them for their help.

I offer thanks to my daughter Melanie who provided her Dad with encouragement and support. May you always follow your dreams.

Thanks also go to my other daughter Vanessa, may your focus and drive lead you wherever you wish to go.

I also must thank my best friend and wife, Amy, for giving me the encouragement and the time to complete this book. Not only did she provide me the unending support needed to write, she also spent many hours giving editing suggestions to shape the presentation and content of this book. I thank her for her very valuable input. The end product reflects her dedication and I could not have completed it without her help.

Amy, I dedicate this book to you. I cannot thank you enough.

Other Thanks

I would also like to thank my extended family and friends for their various sacrifices to allow me time to complete this book.

Thanks to my colleagues and coworkers at my current and past projects for their feedback in helping make this book a reality. I wish to especially thank all the good folks at the Mercury Project for their constant support.

Special thanks to many of the staff members of Grom Associates, TekLink (TLI) and SAP America Inc. for providing me the information and support needed to complete this book.

Contents

Introduction 19

1 The BW Project Lifecycle 25

1.1 ECC vs. BW Implementations 26
1.2 BW from A-Z 26
    1.2.1 Extraction 27
    1.2.2 Staging and Storage 27
    1.2.3 Transformation 28
    1.2.4 Presentation 29
1.3 External Data: What is the Big Deal? 29
1.4 Build for the Present, Keep an Eye on the Future 30
1.5 Dirty Data 32
1.6 Can't BW Just Clean the Data? 33
1.7 Understanding BW 33
1.8 Reasons for Implementing SAP BW 34
    1.8.1 Analytical System Access from the Transactional (ECC) System 34
    1.8.2 Transition to a Single Version of the Truth 37
    1.8.3 Consolidation, Harmonization, and Centralization of Information 38
    1.8.4 Establish an Enterprise Data Warehouse (EDW) ... 40
    1.8.5 Competitive Advantage 41
    1.8.6 Provide Flexible Analysis of Information Assets .. 41
    1.8.7 Business Information to More People in the Organization 42
1.9 Why Not Another Data Warehouse? 43
    1.9.1 Data Extraction From ECC is Much Easier with BW ... 44
    1.9.2 BW is Already Part of the Landscape 44
    1.9.3 BW is the Foundation for Most NetWeaver Products .. 45
1.10 What BW is Not Designed to Do 45
    1.10.1 BW is Not a Transactional System 46
    1.10.2 BW is Not the Only Reporting System 47
    1.10.3 BW is Not Usually Updated in Real-Time 47
    1.10.4 BW is Not a Silver Bullet 48
1.11 Ingredients for a Successful SAP BW Project Manager ... 49
    1.11.1 Good Communication Skills 49
    1.11.2 Knowledge of BW and Data Warehousing 51

Contents

		1.11.3	Knowledge of Business Processes and Analysis Goals	53
		1.11.4	The Need for Political Savvy	54
		1.11.5	Highly Organized and Quality Minded	55
		1.11.6	Willing and Able to Develop and Enforce Standards	55
		1.11.7	Team Building	56
		1.11.8	Budget Accountability	57
		1.11.9	Willing to Say Both "Yes" and "No"	57
	1.12	Summary		58

2 Defining an Implementation Strategy 59

2.1	Defining an Upgrade Strategy			60
	2.1.1	Landscape Strategy		60
	2.1.2	Think About the Training Environment		64
	2.1.3	Adding a Production Support System		66
	2.1.4	Keep Development, QA, Production Environments in Sync		66
	2.1.5	Assess New Phases of Development		68
2.2	Upgrade Landscape			71
2.3	Transport Strategy			72
	2.3.1	Develop and Communicate the Transport Path		73
	2.3.2	Implement Transport Approval Process from the Beginning		75
	2.3.3	Make Sure Each Developer Locks Objects		75
	2.3.4	Transport Steward Process		76
	2.3.5	Keep Thorough Log of Transports		77
	2.3.6	Develop a Process for Troubleshooting Failed Transports		77
	2.3.7	Some Objects Will be Changeable		78
2.4	New Release Rollout Strategy Challenges			80
	2.4.1	Timing of BW Rollout		81
	2.4.2	Rollout Scope		81
2.5	Upgrade Rollout Strategy			82
	2.5.1	Timing		82
	2.5.2	Features and Functionality		82
	2.5.3	Upgrade Testing Strategy		82
	2.5.4	Upgrade Change Management Strategy		82
2.6	Database Strategy			83
2.7	Enterprise Data Warehouse and Global Rollup Strategies			84
2.8	Query Strategy			86
	2.8.1	Pros and Cons of developing Queries Directly in Production		87

	2.8.2	How Do I Allow Development of Queries in Production?	87
	2.8.3	Developing Queries in Production vs. Development	89
	2.8.4	Visual Composer	89
2.9	Support Package Strategy		90
	2.9.1	Recommendation	91
	2.9.2	Front-End Support Packages	92
2.10	Authorization Strategy		93
	2.10.1	BW Security	93
	2.10.2	Authorizations for Upgrade to NW 2004s	94
2.11	Conclusion		95

3 Common BW Implementation Mistakes 97

3.1	Unclear Definition of Goals and Scope		97
	3.1.1	Develop Clear Project Scope Documentation	97
	3.1.2	Establish Milestones	99
	3.1.3	Avoid Scope Creep	99
	3.1.4	Establish a Scope Change Control Process	100
3.2	Over-Ambitious Scope		100
	3.2.1	Start Small	101
	3.2.2	Be Wary of Implementing BW at the Same Time as ECC or R/3	102
3.3	Unrealistic Timeline		103
3.4	Governance		104
3.5	Communication Issues		107
	3.5.1	Insist on Weekly Status Reports	107
	3.5.2	Encourage Informal Discussion	107
	3.5.3	Locate Centrally	107
	3.5.4	Centralize Issues List and Use It	108
3.6	Ownership Issues		108
	3.6.1	Insist on Signoff of Documents	109
	3.6.2	Have the Power Users Develop the BW Queries	109
3.7	Data Quality Issues		110
	3.7.1	Don't Completely Rely on the Source Systems to Ensure Data Quality	112
	3.7.2	Establish Active Governance of Data	113
	3.7.3	Turn to a Third-Party to Help with Validation	114
3.8	Data Alignment Issues		115
	3.8.1	Master Data Alignment	115
	3.8.2	Transactional Data Alignment	118

3.9	Data Realignment		119
	3.9.1	Realignment Without Reload—Is It Possible?	119
3.10	Performance Issues		121
	3.10.1	Establish Clear Goals for Performance	121
	3.10.2	Measure Against the Performance Goals via Statistics InfoCubes	123
	3.10.3	Establish a Performance Sub-Team	123
	3.10.4	Keep Up-to-Date on Support Packages	124
	3.10.5	Data Model for Performance	124
3.11	Technical and Infrastructure Issues		127
3.12	Resource Issues		128
	3.12.1	Insist on the Best, Not Just the Most Available	129
	3.12.2	The Consultant-Heavy Project	129
	3.12.3	Insist on Interviewing All Candidates	130
	3.12.4	Transition Out Bad Consultants	130
	3.12.5	Avoid Conflict Between Consulting Partners, SAP, and Others	131
	3.12.6	R/3 or ECC Basis Experience is Not BW Experience	132
	3.12.7	Keep the Project Team Physically Together	132
3.13	Political Issues		133
3.14	Over-Customization		133
	3.14.1	Determine If the Customization Can Take Place Outside BW	134
	3.14.2	Develop a "Why not SAP?" Approach	135
	3.14.3	Know Where Many BW Projects Use Third-Party Tools	135
	3.14.4	Validation Tools	139
3.15	Meeting and Decision Paralysis		140
	3.15.1	Slow Decision Making	140
	3.15.2	The Lonely BW Team	141
	3.15.3	The Popular BW Team	141
	3.15.4	What Can be Done?	142
3.16	Change-Control and Change-Management		142
	3.16.1	Change Control	143
3.17	Conclusion		146

4 Project Planning in BW — 147

4.1	The Data Warehouse Lifecycle		148
4.2	The Upgrade Lifecycle		149
	4.2.1	Upgrading on the Existing BW Landscape	151
	4.2.2	Dedicated Upgrade Landscape	151

		4.2.3	Production Support During Upgrade Testing	153
		4.2.4	Obsolete Queries	154
		4.2.5	Upgrade Cutover	154
		4.2.6	How Long Will This Take?	155
		4.2.7	When Should I Upgrade?	157
	4.3	Scope Documentation		158
		4.3.1	What Is a Stakeholder?	158
		4.3.2	Stakeholder Document	158
		4.3.3	Communication Plan Document	159
		4.3.4	Integrated Project Plan	159
		4.3.5	Naming Standards Document	159
		4.3.6	BW Development Standards Document	161
	4.4	Typical Roles Needed for a BW Project		162
		4.4.1	BW Project Manager	162
		4.4.2	BW Business Subject Matter Expert	163
		4.4.3	BW Data Architect	164
		4.4.4	BW Applications Developer	165
		4.4.5	BW Presentation Developer	166
		4.4.6	BW Basis Developer	167
		4.4.7	ABAP Developer	168
		4.4.8	SAP Portal Consultant	169
	4.5	Staffing a BW Project		169
		4.5.1	The Small BW Project	170
	4.6	Outsourcing and BW		177
		4.6.1	When Does Outsourcing Work?	178
	4.7	BW Interview Process		179
	4.8	Training Requirements		184
	4.9	Conclusion		185

5 Gathering and Analyzing BW Requirements ... 187

	5.1	Requirements Gathering		188
		5.1.1	Interviews	189
		5.1.2	Is All Data in SAP ECC or R/3 or in Multiple Systems?	190
		5.1.3	Is Intra-Day or Real-Time Reporting Needed?	190
		5.1.4	What Else Do You Know About the Requirement?	191
	5.2	Gathering a Report Inventory		193
	5.3	Functional Model Document		195
		5.3.1	How Many Functional Model Documents are Needed?	197
		5.3.2	Sections of the Functional Model Document	198

	5.4	BW Key Figure or KPI Matrix	204
	5.5	Budgeting or Estimating BW Timelines	204
	5.6	BW Physical Model	210
	5.7	Business Content Evaluation	213
		5.7.1 Business Content as a Learning Tool	214
		5.7.2 Evaluating Business Content for Your Needs	215
		5.7.3 Using a Subset of the Business Content	218
	5.8	Design Reviews	219
		5.8.1 Functional Model Review	220
		5.8.2 Conceptual and Physical Model Review	220
		5.8.3 Data Model and System Review	220
		5.8.4 Final Check	221
	5.9	Conclusion	221

6 Sound BW Development Strategies ... 223

	6.1	Extracting and Loading Data from SAP Source Systems	224
		6.1.1 Service API DataSources	225
		6.1.2 Generated DataSources	227
		6.1.3 Generic DataSources	227
		6.1.4 Custom ABAP DataSources	228
		6.1.5 Testing the DataSources	228
		6.1.6 Filling In Missing Data in Extractions	229
	6.2	Loading Data from Non-SAP Source Systems	231
		6.2.1 Flat File Interfaces	231
		6.2.2 DBConnect	233
		6.2.3 UDConnect	234
		6.2.4 XML Interfaces	235
		6.2.5 ETL Interfaces	235
	6.3	Extracting Data From the BW System	235
	6.4	Loading and Transforming Data into BW	237
		6.4.1 Transformation and Mapping of Data in BW Version 3.x	238
		6.4.2 Transformation and Mapping of Data in NW 2004s	243
		6.4.3 Start Routines	244
		6.4.4 End Routines	245
		6.4.5 Expert Routines	245
		6.4.6 Implementing Transformations	245
		6.4.7 Auditing Transformations for Efficiency	246
		6.4.8 Converting from Version 3.x to NW 2004s Transformations	246
	6.5	Appending or Changing Standard BW Objects	249

Contents

6.6		Data Modeling	251
	6.6.1	Loading into an DSO or ODS	251
	6.6.2	Create a Consolidation Layer for Data	252
	6.6.3	Extract Once, Use Many Times	252
	6.6.4	Use the Right Object for the Job	253
6.7		Issue Resolution and Issue Tracking	255
	6.7.1	Reporting Issues via SAP's Service MarketPlace	255
	6.7.2	Response Delays	256
6.8		Query Performance Analysis in BW	257
	6.8.1	Data Model Does Not fit the Data Volume	257
	6.8.2	Poor Query Definition	258
	6.8.3	Lack of Aggregates	259
	6.8.4	OLAP Cache	261
	6.8.5	Partitioning Not Set	265
	6.8.6	Database Statistics Not Up-to-Date	266
	6.8.7	Virtual Characteristics and Key Figures	266
	6.8.8	Time-Dependent Master Data	267
	6.8.9	Complex Authorizations	269
	6.8.10	NW 2004s BI Accelerator	270
6.9		Conclusion	271

7 Preparing for Go-Live and the Go-Live Process ... 273

7.1		Data Model and System Review	273
7.2		Documenting BW Configuration	275
	7.2.1	BW Functional Model Document	275
	7.2.2	DataStore Object/Operational Data Store (DSO/ODS) Technical Design Document	276
	7.2.3	InfoCube Technical Design Document	276
	7.2.4	Extraction, Transformation, and Loading (ETL) Technical Design Document	276
	7.2.5	The MetaData Repository	278
	7.2.6	SAP Solution Manager	279
7.3		Transport Management in BW	281
	7.3.1	BW Transport Management System Tips	282
	7.3.2	General BW Transport Tips	283
	7.3.3	Separate BW Transports into Logical Groups	283
	7.3.4	Keep Careful Watch of Transports—Take Good Notes	285
	7.3.5	Never Leave a Transport Behind	285
	7.3.6	Final Cutover Recapture of Transports	286
	7.3.7	The Mock Cutover	287

Contents

7.4	Testing in BW		288
	7.4.1	Develop at BW Test Plan	288
	7.4.2	Developing Test Scripts for BW	289
	7.4.3	Automated Testing Tools	290
7.5	Organizational Change Management		291
	7.5.1	Training	291
	7.5.2	A Separate Training System	292
	7.5.3	Do I Really Need Hands-On Training?	293
	7.5.4	Training Budget	293
7.6	Cutover Planning		294
7.7	Go-Live Checklist		296
7.8	Run Initial Loads in BW		298
	7.8.1	Create and Schedule Process Chains in BW	299
	7.8.2	Schedule ECC Jobs	300
	7.8.3	Portals and BW	302
	7.8.4	Developing a Portal Strategy	303
7.9	Conclusion		306

8 After BW Go-Live ... 307

8.1	Building a Production Support Center of Excellence (COE)		307
8.2	Transitioning from BW Development to Production-Support COE		309
	8.2.1	Transition the Knowledge	309
	8.2.2	Determine Measurement Criteria	310
8.3	Ongoing BW Reconciliation and Validation		313
	8.3.1	Develop a Reconciliation Strategy	313
	8.3.2	Reconciling the Data to ECC or R/3	315
	8.3.3	Reconciling Data to External Systems	316
8.4	Periodic Jobs to Run in a BW Environment		317
8.5	Develop an Ongoing BW Support Package Strategy		319
	8.5.1	Front-End Support Packages	322
	8.5.2	Conduct a Lessons-Learned Session	323
8.6	Retaining and Motivating Staff for Future Rollouts		325
8.7	Prepare for Future Rollouts		326
8.8	Conclusion		326

9 Epilogue ... 327

9.1	Using this Book	327
9.2	Common Issues and Challenges	328
9.3	Important Things to Remember	328

		9.3.1	More Challenging than an ECC or R/3 Project	329
		9.3.2	Management Commitment Needed from the Beginning	329
		9.3.3	Project Management: User-Focused, Not Technology Focused	329
		9.3.4	Clear Methodology Needed to Determine Requirements	329
		9.3.5	Understanding Data Load Volume and Granularity	330
		9.3.6	Manage Expectations for BW	330
		9.3.7	Fix Bad Data at Its Source	330
		9.3.8	Build a BW System, Not a Series Of Data Marts	330
		9.3.9	When the BW System Is Live, the Solution Isn't Finished	331
	9.4	Conclusion		331

Appendix 333

A	Sample Project Plan			335
B	Important Checklists			351
	B.1	New BW System Validation Checklist		351
	B.2	Preliminary Checks (Prior to Any Transports)		351
	B.3	Query/Portal Checks		352
	B.4	Loading Checks		352
	B.5	Transport Settings		352
	B.6	BW Query Development Checklist		353
	B.7	BW Data Model Conceptual Review Checklist		355
		B.7.1	Items Needed Prior to Conceptual Data Model Review	355
		B.7.2	Conceptual Data Model Review	355
	B.8	BW Data Model Review Checklist		357
		B.8.1	Items Needed Prior to BW Data Model Review	357
		B.8.2	Items Checked During BW Data Model Review: Overall	357
		B.8.3	DataSources/Feeds	358
		B.8.4	DSO	358
		B.8.5	InfoCube/InfoSets/MultiProviders	358
		B.8.6	Query Processing Checklist	359
	B.9	Cutover Plan Checklist		360
		B.9.1	Administrative Tasks	360
		B.9.2	Security Requirements	360
		B.9.3	System Requirements	360
		B.9.4	Transport Requirements	361

		B.9.5	Portal Requirements	361
		B.9.6	Prior to Load Checks	362
		B.9.7	Prior to Query Testing	362
		B.9.8	Validation	362
		B.9.9	Data Loads	362
	B.10	BW Performance Checklist		363
		B.10.1	Overall Tasks	363
		B.10.2	Query Performance	363
		B.10.3	Load Performance	364
C	Document Templates			367
	C.1	Functional Model Template		367
	C.2	DSO Document Template		373
	C.3	InfoCube Document Template		376
	C.4	ETL (Extraction, Transformation, and Loading) Document Template		379
D	Common Issues When Upgrading from BW Version 3.x to NW 2004s			383
	D.1	System, Basis-Related Issues		384
	D.2	BW Application-Related Issues		385
	D.3	Security-Related Issues		386
	D.4	Portal-Related Issues		387
E	Sample BW Naming Standards Document			389
F	BW Integration Test Script			393
G	Bibliography			397
The Author				399

Index 401

Introduction

I was excited about the opportunity to write this book for so many reasons. I am fortunate to have been involved with the Business Information Warehouse (BW) product since its inception. I've worked with several version BW 1.2B projects, and even participated in early discussions at SAP about BW, when the product didn't even have a name. SAP BW is now called SAP NetWeaver BI. However, in this book, I will be referring to earlier versions of the product that I have worked with from its earliest release as BW or SAP BW.

For over nine years, I worked for SAP, initially as a Sales and Distribution (SD) consultant, working with the Logistics Information System (LIS) and the Sales Information System (SIS) modules. I did not know it then, but these modules would later serve as the foundation for developing the BW product. After working in those areas, it was natural for me to begin working on the BW product when it was introduced.

Much of my work with SAP, and now after leaving SAP, has been in implementation and project management of the SAP BW project. I have also presented sessions at several ASUG conferences, Sapphire events, BW Portals Conferences, and Managing SAP Project Conferences. This allowed me to meet SAP clients and understand the challenges that they faced during their struggles to understand and implement BW.

As a BW consultant, I have been directly involved in over 50 BW projects. Some of these were short engagements, which were needed to validate project plans or solidify strategy for implementation. Others were as a long-term consultant working on the project from beginning to end. I've also been a key participant in countless conference calls, email issues, and short visits to customer sites. In a word, BW has been the *mainstay* of my professional life for years.

I had a unique opportunity as a Platinum consultant for SAP to be a part of many projects, some well managed, others with severe challenges. This allowed me to see and communicate with many clients at different stages of their project lifecycles. As I saw more and more projects, I realized that there were many common issues and mistakes made during these projects.

Over the years, I have authored articles and whitepapers on technical issues and implementation advice. Many articles about these technical and advanced topics can be found on either the BW Expert publication (*www.bwexpertonline.com*) or on the SAP SDN (*sdn.sap.com*).

Early in my consulting career, I started keeping a small notebook of the common issues I had mentioned earlier. At first, the goal of this notebook was to help me make sure that I could avoid these issues when working with future customers. As you can imagine, this notebook—and many others—was quickly filled, until I had a large list of common trouble areas of a BW implementation.

Many of the issues were technical and product related. Others were project and organization related. The goal of this book is to understand and overcome the latter. I felt I could write a very useful book that walks through the common BW application workarounds, even going to the extent of providing configuration and coding advice. But, the problem with that type of book is that the releases and features of the product change so quickly from one release to another and even from one support package to another. That kind of book would quickly become obsolete.

Putting my own experiences and expertise together I am happy to have written this book. I would now like to give you some idea of how you can use the information contained in this book.

How to Use This Book

Because seeing successful, efficient implementations is of utmost priority to me, I wanted to write a book that provided valuable, timely advice. Therefore, my goal for this book is to give project advice to those who are implementing BW, regardless of the release. To give this type of advice, I tried to stay away from specific advice on configuration, transformation, userexits, etc. Doing that, allowed me to keep the content of this book something that could benefit a wider audience and make the advice more universal.

In keeping the advice more project-related, I want to make sure you know that a well-planned project can quite easily attract the best and brightest developers and data architects. These individuals can provide the specific workarounds and configuration experience to help in the day-to-day issues that arise in any project. They should allow a project to overcome the software issues, and this book should help in the process issues.

The advice in this book should be useful to project management and project members on the BW team, but also to those who are in the business of trying to understand the potential of the BW project in their organization.

I would like to give you a quick overview of the contents of this book so you can determine how to go about reading it and using the information contained in it.

Quick Overview

This book is divided into nine chapters (apart from this introductory one) and six appendices. Let me give you a quick rundown of what is included in each of these components so you can better determine how to go about reading this book and using it for your own BW project.

- **Chapter 1: The BW Project Lifecyle**
  This chapter gives you an overview of the BW Project Lifecycle. You will get an understanding of the various complex challenges involved in such projects and will gain insight into the various steps involved in the implementation lifecycle. This chapter is the first step and helps establish the contents of the rest of the book.

- **Chapter 2: Defining and Implementation Strategy**
  This chapter helps you set your own implementation strategy. It does so by helping you understand the importance of a sound strategy, while also taking you through the series of useful plans, steps, and actions needed to create a sound BW implementation strategy.

- **Chapter 3: Common BW Implementation Mistakes**
  Few things are harder than having projects fail because of avoidable mistakes. You will gain from my own experiences in this chapter which takes you through commonly made BW implementation mistakes. This chapter will help you avoid these common issues.

- **Chapter 4: Project Planning in BW**
  This chapter will help you understand and prepare for the various challenges that come up in BW implementations. This chapter on project planning takes you through the steps of planning that should help you in your own project planning endeavors.

- **Chapter 5: Gathering and Analyzing BW Requirements**
  For BW projects to succeed, you need to know how to best gather and analyze requirements. In well-run BW projects, people work together and

use the information gathered to analyze and come up with the best methods and models needed.

- **Chapter 6: Sound BW Development Strategies**
This chapter continues where Chapter 5 leaves off. It explains sound BW development strategies. How to extract and load data, how to load data from non-SAP sources, how to extract data from SAP systems, and loading and transforming data into BW are some of the issues covered in this chapter.

- **Chapter 7: Preparing for Go-Live and the Go-Live Process**
You are now almost at the go-live stage and this chapter helps you see what's in store for you now. It helps you see what needs to be done while preparing for go-live and to understand the go-live process itself. It covers topics like documentation for BW configuration, transport management, and testing, to name a few.

- **Chapter 8: After BW Go-Live**
Your work on a BW implementation project is not complete after go-live. There is still important work to be done and this chapter shows you what and how to go about doing this. From setting up a Center of Excellence to transitioning from BW development to production support and establishing a help desk, this chapter is packed with valuable information.

- **Chapter 9: Epilogue**
This summarizes the book and gives you important takeaways that you can use for your own BW projects.

- **Appendix A: Sample Project Plan**
The sample project included in this appendix can be used as a template or a model for developing a plan for your own organization. The sections and subsections walk you through the BW project plan, letting you know what needs to be done at each stage.

- **Appendix B: Important Checklists**
This appendix contains various important checklists that you can use to track the progress of your BW project. These include: New BW System Validation Checklist, BW Query Development Checklist, BW Data Model Conceptual Review Checklist, BW Model Review Checklist, Cutover Plan Checklist, and the BW Performance Checklist.

- **Appendix C: Document Templates**
This appendix gives you detailed information about the various documents that need to be created for your BW project. It presents these as templates that you can use to create your own documents. They include:

Functional Model template, DataStore template, InfoCube template, and the ETL template.

- **Appendix D: Common Issues When Upgrading from BW Version 3.x to NW 2004s**
  As the title of this appendix suggests, it lists commonly encountered issues during a typical upgrade from 3.x to NW 2004s. These include system-based issues, security-related issues, and portal-related issues.

- **Appendix E: Sample BW Naming Standards**
  Naming standards are important to maintain consistency in the approach to naming custom objects in SAP BW. This appendix lists some commonly used naming standards for your review and will act as a guide to creating your own naming standards document.

- **Appendix F: Integration Test Script**
  This appendix gives you a document that can be used as an integration test script for the BW data against the source data being loaded.

These chapters and appendices work together to give you a clear and practical understanding of how BW projects work (and should work) and how to best implement BW projects.

Conclusion

I hope you find great value in this book. It gives me pleasure to allow the information that has been kept in those notebooks so long to be shared with people who can put it to good use. I do welcome any questions or comments on the book and hope you enjoy reading it.

SAP BW can be a very complex product. Its complexity lies in the many choices that are available when using it to provide business information. Understanding the product and its advantages and disadvantages is important for leading a project to success.

1 The BW Project Lifecycle

The SAP Business Information Warehouse (BW) solution has had many iterations and versions, but the core intention of the product and its designs have remained relatively unchanged since the first widely available version, 1.2B. The product now officially goes by the name SAPNetWeaver BI. However, most industry professionals and consultants still refer to the product as *Business Warehouse* or simply BW.

Implementation of BW has its challenges. There are many different sources of documentation that walk us through the functionality available in the product, but often the most difficult task is not *understanding* the functionality of the BW product but rather *applying* that functionality to business situations and implementing the product to its fullest potential. Using the product is what allows us to provide the best advantages to the business for reporting and analysis.

There are many corporate uses for BW; most involve gathering various data from different sources and analyzing this data in one place, the BW system. Because BW is fully configurable and quite flexible, the possibilities for reporting and analysis are virtually limitless. Among other things, companies use BW to analyze sales in order to determine profitability, analyze headcounts, identify slow-moving materials, and track vendor performance.

The best way to start to look at the BW product is to compare its related core transactional system R/3, or the more recent version of that transactional system, ERP Central Component (ECC). The R/3 or ECC systems are implemented to provide optimal transaction processing in the organization while the BW system is designed to provide optimal analysis of this transactional data. This data can source from the ECC or R/3 system or from other systems in the company's landscape. We refer to these sources of data by the BW term *DataSources*.

1 The BW Project Lifecycle

1.1 ECC vs. BW Implementations

A very common analogy is often used to compare implementing ECC or R/3 vs. implementing SAP BW: Implementing ECC is science, while implementing BW is art. On the surface, this analogy sounds like a ploy to allow BW project managers to make their projects sound more exciting (and perhaps gain more of the IT budget). However, as you examine the analogy, it does prove to be very true in many BW projects.

The art of implementing a BW project lies in the extreme flexibility of the product and its diverse methods of delivering data. BW was deliberately designed with this flexibility to allow maximum use. This flexibility of BW allows many more choices in the implementation process than exist in a typical ECC project. BW can be implemented many different ways with very little constraints on the sources or quality of data that is loaded. This allows a lot of creativity when solving business problems using BW.

To compound the complexity, measures of success are less concrete with BW projects. Most ECC or R/3 transactional systems have clear-cut requirements. For example, a common sales-system requirement might be to provide an order-to-cash process in support of business operations. The goal of a BW implementation—i.e., "to help people make decisions faster and better"—is more subjective. This lends itself to a much more unstructured environment, thus, a more difficult project to implement and manage than those of a transactional system.

BW lets the organization manage data from multiple sources to answer questions that previously may have been very difficult or even deemed unanswerable. Thus BW itself, in many ways, should be considered a process, not a product. This complexity makes for a challenging implementation environment. To understand the environment, we must first understand the product, its strengths and weaknesses, and its overall development lifecycle.

1.2 BW from A-Z

Simply put, BW is a data warehouse. A data warehouse is defined as a logical collection of information gathered from many different operational databases and used to create business intelligence that supports business-analysis activities and decision-making tasks. Primarily, it is a record of an enterprise's past transactional and operational information, stored in a database designed to favor efficient data analysis and reporting.

BW, as with other data warehouses, requires that data undergoes specific steps: be gathered from the source system, put into a consistent state, stored, and presented to the end user for analysis. The main steps in the lifecycle of information in BW are, given in order below:

1. Extraction
2. Staging and storage
3. Transformation
4. Presentation

Let us look at these in more detail now.

1.2.1 Extraction

Data can be extracted from source systems in a variety of ways. If the data required is in an ECC source system, this data can be extracted via the *service applications and programming interface* (service API). In simple terms, the service API is the collection of pre-delivered extractors in ECC. Almost all standard data in ECC have delivered extractors called *DataSources*. These DataSources can be used to load data into BW.

External systems do not have these DataSources, so this data must be extracted from these non-SAP systems in some other way. Typically, this is done via a custom extraction program on the external system that outputs files in a flat file format for loading into BW. It can also be done via a direct connection to another non-SAP database to allow BW to read data directly from these sources for a more direct loading. This extracted data can then be merged with other external data or ECC data for reporting and analysis.

1.2.2 Staging and Storage

Staging and storage of data means that the data is kept in an environment that can handle large data sets and house them for further loading or for presentation to the end user. As you might expect, BW implementations typically take up a lot of disk space.

A small BW implementation can be as small as 50–75GB, while more complex environments can involve up to several terabytes of data. According to SAP, the average BW implementation supports 200 users and is between 100 and 200GB in size.

A majority of this disk space is taken up with the Data Store Objects (DSO), formally known as an Operational Data Store (ODS), and the InfoCubes. Typically, the DSO is a repository for storing detailed, typically transactional data in the BW system. The InfoCube typically contains aggregated summary information fed from either the DSO or other sources designed to present data in a clear and efficient manner.

> **Note**
> Data-modeling decisions can severely affect the volume of data in BW. This can have an adverse effect on performance. These data-modeling decisions should always take into account the overall effect on data volume and system performance.

The DSO and InfoCubes set the foundation for data storage in BW. Usually, the more voluminous the source, the more storage space is needed in BW. However, this is not always the case. Decisions regarding redundancy of data and data granularity can either reduce or even exponentially increase the data volume in BW.

1.2.3 Transformation

Data transformation is a large part of any BW implementation. It is through data transformation that data from differing sources can be married to provide some meaningful analysis. This transformation is necessary both for adding values that are not in the source data or altering values that may not be consistent with others. For example, users need to analyze data from both the legacy system orders and from the ECC system orders. These two data sets exist on separate systems. They both use completely different customer numbers, material numbers, etc. Users want to be able to see order history across the two systems. How can we provide this?

The only way to do this is to combine and harmonize the data together as if they all came from one system. This can be quite a difficult task. The customer numbers must be converted to a consistent number format from one source system. This must be done with all transactional fields until the data is stored in a consistent format.

This transformation is done in the BW system using either update and transfer rules in BW versions 3.0 to 3.5 or with the transformation area in the NW 2004s system. Data transformation can be time-consuming and complicated, depending on the data that needs to be altered or appended.

Understanding and implementing harmonization of data requires a clear understanding of the sources of data. It involves combining the data in a logical format that can be re-used often for other reporting purposes. We also need a clear understanding of all the data analysis needs of the organization. Fully understanding all these areas can be quite challenging. Thus, transformation of data is a large task that often requires several iterations before the final version is complete.

1.2.4 Presentation

Presentation of data can come from a variety of different formats and methods. Simply put, the presentation of data in BW involves providing the data to the end user in a meaningful way. There are several different ways to present data in BW, as seen in the following list:

- **BEx Reporting**
  A tool to provide data analysis using Microsoft Excel as the basis for the delivery of the data.
- **Web Reporting**
  Analysis using reports with an HTML or Java front end and typically launched from a portal.
- **Third- Party Tools**
  Various third-party tools provide information analysis in BW.

1.3 External Data: What is the Big Deal?

In most BW projects, there are multiple sources of data. This data needs to be analyzed with various methods of discovery by a wide variety of users. To add to this complexity, most projects involve bringing the data from multiple sources and combining this data so it appears to come from one single source. This harmonization of data can require significant analysis as well as transformation of data to allow the analysis to take place.

Although some customers use BW without any SAP data loaded into it, most BW projects source a large majority of their data from the associated SAP transactional systems. This is because the transactional system of record for most projects involving BW is usually SAP ECC or R/3.

Most BW implementations do not rely only on the SAP ECC system as their sole DataSource for BW. The reason for this stems from the best of breed and lifecycles of most IT organizations. Many IT organizations have multiple systems spanning many different processes and functions in their landscapes. Because these systems need to be analyzed together, BW is often called upon to provide this analysis.

> **Example**
>
> A large pharmaceutical company needs to analyze sales, shipments, and on-time delivery statistics. The ECC system provides the sales and shipment data via the Sales and Distribution (SD) system. However, a legacy system provides the on-time delivery statistics. This on-time data must be loaded into BW and *married* with the ECC data so the analysis can span the entire data set. When users request this analysis, they should not need to know or care that the data came from a variety of systems. They simply expect a meaningful analysis of this data, regardless of its source.

1.4 Build for the Present, Keep an Eye on the Future

The BW system must not only be designed with the current requirements in mind, but must be flexible enough to allow for analysis of future data with requirements that may not even be known today. This is because the organization is constantly changing, and new ways of analyzing data emerge with the evolution of the users and the transactional source systems.

Implementation decisions that are made early in the BW implementation cycle can provide significant challenges in the future. Much of the configuration in BW is not easy to fix once data has been loaded. Data loaded into BW InfoCubes or DSO structures can require a significant effort to redesign.

Any significant changes usually require a purge or dump of the DSO or InfoCube in BW, and a reload of this data. In many cases, a full reload of data in BW requires the source system to be *quiet* during the reload. This would mean that no users could perform transactions during this time.

As more and more organizations migrate toward a 24x7 uptime environment, it is much more difficult to schedule downtime on the transactional system. This type of disruption of business may not be possible in a very dynamic environment or in one where the uptime of the system's transactional system is mission critical.

The challenge is to anticipate the core data that is needed for future requirements, then build it into the data model to prevent a scheduled outage of the transactional systems and reload of the BW system. This can present a burden on the BW team to "get it right the first time."

> **Example**
>
> A field in the sales order called *batch number* was not deemed appropriate for the sales-order reporting requirements, so the implementation team decided not to pull this field into BW. It does not exist in the DSO order structures and therefore does not exist in the InfoCubes. Because it does not exist in the BW environment, it cannot be used for reporting and analysis. The business users decide they now want to perform reporting in the batch number. How do we get the batch number into BW?

Let's examine this example more thoroughly. If the data has not been mapped into BW, and the batch number needs to be populated in all existing orders, including the history in BW, we have some significant work to do. We must first purge the data in the BW DSO and InfoCubes. We then need to add the field for the batch number to both the DSO and InfoCubes relevant for the reporting needs. Now, we have a place to store the batch number. We need to re-populate the InfoCubes and DSO to include the batch number.

To extract the data from ECC, we must shut the users off from the ECC system while we re-initialize the data and reload the data into BW. This downtime on ECC is required to make sure that the data is static in ECC and the initial set-up of data is consistent and correct. There is no way to do this set-up while users are busy changing and adding sales orders. Depending on the volume of data in the ECC transactional system, this downtime could be significant: several hours or even days. This downtime is only required for the initial loading and setting up of the data; it is not required for each day's delta load into BW.

This downtime can quickly become quite a burden on the transactional system, if a shutdown is required for each new data field that had not been mapped. Thus, the only way to prevent these outages is to anticipate the future needs of the analysis users and make sure that the fields that they *might* need are incorporated into the design.

The main storage of data in BW is in the DSO structure. This DSO can contain a large volume of data and thus should be used to store the majority of the fields that are either specifically needed or may be needed into the future.

InfoCubes in BW provide the main analysis structure for reporting in BW. When the DSO data is loaded into the InfoCubes for eventual reporting, subsets of the DSO data are typically chosen based only on the current analysis requirements. This is useful, because the InfoCube can then contain only the data that is most pertinent for analysis. If the InfoCube is missing data needed for analysis, it can simply be reloaded from its source DSO in BW. This does not require downtime on the transactional system. It simply requires some downtime of the BW InfoCube. This is usually much less disruptive for the organization.

> **Note**
>
> The more complete the anticipation of future needs during the data-modeling process, the less impact new needs and changes will have on the transactional users and the more quickly and easily they can be implemented.

1.5 Dirty Data

Compounding the challenges facing a BW project is that the source data has differing levels of quality. Delivering a BW system with high-quality data is of utmost importance because once users determine that the data warehouse has data inaccuracies, it is very difficult to win back the users' confidence.

The number one axiom for a BW data warehouse must be: Get the data right, right from the beginning.

The Data Warehousing Institute estimates that data-quality problems cost U.S. businesses more than $600 billion a year. Yet, most executives are oblivious to the data-quality lacerations that are slowly bleeding their companies to death.

The challenge with data quality most often lies in the source of the data itself. This is best illustrated with the old (and often overused) analogy of garbage in/garbage out. Obviously, any data warehouse is a reflection of the quality of the source data that is loaded into it. However, because data in BW is harmonized, the BW user does not know or care where the source of data lies.

This presents an issue. If a user providing analysis in BW sees incorrect or inconsistent data, he or she typically decides that BW is wrong. Usually, this user does not understand or even care that the issues are often with *dirty* data at its source.

A colleague of mine, Richard Dunning, once summed this up with the simple statement: "When a transactional system coughs, BW catches a cold."

Data in a typical organization rolls downhill, and unfortunately BW is at the bottom. Thus, any anomalies in the data that may not have surfaced in the transactional system now become part of BW's territory.

Source-system data issues provide a severe challenge to any project. Much time in a typical BW project is spent analyzing data issues and meeting with the owners and representatives of the various source systems to get this data fixed. This significant part of the BW implementation is difficult to quantify, yet must be budgeted as part of the BW implementation lifecycle.

1.6 Can't BW Just Clean the Data?

This question comes up frequently in a typical BW implementation. The root of the question lies at the very foundation of BW. Is BW simply a mirror of the sources of data in the various InfoCubes and DSOs? The answer to this question should be a resounding "yes." This is because BW is designed to house data from various source systems and present this data the way the data is in those systems, right or wrong.

Because BW does allow transformation of data, there are those who try to use BW to *clean* data as it arrives in BW. This is a mistake, because if the mission of a BW project is to clean all data as it arrives in BW, the project team will spend a great deal of time on this process. The best way to approach data is to expect that the data is clean at its source. This will allow the BW team to concentrate on getting the data extracted and loaded into BW, without worrying about keeping this source data consistent or correct.

1.7 Understanding BW

It is difficult to talk about implementing software like SAP BW without clearly explaining what BW does well and is designed to do, and to explain some things that BW is clearly not designed to do. Simply put, BW can provide aggregated reporting from one or many different DataSources. Typically, BW is used for a more strategic view of data, while ECC is designed for a more operational view of data. Although this is not mandatory, typically BW fits better in the organization when it provides summary strategic data across the enterprise.

33

1.8 Reasons for Implementing SAP BW

Some popular questions often asked about SAP BW are: Why do I need SAP BW? Doesn't ECC have reporting? Why do I need a separate system for reporting?

Understanding the strengths of the product and why most customers implement BW allows us to gain a better understanding of its strengths. This allows us to make sure we implement in ways that optimize those strengths. The main reasons for implementing BW are as follows:

- Concentrate the analytics on BW rather than ECC or R/3
- Provide a single version of the truth
- Consolidate, harmonize, and centralize information
- Establish an enterprise data warehouse (EDW)
- Provide a competitive advantage
- Provide flexible analysis of information assets
- Make information available to more people in the organization

In order to understand each of the above points, we can explore each reason for implementing BW to reveal the motivation and how BW provides the solution.

1.8.1 Analytical System Access from the Transactional (ECC) System

The reasons for implementing BW vary but the premise is the same. ECC by its nature is an on-line transactional processing system (OLTP). The system is designed for providing fast and efficient entering and retrieval of transactional data across the enterprise.

OLTP systems excel at transactional data processing and the timely delivery of data to support the transactional volume and users. Thus, most transactional systems use a relational database structure with multiple tables and fields, all connected by key fields and a complex number of join tables. This relational structure allows for fast transaction processing as the data is saved into the many tables in the OLTP system.

Figure 1.1 shows a common relational database view. This gives a view of the relationships among the tables in the R/3 or ECC systems. The volume of tables and their relationships are quite complex.

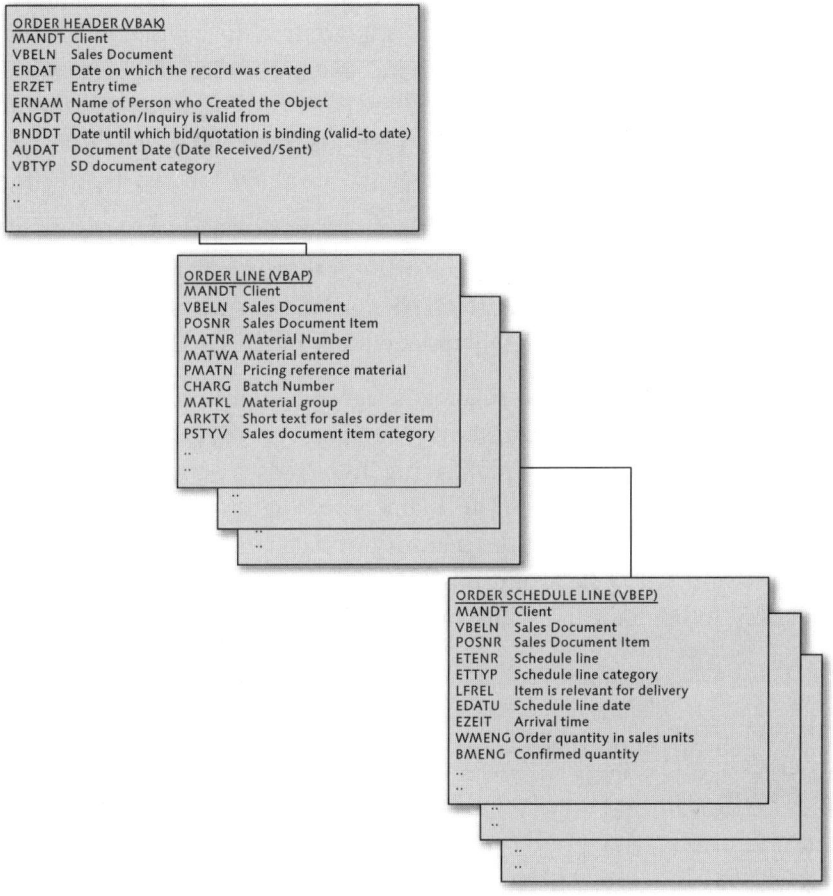

Figure 1.1 View of Subset of ECC Sales Relational Database Tables

Often after an organization has been using the ECC or R/3 transactional systems for a while, it finds itself with a need to analyze the great volume of data that has accumulated. It is at this time that BW is often considered as a solution to the need for analysis.

The reason BW is chosen is because in any OLTP system, it is very difficult to provide fast and efficient transaction processing while at the same time providing fast and efficient reporting. The two goals work against one another. Someone trying to enter transactions cannot afford to be slowed by a high-volume report analyzing data. However, the reports must be run. How can we make sure that we are able to analyze large volumes of data while also allowing ourselves to create many diverse transactions in one system?

The answer is to remove the analytical data from the transactional environment and move it to a more suitable place to provide the analysis that is required by the users. Because there is no way to tune the transactional database optimally to serve both uses, it is vital that separation of the two systems provide both user groups what they were seeking. The separation allows each system to optimally provide their assigned tasks. The OLTP system (typically ECC) continues to be designed to allow for fast transaction processing.

In contrast, BW is considered an online analytical processing system (OLAP) system. Data retrieval in a separate OLAP system can provide a quick and efficient analysis of data completely independent of the OLTP system.

BW's database structure is a star schema design. See Figure 1.2 to get an idea of what this looks like. The figure shows the main reporting structure in SAP BW. This means that rather than having hundreds of transactional data tables, BW provides very few. The main reporting structure in BW, the InfoCube, is designed to allow the majority of data to sit in the central fact table. Dimension tables surround this fact table, the combination of whom provide a key to the data and a link to the shared master data.

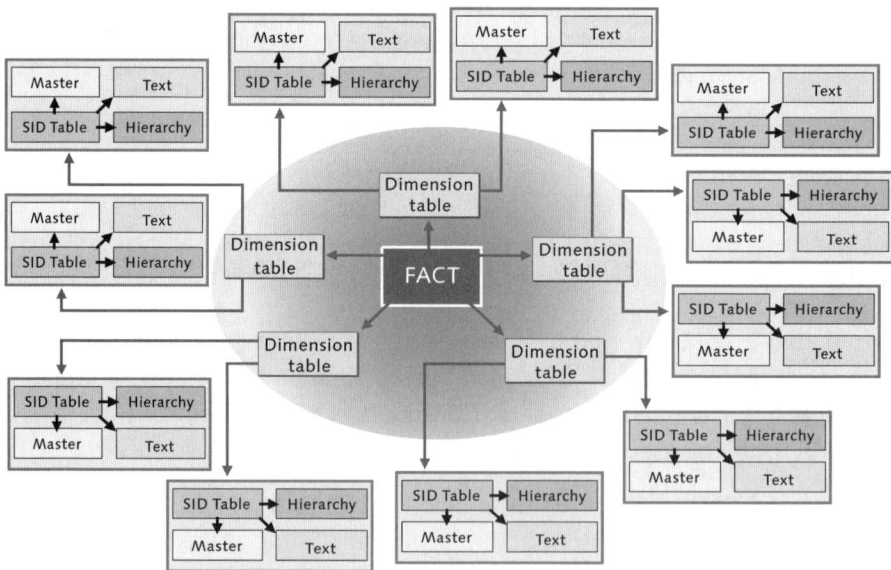

Figure 1.2 Star Schema of InfoCube in BW

1.8.2 Transition to a Single Version of the Truth

Many organizations look to their data warehouse, in this case BW, to help them provide a consistent view of the data in the organization. Because BW can bring in data from multiple sources and harmonize this data, it can enforce one version of the data across the enterprise.

> **Example**
>
> There are many common statistics across an organization. To illustrate this fact, we can look at all the sales reports that report the key figure *net sales*. In an organization, many different reports often show net sales as a value on the report. However, net sales may be understood (or seemingly understood) in many different ways.

Some net sales values might include tax; others might exempt tax from the net sales value. Some may include returns values, while others may exclude these values. This situation can provide a very unclear view of the organization. If many people are looking at one key value and defining it in different ways, this leads to incorrect assumptions and may, in turn, lead to invalid strategic decision-making. How can we make sure that everyone in the organization who refers to a net sales value is always including the same values in their calculations?

This can be done by simply providing the data in BW and mandating that the *net sales* value is always shown to have a consistent calculation to determine the results.

Thus, BW does not necessarily itself provide a *single version of the truth*, but it does allow, through its implementation, an opportunity to enforce this thinking and keep the organization thinking of data in the same way. If everyone is running the same reports from the same systems, it is quite clear that their decision-making would be the result of one set of agreed-upon measures. The organization can then focus more on the decision-making process and not on the makeup of the statistical key values.

This consistency must be enforced from the beginning of a BW project. It is very difficult to retroactively make the BW environment consistent after the implementation has become mature. In our example, gathering up all net sales key-figure values and determining what calculation is used to show these values and then fixing them is quite time-consuming after implementation.

However, if these standards are determined and planned from the beginning, the data can be made consistent in the design. This allows for a firm data foundation for future analysis as more complex key performance indicators (KPIs) are developed.

1.8.3 Consolidation, Harmonization, and Centralization of Information

Consolidation, harmonization, and centralization of information simply refers to getting data from multiple places and merging that data cleanly so that it appears to have come from one source. Many companies meet information needs with small caches of data to support a number of small user groups. We usually refer to these small data stores as data marts.

Data marts may take the form of flat tables, spreadsheets, small data warehouses, MS Access tables, etc. These help to provide some type of raw analysis for the power users and even the end users. Depending on the environment, these data marts may exist all over the organization with many different sources and uses.

Figure 1.3 Completed vs. Planned Consolidation

Figure 1.3 is based on a survey of 521 respondents conducted by Wayne Eckerson, Director of Research, TDWI. This figure shows that organizations have only consolidated about a third of the analytic structures that exist in their organizations. The chart shown in Figure 1.3 gives an indication that organizations have many different data warehouses, independent data marts, data stores, and spreadsheets or *spreadmarts*. Many are in the process of consolidating and/or eliminating these data marts. This is especially true of the most common and most flexible spreadmarts.

The problem with having many different data marts is that the information in the data marts may not always follow a consistent format or standard. This becomes an even more complicated issue as people begin to combine and aggregate data marts to make business decisions. Sometimes the data they are combining or aggregating is not consolidated properly, and thus business decisions are based on incorrect premises.

> **Example**
> A user may want to combine sales information with the accounts receivable information in order to get the full picture of the customer's information in the organization. Because the data for sales is stored using the customer's sold-to information and the accounts receivable is stored based on the payer information, the two streams of data cannot always be meaningfully combined.

Sometimes assumptions are made on the data as it is combined, and thus confusion results from these decisions. For example, if the user of the combined data mart data forgot to eliminate *intercompany sales*, this could skew the numbers improperly.

The only way to reduce this confusion in the organization is to centralize this data and establish some standards for extraction, loading, transformation, and presentation of the data. The next step is to eliminate the data mart completely.

There is an old legend about the pirate Blackbeard that says he would sometimes burn his own ship when engaging in combat with another ship. He did this, they say, so that his crew would have to fight harder to survive. Although we are not doing something as drastic as fighting another ship's sailors when implementing BW, it does help to *burn the ships* in regard to data marts and reduce the number of places to go for information in the organization. We just have to make sure that those who relied on the ship that was burned can stay afloat elsewhere.

BW allows for data standards to be created, and these standards can help in the eventual reduction or elimination of these data marts from the organization. Thus, various users with differing goals for analysis can use one central tool for reporting.

That central tool, in this case BW, then reduces the training needed for users to understand different tools for mining data from various data marts. It also makes sure that these users are all looking at the same data that has been consistently joined. This sets a firm foundation for information in the organization.

1.8.4 Establish an Enterprise Data Warehouse (EDW)

The next step in reducing the data marts is to have one and only one data warehouse in the organization for all reporting. This central or enterprise data warehouse (EDW) would be used not only for regional reporting but would also allow the data to be *rolled up* or aggregated for a global view of the data.

Many companies are facing more and more requests to view data at a global level. This presents a challenge in many organizations, especially those that do most of their data analysis locally rather than globally.

Many companies have data scattered across the organization or siloed in systems that do not allow for quick and easy roll-up to a global reporting instance. This often occurs because development of different systems took place at different times and with different objectives, without proper global governance and vision to assure that this data rolls up properly to a global EDW. Thus, data becomes difficult to analyze consistently and even more difficult to combine or harmonize.

This also happens when there are multiple BW or multiple ECC instances in the system landscape, because these systems often do not share common configuration or common master data.

Most companies, even without an EDW, are doing global reporting. However, this often involves a manual gathering of data from the various source systems and a manual synchronization of the data to a global view. This is typically resource-intensive and time-intensive and lends itself to errors because it is not always performed consistently.

To standardize this practice, and to get more visibility of data across the organization, companies either consider or actually implement an EDW so as to perform global reporting. This EDW would gather data from differing source systems and provide reporting at both an enterprise and an operational level.

Figure 1.4 shows an example of an EDW that combines data from multiple ECC systems and legacy systems into three separate BW systems and one legacy data warehouse. This data is consolidated into one enterprise data warehouse, and all reporting is then run from the enterprise data warehouse. This provides one version of the data and one place to go to gather data from the multiple sources.

Enterprise Data Warehouse Architecture

Figure 1.4 Example of Enterprise Data Warehouse using SAP BW

It is not necessary that multiple BW instances or legacy data warehouses be used to gather the data in order to consolidate. Many projects also provide one enterprise data warehouse that gathers data directly from the various source systems without an intermediate BW system. The main goal is to consolidate data across the enterprise, and this can be implemented in many ways.

1.8.5 Competitive Advantage

It has long been known that better information can mean a huge competitive advantage in business. There is no better example than Wal-Mart. Wal-Mart has one of the most sophisticated IT departments in the world. It not only gathers its own but also collaborates with customers and vendors to provide forecasting, planning, and logistical information.

Through Wal-Mart's constant focus on better information and better visibility in all phases of its supply chain, the company has forced many other organizations to also increase their information requirements. Remember: Better analysis means better decision-making

1.8.6 Provide Flexible Analysis of Information Assets

ECC as a transactional system gets very few fundamental criticisms. The system is extremely well engineered and very flexible. The problems that organizations most frequently encounter with ECC are summed up in this quotation: "I know that the information that I need is somewhere in that huge system. I just can't seem to get it out."

BW is designed to help gather up this transactional data in a more meaningful and summarized way than ECC can provide. This gives the users the information that they need to analyze data. It should be noted that BW is not designed to provide simple flat reports that might be long and cumbersome to read and distribute.

BW is designed to present the data in a drill-down format that allows users to take the data and slice and dice in the fashion that makes the most sense for their analytical need. By pre-aggregating the data in a wide variety of ways, BW lends itself to flexible analysis and thus to better visibility of the voluminous data in both the ECC system and other legacy systems.

1.8.7 Business Information to More People in the Organization

Another advantage of BW is that by providing one common tool and one common place to look for information, you can make the data in the organization available to more people. You may not want a large population of users getting access to the transactions to perform accounts receivable and ordering activities in your organization. However, if this data is extracted and stored in a meaningful format elsewhere, you may choose to allow the access of this data for strategic and even operational analysis.

Because the reporting in BW can use one standard toolset, many users can be trained and have this functionality rolled out to them quickly. If the same users went to the transactional system reporting for this data, they would be forced to learn a variety of transaction codes to get the reports they desire. BW allows these reports to be rolled out in a consistent format on an enterprise portal and even as web reports.

SAP ECC or R/3 does not excel at providing strategic analysis of transactional data. It cannot easily provide the organization with comparisons, trending, and graphing that is needed for strategic decision-making. Without a great deal of customization, ECC cannot provide the strategic data in a usable format that most companies need. It works well with the operational reports such as, "Give me all the deliveries that shipped yesterday." What it does not quickly and easily answer is, "What were my total sales for this product in the state of Pennsylvania last year vs. this year?"

ECC keeps data at its most detailed form. In other words, virtually all data stored in ECC is at the transactional level. Thus, in order to perform aggregated high-level reporting, the data must be aggregated by an ECC report each time the report is run.

For example, in the report described above— "What were my total sales for this product in the state of Pennsylvania last year vs. this year?"—the system would have to go into the multiple sales tables, headers, detail and other fields, gather up the various sales, filter out those for the state of Pennsylvania, and gather this data for two years.

Once the user finally gets back the totals that they requested, the next question the user might ask is: "Now let's see the same comparison for New Jersey." The system must then plow through the same volume of data to provide this analysis. Because each of these reports takes place on the transactional system, the transactional database server must be tuned to allow fast entry and saving of these transactions to provide the quickest turnaround of the system for the next transaction.

The gathering of the data in an aggregated format requires an on-the-fly joining of the data. In the case of analyzing the sales data in ECC for the state of New Jersey, this can mean joining up of 15–20 separate tables, gathering of data, sifting out the records that are irrelevant, and providing those sales for only New Jersey. This is a big load on the transactional system. Typically, this reporting would take place during the work day, at the same time the organization needs to process transactions. Thus, organizations limit the use of the transactional systems (typically ECC) for large-volume data analysis.

We also should note that most large organizations do not have all data in ECC. Thus, only one small picture of the entire organization would be reported if all strategic analysis were done in ECC. Because BW allows for data to be brought in from many different DataSources, this provides a clearer and more complete picture of the enterprise. One of the most important features of BW is that this data can be harmonized so that during reporting and analysis the user does not need to be aware, or even care about the original source of the data.

1.9 Why Not Another Data Warehouse?

There are several reasons why SAP customers choose BW over other third-party data warehouse software. Let's examine these reasons in the subsections that follow.

1.9.1 Data Extraction From ECC is Much Easier with BW

In each ECC system, there is a package installed called a *plug-in*. These plug-ins can vary in their release levels and breadth of functionality, but each performs the same task. The plug-in houses the BW DataSouces. A DataSource is a pre-delivered package on the ECC system designed to extract data for loading into BW. The advantages of these DataSources are vast. SAP has already provided an easy path to take data out of ECC and into BW. In the ECC 6.0 version, the plug-in has been eliminated; the DataSources are incorporated as part of the releases of this version.

If the external data warehouse package cannot take advantage of the BW DataSources, the effort becomes burdensome. In the absence of these DataSources, the data must be extracted manually out of the ECC system. This is not an easy task in a relational database system. Often, complex function modules and ABAP programs are required to extract and gather the ECC data in a meaningful way.

A great deal of knowledge is required to gather data from the various tables in ECC and extract this data in a consistent form. The DataSources perform the task of gathering data for extraction. This significant task makes the implementation of BW much easier than it would be for another data-warehouse software package.

1.9.2 BW is Already Part of the Landscape

In most cases, BW is already owned (and paid for) as part of the licensing of the ECC system. When an organization already owns the software, it makes little fiscal sense to purchase another data-warehouse software package. Thus, many opt to use SAP BW for their data analysis and data warehousing needs.

Those who do not choose to use BW sometimes take a hybrid approach to data warehousing in the organization. They may use the DataSources in BW to gather data from ECC and use functionality in BW called the *open hub* or *InfoSpoke* to extract the data out of BW and load this to another data-warehouse software package.

This technique is typically employed only by companies that already have a non-BW data-warehouse package. Often, they need to provide some data from ECC to an existing data warehouse, but do not want to migrate to SAP BW. In these cases, the company might decide that the lengthy learning curve and implementation costs of transitioning completely to SAP BW from their legacy data warehouse make it too difficult. Otherwise, BW is often used as the enterprise data warehouse.

1.9.3 BW is the Foundation for Most NetWeaver Products

BW should be the cornerstone for many more products in the future. Some of the products that rely on BW include, but are not limited to: Customer Relationship Management (CRM), Advanced Planner and Optimizer (APO), Strategic Enterprise Management (SEM), and Supply Chain Management (SCM). Simply put, many existing and new products exist either in conjunction with or completely outside of the ECC transactional environment. The reporting for these packages are usually best performed in the BW environment rather than its source.

> **Example**
> SAP APO is used for creating plans for manufacturing or procuring products. This planning data is only useful if it is compared to actual data for analysis of the accuracy of the plan and for budgetary and manufacturing purposes. The actual data resides in BW because this data is fed from the ECC transactional system.

To compare the actual data to the plan data, the plan data is extracted from the APO system and combined with the actual data extracted from the ECC system and used for reporting. The end user does not need to be aware of the source of this data, because plan and actual data are presented together in BW.

In the absence of BW, the user would be forced to go to APO for the planned data, then to the ECC system to get the actual data and then manually harmonize and compare this data. This would be quite labor-intensive. It also forces APO to do something that it was not intended to do. APO is designed for planning. BW is designed for reporting. By passing the data from APO to BW, we take advantages of the strengths of both products.

1.10 What BW is Not Designed to Do

A complete understanding of BW includes understanding what BW is not designed to do, and the tasks at which BW does not excel. Read the following subsections to understand what BW is not.

1.10.1 BW is Not a Transactional System

Transactions should all be performed in the source systems and BW will capture the transactional and associated master data values from these transactions. The best projects make it clear from the beginning that BW is not the system of record for data. The system of record in the organization continues to live in the transactional systems that feed BW. In most cases this is ECC, but it could be any other legacy system.

Projects fall into a trap when they try to use BW to perform transactions. Sometimes this comes in the terms of fixing missing data. For example, they ask: "Can't we just load the data into a table in BW, manually fix that table, and then load the data into an InfoCube in BW?" The answer to this kind of request should *always* be "No." Alter the data in the source system in its original source transactions and the changed data can then flow into BW. BW is simply not designed as a transactional system for data.

Another common request is to provide transactions in BW for entering data, or for tracking it against other data already in BW. Because BW is not designed to be a transactional system, these requests should be implemented in the transactional systems. Once these processes have been implemented in the transactional systems, BW can be used to extract and store this data and even provide some analysis of the data. The main goal is to keep BW as an analytical system and not as a transactional system.

The more BW's focus gets drawn away from its core value of storing, staging, and presenting data in an aggregated form, the more problems can arise with the project. To avoid these situations, it is important that everyone working on the project understands that BW's role is to deliver information and that all transactions take place on the source system.

The only exception to this rule is planning. BW does allow for planning transactions to take place directly in the BW system. This allows the user to enter planning data. This planning data is saved directly into the BW environment for analysis. Planning is usually done in a very limited set of circumstances in BW. This planning must be configured through either NW 2004s Integrated Planning module or Business Process and Simulation (BPS) functions in BW.

For example, while analyzing the current year's actual sales values, it may be necessary to also plan next year's projected sales figures. This planning is performed by entering this planned data directly into the system. Although this is a transactional entry, it can and usually does occur in the BW system itself.

1.10.2 BW is Not the Only Reporting System

Although BW does provide reporting it should not be considered the only place to provide reporting in the organization. The source system's reporting is not automatically replaced by BW. For example, a report such as *Credit Hold Orders* that shows all orders currently on credit hold is a report that would be better run in the ECC system than BW. BW is typically updated in batch mode once a day. Information on which orders are on credit hold usually needs to be up to the minute. This report would not work well in BW.

It is imperative that your organization understands that BW does provide reporting, but there will always be some reporting requirements that should be met in the source transactional system. This situation will never go away. Not all reporting requirements are automatically BW requirements.

1.10.3 BW is Not Usually Updated in Real-Time

BW was designed as a batch system to gather data from source systems. In fact, if you were to survey all customers and their data in BW, you would find that more than 99 percent of the data arrives in batch, not via real-time loading.

Recently introduced functionality has allowed BW to get some data near real time. This should only be used in the applications that absolutely require very up-to-date, fresh reporting. Usually this real-time reporting is better handled directly in the source system.

It is a significant challenge to verify the validity of real-time data, simply because the data is so dynamic. Users often have trouble performing analysis because the underlying data is changing even as the report is being run. A quick refresh of the data could yield completely new results. This can make for a difficult environment for decision-making. For this and other reasons, many companies prefer an analysis method geared more toward a place in time than toward real time.

Extracting data in real time or in near to real time can involve difficult configuration and decision-making. To avoid confusion, it is usually recommended that teams with new projects not even talk about real-time reporting in BW. They should convey the fact that BW does not do real-time reporting at all.

This avoids confusion and assumptions that people new to BW sometimes make. If those gathering the business requirements assume that the data is updated in real time in BW as a rule, their analysis requirements reflect this real-time requirement. If, on the other hand, everyone assumes that BW is not real-time but rather updated at most once a day, the BW team can deal case by case with any circumstance where the data needs to be updated more frequently. In practice, this need turns out to be extremely rare.

1.10.4 BW is Not a Silver Bullet

Let's take a simple example to illustrate this premise.

> **Example**
>
> A large company wanted to use BW to provide global reporting. The company had a very complex environment with many different source systems. These source systems included multiple implementations of ECC and several legacy systems. Therefore, the company wanted BW to help provide some global reporting from these systems.

BW is a perfect solution to provide the kind of reporting described in the example. However, this company thought that simply by implementing BW it would automatically get global reporting. The company did not clearly understand that BW can bring in data from many different sources, and this data can then exist together in one BW system. In order to have true global reporting, the data from the various sources must be harmonized into one common master data and transactional DataSource.

This can be quite a daunting task in some organizations. In this particular company, the different ECC systems used different material codes for the same material. One ECC system called a product A1, while a second ECC system called the same product F1. Clearly, this data cannot be reported together as one unless there is some link between the two products.

This rule is also true for transactional data. There is no easy way to combine transactional data from many different systems with different configurations. Thus, a transformation process is required in BW to create the harmonization, and in many cases this can be quite tedious.

When this company realized the level of effort required in BW, it was rather frustrated with what it perceived as a limitation of the BW product. I pointed out that there was no system that can automatically harmonize and combine data from multiple sources. Any data warehouse would require this work in order to bring this data together.

1.11 Ingredients for a Successful SAP BW Project Manager

Now that you understand what the product is and what it does well, you can focus on how to implement BW. The first step in any BW project is to pick a BW project manager. Nothing is more integral to the success or failure of a BW project than the project manager. The project manager's many responsibilities are as follows:

- Gather requirements from business users
- Set priorities among business requirements
- Build a capable BW team
- Oversee extraction data from various systems
- Implement BW functionality to stage, store, and present information
- Communicate BW scope and functionality to the organization
- Manage and organize transports between systems
- Manage testing and validation
- Track and resolve issues
- Coordinate go-lives
- Manage production support transition
- Filter, prioritize, and implement new requirements

The tasks shown in this bulleted list are diverse. These tasks require a broad skill set. The remaining pages in this section discuss the most important qualities of a BW project manager, in order to help you choose a project manager to manage your new project or upgrade. These skill sets are identical for a new implementation and for an upgrade project. This is because upgrade projects and new implementations go through the same tasks shown above, just at different levels of detail and timing.

1.11.1 Good Communication Skills

Communication skills are imperative when implementing any large-scale change in an organization. BW is no exception. A major part of implementing or upgrading BW is the selling of the system. It is up to the project manager to keep the steering committee, project sponsors, and business users in on the decision-making process of BW. These people must understand what will be delivered with BW and they must be involved, as much as possible, in order to give them some ownership of the system.

The only way to foster ownership among others is to make sure that there is constant communication about the implementation. This communication can come from status reports, one-on-one meetings, and even prototype demos of the system. The project manager should do anything to make sure that the BW project is not seen as an IT project run completely by the applications BW team. The goal is for the business and project sponsors to become part of the process so that when inevitable issues arise, they are willing to work together toward a common solution, rather than waiting for the BW implementation team to solve all issues.

Continued and ongoing prototype demonstrations and design interviews help ensure that there are no surprises during the eventual handoff of the system to the business users. The more involved the business users and project sponsors are during the planning and development process, the more the BW implementation will reflect their analysis needs.

It is not enough to simply foster the communication. The next step in the communication process is to have clear governance and documentation templates. These allow the BW team to speak with one voice to the business and other units of the organization. This helps stop the scope assumptions and limits the scope creep that can cripple a project or cause project delays.

Once the documentation is complete, the best projects also require signoff on all major documents to make sure that the understanding of the business requirements are clear to all involved. This does not completely prevent the scope and design issues that arise. However, the signoff does help to mitigate and reduce the confusion.

Part of the communication process is the selling of the BW project to the business. This involves generating excitement over the new features and functionality that may not currently be available in the reporting environment. After the initial implementation, the communication usually evolves into recruiting some *BW champions* in the organization to help get the word out about BW and create momentum in the organization. Simply put, the more users who rely on the tool and the more universal the acceptance of it, the more value in the implementation. This acceptance is only gained through awareness. The ultimate role of building this awareness falls on the BW project manager.

1.11.2 Knowledge of BW and Data Warehousing

There no way to avoid the need to understand the BW product and the various sources of data that are loaded into the system. Although this is not necessary right away, the quicker the project manager can become proficient with the BW system and the various source systems that feed BW, the more effective he or she will be.

This knowledge of the product helps when trying to quickly understand issues and their impact on the project. Suppose, for example, that a new requirement surfaces late in the development phase of the project. How quickly your project manager can determine the level of effort and impact of this change can help to determine if that requirement can be added to the scope of the project or delayed until a future phase of the project.

If the project manager has no BW knowledge, this new requirement must be communicated to a product specialist, scoped, assessed, and then communicated back to the project manager for a decision. This can add significant time to the project.

Product knowledge is especially helpful because it provides another set of eyes on the issues. This can lead to quicker resolution of a problem and, if needed, a more appropriate escalation of an issue because of the understanding of its impact. If possible, it helps if the BW project manager does some hands-on configuration of BW. Depending on the scope and timeline, this is not always possible, but the more detailed the knowledge of the manager the better the understanding of the issues faced.

> **Example**
>
> I worked with a BW project manager who bragged that he was going to complete and entire BW implementation without logging into the system. He did all he could to stay away from the actual product. He saw his job as *managing* a BW project. Despite my constant prompting, he did not want to know the specifics of the product. Thus, when issues would arise that we would have to escalate to SAP or the business management, it always slowed the process; we would have to explain the issue, explain the impact, and the severity. We found ourselves keeping the project manager out of many of the issues because it simply took too much time to keep him up to speed. This made for an extremely ineffective manager, and as a result the project moved slowly.

There are many sources that a product manager can go to for BW knowledge. The best place to start is with the SAP education tasks. At minimum, the manager should attend SAP BW classes on the following:

- Data warehousing
- Data modeling
- Data extraction
- Presentation

This will provide a background of the product that should aid in the decision-making process. Make sure significant time is allocated for this training. With the current structure of the classes listed above, this involves more than 18 days of training. When you factor in travel and schedule time for these classes, you realize there is a large time allocation for BW training. This illustrates the rather steep learning curve for the BW product.

It is very important to make sure that the classes are representative of the release that will be used for development and go-live. There is very little functionality difference between Versions 3.x and 3.5. Thus, those organizations that are planning a BW release in Versions 3.0, 3.1, or 3.5 can attend the 3.x training. Any customer that plans to use the NW 2004s release of BW should make sure that the class is specifically tailored to this release. There are rather significant changes between the 3.x releases and the NW 2004s release.

The next source of information on any project should come from the product and implementation know-how of the consultants on the project. As a consultant, I always feel that my number one priority is knowledge transfer. This is an advantage in many ways for me. If I can make sure the project manager and other employees are competent with the system, it makes issue resolution much easier and allows the client to take responsibility for issues and design concerns. It also means that when I leave, I feel confident that the BW team can satisfactorily manage the system and deal with the inevitable issues that arise.

A good project ensures that there is time allocated throughout the implementation process to allow for this knowledge transfer. I have worked at many projects where I am told that my number one job is to make sure the employees (not the consultants) are doing the actual BW configuration. However, the timeline does not allow time for me to keep the employees up to speed on the configuration that is needed. Thus, the project ends up being almost completely consultant led and executed, with employees watching the configuration and helping with the documentation.

> **Note**
> If the deliverables are the number one concern, then knowledge transfer is usually not considered a deliverable. This is a mistake. Knowledge sharing should always be considered a deliverable.

When it is time for consultants to be moved off the project, some project managers expect several months or even a few years' worth of knowledge transfer will take place in a few weeks. With a consultant who has one foot out the door, this will not happen. A roll-off knowledge transfer simply does not take place with the quality that would occur if the employees are part of the configuration from the beginning, have some ownership of the configuration, and stay involved in the process.

1.11.3 Knowledge of Business Processes and Analysis Goals

Knowing the business analysis goals can sometimes be a daunting task for a project manager. Many times even the organization itself does not completely understand its goals for data analysis. It is the job of the project manager to make sure that these goals are clearly defined and the implementation of the BW system satisfies those goals. Thus, the more the project manager knows the business, the better he or she is able to be a voice for the business in the scoping and implementation of BW.

I have worked with some outstanding project managers who can quickly understand and evaluate the business user's requirements and help to explain them to the BW team. I usually know project managers are especially effective when I hear them say: "The business users may say they want X, but I know what they really want is X+1 or even Y." I should note that this is not replacing the user's needs with something they do not want, but more clearly understanding the goals of the business and helping them to get their needs communicated to the team.

It is this type of understanding of both the BW tool and the business users' needs that help to make sure that the business is not only satisfied but also delighted with the implementation of the BW product.

Knowledge of the organization is also helpful when there are leveraging opportunities. There are many circumstances where two groups in the organization are looking for the same type of information, but with a slightly different view. BW is outstanding at providing this kind of flexibility. Knowing the business helps to get several groups interested in the BW data. This not only expands the user base, but also helps in funding the project across the organization.

1.11.4 The Need for Political Savvy

There is no way to avoid these inevitable political issues. BW projects usually are quite political. This is because ownership of information in an organization makes one's position more powerful. BW, if implemented properly, can be a powerful tool.

Setting the scope and priority of any project can cause political battles in many organizations. I have witnessed many projects delayed because of simple decisions that could not be made due to an intensely political environment. Failure to properly escalate or champion issues though the political environment of any organization can cause significant delays that adversely affect the project. The project manager must be able to negotiate through these political hurdles.

> **Example**
> I consulted with a client in an early stage of a BW implementation. They spent several months deciding where their development and production servers should be physically located. This decision does not add any value to the implementation. However, in this organization, the location of the servers denoted the ownership of the box. This translated into resources for the technical and sustaining organizations. Each group was fighting for the servers to be located in their location in order to get some of that budget money.

The problem in the case described in this example, was not as much the fight, but the length of time that this delayed the project. The BW project manager felt that this battle was too political and outside his domain. He decided the best approach was to wait until the various technical groups determined the location for the servers. This decision lasted a long time, and we wasted a great deal of time when we could have been productive. If the project manager had a clear path to the steering committee and/or project sponsors, they could have escalated this issue and forced a quicker decision, thus saving time and money.

The opposite is also true. Not including groups in discussions or not following the proper escalation channels can also land a project in a difficult situation. I have been in many situations where potential allies in the implementation process were alienated early in the project because of a political squabble and thus did not give our project team the extra help we could have used later.

The project manager also needs to be able to balance the team's strengths. For example, the best use of a BW developer's time is as a tool to aid in the implementation of the BW product. Typically, developers like to stay close to the product and work on the system because they do not like the day-to-day project management and the political struggles that come with a project. The better the project manager is able to keep these political issues from the developers and keep them focused on delivering and implementing the software, the more productive the team will be.

Often, you can spot a well-run project when developers find out about large political issues only after completion. This means that the project manager was sheltering the developers from those battles and keeping the team focused on delivering the BW system.

Keeping this delicate balance is a very difficult and often overlooked talent that a BW project manager must possess. However, the more politically in tune this manager is with his or her surroundings, the more efficient the entire implementation of BW can become.

1.11.5 Highly Organized and Quality Minded

The multitude of issues, meetings, and requirements that are involved with a typical BW project requires a detailed and organized and quality-minded individual. Developing a methodology to track requirements and issues is vital to a successful project.

1.11.6 Willing and Able to Develop and Enforce Standards

Any BW project should be considered a foundation for the future. To ensure that this foundation is sound, governance must be established to make sure that the decisions of the past do not cause issues in the future. For instance, naming standards are very important in BW. The system allows for an extremely flexible naming of the InfoCubes and DSO structures.

It is up to the project manager to not only make sure that the naming standards are developed but also that these same standards are enforced in the BW implementation.

As the number of InfoCubes and DSOs grow, the naming conventions become more important to track and understand the contents and purpose of the data in an InfoCube or DSO. The naming of the DSO and InfoCubes can also be used for security and authorizations. Thus, a well thought-out naming standards document and enforcement of the standards can make for easier authorizations.

Many projects wind up with a naming standards document that is not enforced. One project I reviewed had a naming standards document, yet most of the InfoProviders (InfoCubes and DSOs) did not follow the standards because there was no enforcement. Later the project team wanted to implement security based on their naming standards for each InfoProvider but, because of the lack of governance, it was much more difficult. These standards need to be built and enforced by the project manager.

1.11.7 Team Building

Building a good BW team is a critical task for the project manager. Keeping a good mix between consultant resources and employee resources, and making sure these personalities work well together and fit into the overall corporate culture, is very important. The project manager must be able to choose a productive team. This team consists of a BW internal team and an external team. Let us discover what is involved in building these teams next.

Building an Internal Team

In a typical BW project there are two main groups helping on the implementation. These are considered *internal team* members, because they are performing the day-to-day implementation of the product.

These are usually called the applications and Basis teams. The applications team is focused on the day-to-day configuration of the BW product. This includes the configuration, loading, testing of the product. The Basis team handles the infrastructure of the implementation. This includes creating the environment, handling transports, patches, administering security, upgrades, etc.

The Basis and applications teams have a fundamental conflict in their goals. The Basis team is responsible for keeping the system at a stable, steady state, with maximum uptime. The applications team, when performing large data loads in BW, can test the limits of the system environments in memory and disk space, thus placing a strain on the Basis goals of maximum uptime and steady state. This can cause conflict in some teams between the Basis and applications teams.

In a typical project, the Basis team and BW application team must work together more closely than the ECC teams and their Basis counterparts. This is because of the nature of the BW product. It requires the Basis team to aid in connecting to the various source systems and handling file management, index creation, transport issues between systems, etc.

The project manager needs to bridge the gap between the Basis and applications team, and aid in the issue tracking and issue resolution between the two teams. This will help make sure that the ownership of issues is clear and the constant communication keeps the priority issues on track for resolution.

Building an External Team

All projects have not only a BW implementation team but also have various stakeholders who guide the requirements for the BW project. Identifying and keeping these stakeholders part of the extended BW team is very important in making sure that stakeholders are satisfied with the implementation. These stakeholders might take the form of sponsors, users, managers, or other individuals or groups that have a stake in the success (or failure) of the BW project.

The project manager must be able to understand the stakeholders' motivations and goals and make sure the BW project meets the various changing needs of these extended team members.

1.11.8 Budget Accountability

BW as with every project has budget concerns. These include hardware, consulting, application, and production support. There are no available figures that detail the average total budget amounts for BW projects. However, there are some surveys that give these figures for data warehouses in general. BW projects are generally large, as compared to a typical data warehouse, because the volume of the source data is usually rather large.

The BW budget, like the ECC budget, is usually set at the beginning of the project before the scope is clearly established. As the scope gets more refined, the budget is typically not in line with the requirements. This means the BW project manager is forced to re-allocate the resources based on the budget that has been allocated or seek to redefine the budget.

1.11.9 Willing to Say Both "Yes" and "No"

This is where the project manager needs to walk a very fine line. If scope is set too rigidly and no changes are allowed, opportunities can be missed. For instance, a minor change in BW could allow for a much more useful environment. I worked on a project building a sales reporting environment. We did not have any cost information planned into our InfoCubes, because it was originally deemed out of scope. However, late in the implementation process, the cost values were requested by the project sponsor.

Adding the cost values to the InfoCubes would not have involved a large effort, but the scope was very rigid, and the project manager declined the request. If the project manager had paused and assessed the workload of the new change, we could have included a much larger user base in BW. In turn, we would have made BW more useful to the organization without a large budget impact. We were already planning a full regression test on the BW data. This testing could easily have been adapted to include the costing figures and costing requirements.

There is another side to the same story. On one project, each small change that was requested was incorporated into the scope, even as we were late in the build phase of the project. This caused us many more hours of work as we added the new requirements and re-tested the changes needed to fulfill the scope. For many of these requests, the project manager should have said "No" or should have taken time to reassess the scope as a whole rather than adding each request individually.

The only way to handle these requests is to have scope clearly documented. Thus, any new requirement can be clearly shown to be out of scope. All initial judgment should be withheld until a formal scope-management process can assess impact and benefit. Only through a formal process can a decision be made to include or exclude a request. The project manager is the one to head up the authorization of these requests.

1.12 Summary

In this chapter, I tried to give you a practical understanding of what is involved in a typical BW project lifecycle. I hope that you can plan your own BW implementation project with knowledge of the potential pitfalls. After reading this chapter, you should know what BW can and cannot do and what your organization and project manager should be prepared for.

Now, we can proceed to Chapter 2, in which we will look at defining an implementation strategy.

"Strategy is a style of thinking, a conscious and deliberate process, an intensive implementation system, the science of insuring future success."
– Pete Johnson

2 Defining an Implementation Strategy

The first step in a project is to set the overall strategy. There are many factors that go into these decisions. Understanding the process and pitfalls in setting the strategy can make sure a project has the best opportunity for success.

A BW implementation strategy is a series of useful plans, steps, and actions in order to arrive at a clear and effective use of the BW product. An implantation strategy of BW can become quite complex. There are many factors involved in the decision making.

Common decisions that make up the implementation strategy involve scope, resources, technology, politics, culture, and change management. A sound implementation strategy should be able to answer the following questions:

- Who can leverage and get the most advantage from implementing BW?
- What are the business questions that BW is to help answer? What are the assumptions?
- What are the business and project risks?
- Is there sufficient commitment and involvement from the steering committee, project sponsors, and user community?
- What is the scope of the data that will be in BW?
- How will the current reporting enviornment be affected? Will it be retained, phased out, or replaced?
- What are the volume and sources of the data to be loaded into BW?
- How granular is the data to be in BW, and what is the frequency of the update of data?
- What type of presentation is expected for the end users?

- What SAP ECC data is in scope? Is BW being implemented at the same time as ECC? Is BW going live at the same time as ECC? How will BW interact with ECC?
- Who will be implenting BW? How will these people become proficient with the product?
- What time frame is expected for BW?
- How is the scope to be documented and how will this be communicated to the business community?
- What is the technical landscape: hardware, software, network, etc?
- What testing and validation will be required?
- What production support will be planned after go-live?

2.1 Defining an Upgrade Strategy

A sound upgrade strategy should be able to answer the following questions:

- What version will be implemented?
- Why are we implementing the new version?
- What is the technical landscape? Will the upgrade take place in a new development environment, or will the upgrade take place on the common development environment?
- What is the timeline for the upgrade?
- What new functionality (if any) will be implemented immediately?
- What testing and validation are required?
- How does the upgrade affect other components of BW?
- Is a conversion function needed to use new functionality in the release?
- How does this affect other components in the landscape? Will other components need to be upgraded too?
- What are the plug-in requirements in the ECC system for this upgrade?

2.1.1 Landscape Strategy

The new system landscape strategy involves the following:

- The number of systems in the BW landscape
- The purpose of each system

- Strategy for keeping the systems synchronized
- Strategy for development
- Srategy for production support

The choice of the landscape for the BW environment is one of the most important decisions made in a BW implementation. In BW, as with ECC, systems are set up, each with their own purpose. The typical systems and their purpose in a BW landscape strategy are as follows:

- **Development**
  As the name implies, the development system is the BW system where all new configuration and development is performed. Everything that will be eventually rolled out to the production user will begin here.
- **Testing and Quality Assurance (QA)**
  Transports from the development environment typically land here first. All validation testing of the configuration takes place here before it is moved to production.
- **Production**
  The production instance. This is where all *live* analysis will occur.
- **Training**
  This is an optional system used to train the end users.
- **Sandbox**
  This is an optional system used for prototyping and *playing*.
- **Production Support**
  This is an optional system used for testing production issues. This system is refreshed by copying the production system periodically.

There are several important elements that you can incorporate into your landscape strategy that will make a positive impact on your project. My recommendations for developing a landscape strategy are given in the subsections that follow.

Insist on a Sandbox System

When a BW landscape is being determined, many feel that a sandbox is a luxury. They feel that having a three-tiered landscape environment (Development, QA, and Production) is enough to satisfy the needs of the development team.

The main advantage to the three-tiered landscape option shown in Figure 2.1 is in its simplicity. There are only three systems to install, maintain, back up, etc. This is the least expensive landscape option from a maintenance standpoint. It works fine if there is an extremely simple project with a tight timeline and a well-understood scope.

DEV QA PRD

Figure 2.1 Typical Three-Tiered Landscape in BW

However, this is rarely the case. Most configuration in BW requires some level of prototyping and building up of several scenarios to determine which is best. In the environment seen in Figure 2.1, there is no sandbox system for performing these prototypes. Because these are needed, the only place to do them is in the development system.

Quickly, the development system can become filled with many different prototypes and test objects, which pollute the environment with much unneeded configuration. The best way to prevent this is to have a sandbox system that allows configuration outside of the development environment.

I worked with a client who had a Basis BW sandbox but no development sandbox. In other words, they wanted a sandbox to be used to test support packages, upgrades, etc. only. This sandbox was not to be used for configuration testing. We could not convince the Basis team that this added little value to the project.

They did not understand that any testing of support packages and upgrades needs to occur in conjunction with the development team and that having one sandbox for both teams would have made for a more useful prototyping environment for both the Basis and the development teams.

Figure 2.2 shows a landscape environment including a sandbox. In this environment, prototyping and testing can occur in the sandbox system outside of the development system and away from the final configuration.

Figure 2.2 Typical BW Environment Using a Sandbox

Unlike ECC or R/3, BW does not support a multi-client system for doing some testing. For example, in ECC it is possible to create another client on an existing development system that could be used for some configuration and/or testing without impacting the development client. These clients allow for separate sets of master and transactional data on the ECC system using the same set of configuration.

This is not possible in BW. BW allows only one client per BW instance or system. This is an important distinction and one that somewhat limits the BW system because multiple clients allow a lot more flexibility in the ECC or R/3 systems.

Since there is no way to have multiple clients, and because we do need an area for prototyping, a completely stand-alone sandbox system should be created for the prototyping.

> **Tip**
> Any BW project with significant scope should have a sandbox for prototyping.

Of course, this sandbox can be refreshed as often as needed. This usually is accomplished via a client copy from either the development or the QA system. The assumption is that any configuration done in the sandbox will need to be manually replicated in the development instance.

The process of sending a configuration from one BW system to another is called the transport process. This allows for the approved configuration to be moved from the development system to the QA system and then onto the production system. This is designed to make sure that only the functionality that was approved moves to the production and/or QA systems. The sandbox system is designed strictly for prototyping, therefore, transports should never be created from the sandbox system.

It must be clearly understood that any configuration done in the sandbox is fleeting and can be lost at any time to a system refresh. I have worked with team members who did not know of an impending refresh and lost their work. As long as this is understood and the refresh schedule is clearly posted, this is typically not an issue.

Figure 2.3 BW Landscape with Sandbox, Production Support, and Training Systems

Figure 2.3 shows a complete BW environment including a sandbox. This is called a five-system landscape because the sandbox is not typically counted as part of the landscape. It is a stand-alone system that is not part of the transport path.

2.1.2 Think About the Training Environment

Training in BW is a task that is often not planned until well into the project lifecycle. This is a mistake. Because the configuration typically is not in production until cutover, training on new BW functionality must occur outside of the production system. There are two popular strategies to provide BW training:

- Use the Development or QA system for training
- Have a separate training system

There are ramifications to both options. If you plan to provide the training on the development or QA system, conflicts inevitably occur. The queries, InfoCubes, DSO, and master data objects that are needed for training must be filled with valid data and kept fairly inactive during the training. This can be difficult for projects with tight schedules.

Constant changes make for a very dynamic environment. To make matters worse, some of the configuration changes needed in BW require data to be dumped and reloaded. All these factors mean that things are never at a steady state during the development and testing process.

To provide training, a steady state is needed. This causes conflict between the training group that is looking for a static environment to build test exercises, screen shots, etc., and the BW development team that is trying to complete the BW configuration. Essentially, this means that most development on these objects must stop during training.

The only way to alleviate this issue is with a separate, stand-alone training system. Figure 2.3 gave you a view of this landscape. Many companies opt for this landscape in order to have a static place for training. In my experience, this is usually the best option, but there are some drawbacks.

At some point you must build the training system from the QA or development system based on the configuration at a certain point in time. Any changes after that time are not automatically reflected in the training system because that system must be at a steady state in which transports will not change the configuration.

Therefore, some of the issues that have been fixed in the development and QA systems are not included in training. These usually need to be manually fixed or worked around during training. The other most important factor is the time it takes to build a separate training instance. Most projects underestimate the amount of time it takes to get the training system ready.

The end users are getting their first view of BW in this training environment, so it is very important to have this system perform as strongly as possible. This sometimes means creating manual flat file feeds to fill master data tables and InfoCubes/DSO in the training environment because the connected source systems do not yet have valid data.

Some level of performance tuning and testing should also occur on this training system. This is to ensure that the users have a positive view of the system during the training.

These efforts can be quite time-consuming. This significant time dedicated to training keeps the development team away from their development work and testing tasks, and thus can affect the schedule.

> **Tip**
>
> Significant time should be built into the project plan to build the training environment.

As long as the time can be dedicated to this environment, having a separate training system is the approach least disruptive to the project and the one that allows for more successful training of end users.

2.1.3 Adding a Production Support System

Some companies also opt for another system in their environment called a production support system, as shown in Figure 2.3. This system is usually a complete copy of the production system that is refreshed periodically.

This stand-alone production support instance would allow for some limited prototyping and issue testing. For example, suppose a production support issue is reported in the sales InfoCube with return orders for a specific material type. There are very few valid returns in the QA system, and none for that material type. We could attempt to create one in the ECC QA system, but, we might not be able to replicate it exactly.

Thus, in a scenario where there is little production data in a QA environment, it becomes difficult to test production support issues. This is because the data needed to replicate is simply not in the QA environment, and it can be very cumbersome to try to create a specific scenario.

There is no better way of replicating the specific issue than with a copy of the production environment. The production support system serves as that copy. Typically this system is open for configuration so scenarios can be tried to fix problems.

> **Tip**
>
> There should be no transports from the production support system. It is simply used as a system on which to test and re-test issues and prototypes with production data.

Periodic refreshes should occur to keep this system as close to production as possible. For a more complete environment, insist on a production support system in your BW landscape. This system allows for quicker problem resolution and more complete prototyping of scenarios, and thus for a better overall environment for end users.

2.1.4 Keep Development, QA, Production Environments in Sync

One of the most important tasks in maintaining separate systems in a landscape is to keep them in sync. If these systems are not in sync, it is very difficult to troubleshoot configuration, transports, and technical issues. If a function is working in development and QA, there is no reason that the same function should not work in production. If this is not the case, and the problem is not data related, the problem is usually that the systems are out of sync. This can happen for many reasons. For example, changes made to one environment may not have been performed in another. These changes can be manual changes or even transport changes.

> **Tip**
> Never, never, never let anyone pollute the environment by allowing configuration in a client other than the development client.

How can we keep these systems in sync to avoid wasting time chasing issues when something works in one environment and inexplicably does not work in another? The answer lies in having strict rules to make sure that all changes are performed in each system.

This recommendation sounds rather obvious. Anyone who has done any ECC or R/3 development knows that you would never perform any development in a client other than the development client. However, I find it amazing that so many are willing to create exceptions to the rule.

Here is a typical scenario that causes someone to allow the landscape environment to be compromised, even if it unintentionally. A BW developer is trying to build a rather complex InfoCube. He needs to perform significant transformation of data to arrive at a specified calculation and characteristic data in an InfoCube. This requires many iterations of testing to get the configuration correct.

The development system is linked to the development ECC system, therefore all the data that is fed to the development system comes from this system. The developer cannot test his work in development because the real data that he needs to verify the configuration is only found in the production ECC system or QA system. Security and space requirements prevent the Basis team from connecting the production or QA ECC system to the development BW system, and so there is no way to test the new InfoCube transformation.

The developer could simply make a best attempt at the configuration, transport to QA or production, load the data there, and then—if results are incorrect—re-transport, etc. However, this adds a lot of time to the development process.

This is the point at which many project managers allow the development in the QA or productive environment. They ask for promises that any work that

2 | Defining an Implementation Strategy

is done is then put into the development environment and transported again. They think that this will keep the systems in sync. They then ask the Basis system team to open up the QA or production system for configuration temporarily. Opening up the system is a simple process using Transactions SCC4 and SE06 that Basis performs to allow the manual configuration in these environments.

What inevitably happens is that as developers begin to get sloppy they either forget or do not want to be bothered with making sure that all changes done go back to the development system. There is also the risk that they inadvertently change things in the QA or production system without really understanding the changes.

> **Note**
> Any time that you allow any manual configuration in any system other than the development system, you risk allowing the systems to get out of sync. Later this can cause hours of work and troubleshooting issues.

There is one notable exception to this rule. Periodically, issues with transports necessitate allowing spot fixes in the QA or production environment. Read the section later in this chapter on transport strategies to understand more about this exception.

2.1.5 Assess New Phases of Development

New phases and releases of BW cause the BW landscape environment to become more complex. Issues and conflicts occur when you try to do new development in the production support landscape.

> **Example**
> We have a BW landscape like the one we saw depicted in Figure 2.2. We have gone live with the BW system and everything is going well, users are active in our production environment, and the organization is happy. After the system stabilizes, they give us a list of things that they also want implemented into the BW system. We decide to implement these changes and features and call it the resulting system *BW Release Two*.

We can start doing the Release Two development directly into the BW development system shown in Figure 2.2. However, some conflicts can occur with that strategy. If I have done some Release Two configuration changes to the productive sales InfoCube and later get a call from the users that there is a production problem with the very same InfoCube, I have an issue to resolve.

68

The changes that I have already done for the new development are not yet ready to go into production. However, we need to fix and transport the InfoCube in order to fix the production problem. How do we fix the production issue but still keep my newest configuration?

We must first back out any configuration changes to the InfoCube for Release Two, make the change needed for the production support issue, test, and transport the change up to production. We then have to reconfigure the release two configuration back into the InfoCube. This can get very cumbersome if there are multiple production issues with that InfoCube.

We cannot simply avoid the issue by taking the InfoCube, DSO structure, and/or master data object and copy them to newly named DSO, InfoCube, or master data objects. If we try to do this, we would have to implement a new InfoCube, DSO, and/or master data object each time we have any changes to these objects.

This is not practical. Changing an InfoCube technical name means switching the base cube name, which causes all InfoCube queries and favorites from the users to become invalid because they were built on the old technical InfoCube name. This would cause a disruption for the users as their favorites and bookmarks would no longer function and would have to be rebuilt.

The solution to this problem is to create a Release Two development and QA environment. This environment shown in Figure 2.4 and is used for new development. All configuration for Release Two occurs in the DEV2 system. All QA testing for Release Two occurs in the QA2 system.

Figure 2.4 Release Two Development Environment Showing Dual Development and Dual QA

2 | Defining an Implementation Strategy

This allows independent configuration of the system, while still allowing production support to take place. This is a very popular landscape strategy where production support is outsourced to another group. The production support group *owns* the DEV1, DEV2, and the Production (PRD) systems, while the new development team *owns* the DEV2, and QA2 systems.

This landscape design raises an important question: How do changes made to the production support environment get into the new development environment? The answer is that any production support fixes or changes are manually added to the new development environment. This is because we cannot transport from one development to another development without a lot of analysis, and this can even be impossible if the two development releases are on different BW versions.

A process must be put in place to track the production support changes and make sure that these get into the new BW development environment.

Once new development is complete, you are ready to cut over the new development landscape. For this, you shut down production temporarily, transport the new development into the production system, and retire the DEV1 and QA1 systems. The DEV2 and QA2 systems now become the production support environment.

If a release three development is needed, we make DEV1 and QA1 the new development landscape. During cutover, the DEV2 and QA2 are now retired and DEV1 and QA1 become the production support environment. We keep switching back and forth between the systems to allow development and production support to continue simultaneously.

The disadvantage to this approach is that there are more systems to maintain and support. However, this disadvantage is far outweighed by the flexibility of the landscape, if the new development is significant.

> **Note**
>
> If new development is minor, use the development system to perform changes, and manually back-out changes if needed for production support. If the release is significant, create a new development system as shown in Figure 2.4. Upgrades typically require a Release Two-type landscape strategy.

Figure 2.5 showed a Release Two landscape and cutover. This type of landscape is typically required during an upgrade. This is because we must upgrade the system, test the new release, and run regression tests on all parts of the system to make sure that the current configuration still works after the upgrade.

The DEV1 and QA1 systems are retired and the DEV2 and QA2 systems now become the production support systems

Figure 2.5 Release Two Cutover

Unless BW can be shut down during the upgrade, there is really no clear way to provide an upgraded system and also perform testing. When the testing is complete, the production environment is shut down and upgraded. The DEV1 and QA1 systems on the old release are then retired after the production system has been upgraded. Some customers need to perform an upgrade to an existing environment. There are also several specific decisions that need to be made when determining the upgrade landscape.

2.2 Upgrade Landscape

An upgrade landscape refers to the series of systems that will be used to house the new development and production support when the system is being upgraded to a new BW release. Because an existing environment is already in place, many decisions need to be made. A further challenge is that sending transports between systems of different releases is not a recommended practice

The main focus of the upgrade effort should be on understanding how the upgrade can least affect the users who are using the system in production. Keeping this in mind, you need to make sure the upgrade can be fully implemented and tested in a stand-alone environment, away from the end users. This allows for a full regression testing of the new release without affecting these users.

Typically, this is handled by a process known as wave development. This is a process in which two development environments are created and used simultaneously. One is used for production support. The other is used for new development tasks. The team moves from one to the other as new releases are planned. This allows the new upgraded environment to take place in one area and the existing production support to take place in a parallel but separate area.

During upgrades, organizations can opt to upgrade the existing development environment or opt for a new development environment. To upgrade the existing development environment, they must halt all production support fixes during the upgrade process. This is because SAP does not allow transports between different versions of the software.

If no freeze can take place in the production support environment for fixes, a new development environment like the one we saw in Figure 2.4 is often implemented. Once new development is complete, as part of an upgrade or part of a new install, the configuration needs to be moved throughout the landscape. Having a clear and well-documented transport strategy is important to make sure that the systems stay in sync.

2.3 Transport Strategy

Transports are the method used to move configuration from one system to another in SAP systems. If all development is performed in the development system, the only way this configuration (InfoCubes, DSOs, etc.) is created in the QA and production environments is via the transport process.

A transport serves as a record in the system for what has been changed and when the change occurred. Each object that is activated in BW has a development class. The development class is used by the system to track the status and type of development that has occurred. When a new object is created, the BW system, by default, assigns the object a development package of $TMP.

This $TMP development-package indicator means that the development is currently deemed by the system as temporary. When the object is assigned to a transport via the transport system, the object can be assigned to a new development package. Once the object gets assigned a new non-$TMP development package and is attached to a transport, the object is locked for development. No other user may alter that object without being added to the transport that has been created.

In most projects, there is a central group that actually sends the transports from one system to another. Typically, this group is part of the Basis or technical group. In most projects, the applications team is responsible for creating a transport, adding the necessary objects to the transport, testing, and then releasing the transport. The release part of the transport means that the objects are now ready to actually move, and the development lock on the objects is released.

Once the transport has been released, the applications team typically informs the Basis team to send the transport in a formal process or form. The Basis team then typically sends the transport and reports back if there are issues with the transport. The issues are handled by the applications team and/or the Basis team. A released transport is then imported into the desired destination system.

2.3.1 Develop and Communicate the Transport Path

The BW transport path goes hand in hand with the BW landscape. You can see this in Figure 2.6. The transport path is the series of systems that are connected and the sequence in which these systems are involved in transporting configuration.

Figure 2.6 Transport Path of a Typical BW Landscape

When developing a transport strategy, it is important to note the following:

▶ **All BW transports are sourced in the development system**
Although this might sound like a simple statement, in designing landscapes it often is forgotten that all transports are sourced from development. Because we understand that transports are sent to QA, and then sent to production, it is easy to assume that the transport moves from DEV to QA and then QA to production. This is not the case. The transport actually moves from development to QA then from development to production.

To develop a sound transport strategy, we must develop a sound landscape strategy with each system's purpose clearly documented. Typically, the only systems that receive transports are the QA and PRD systems. Most other systems in a BW landscape are developed and refreshed as copies from other systems.

▶ **Transport process can be easier when sending transports to QA is delayed**
Transport issues are minimized when there are fewer transports. There are fewer transports if the same InfoCube is not transported multiple times. This is not always possible, depending on the data. If, for example, I create an InfoCube in development, I unit-test the InfoCube and determine that the InfoCube passes the unit test. If I immediately send the InfoCube to QA for testing, any new requriements that are needed now must be transported.

I have run into scenarios at organizations where we are transporting the same InfoCube 20 times at cutover. This happens because of the multiple issues discovered during testing and changing requirements from the business. The longer the InfoCube is kept in development, the more changes are included before transport to QA and the fewer transports are made. The fewer the transports, the less potential for issues.

Sometimes, keeping the confguration in the development system as long as possible becomes difficult, or impossible. In order to fully complete the development, an integration test must be completed. If the only valid data for testing is in the QA system, the integration test cannot easily be performed. This means that transports are required earlier, and as a result more transports are created and there is greater potential for issues.

So, if valid, system-ready data is available in the development system, some level of integration testing can be run in the development system. This allows many of the issues to be caught and fixed in the development system right away, rather than using the QA system for this work. If the QA system is used, any fixes need to be transported. This adds to the implementation time of the fix.

2.3.2 Implement Transport Approval Process from the Beginning

The approval process for transports is vital because, as many people start to work in a BW environment, there will eventually be conflict in their development work. This is because BW development usually involves sharing some objects and configuration as seen in the following typical scenario.

> **Scenario**
>
> Amy needs a new attribute to track the parent customer. She creates a new custom InfoObject ZPARENT and appends ZPARENT onto the common master data object of 0CUSTOMER. She is not ready to create a transport because she has not tested her configuration.
>
> Another developer, Greg, needs a new attribute ZGROUP on 0CUSTOMER, so he also appends his new InfoObject ZGROUP onto 0CUSTOMER. He tests and is ready to transport, before Amy is ready to send her transport. He adds his new InfoObject ZGROUP and 0CUSTOMER to a transport, releases it, and requests migration. When Greg's transport is sent, it fails because ZPARENT is appended to 0CUSTOMER but has not been transported.

This example illustrates a fairly simple scenario of conflict between developers. This can become more complex when we add DSO and InfoCube structures to the mix. As new fields are added, transformation is modified or configuration is changed in a BW data model, it is easy for one developer to step on another's work. There really is no systematic way to prevent this from occurring, but I will now discuss some of the steps to minimize the problem.

2.3.3 Make Sure Each Developer Locks Objects

Locking means setting exclusivity on an object so no other developer may change it. This occurs automatically if an object has a development package assigned to it other than the default development package of $TMP. Once a user tries to change an object that has previously been locked or migrated, the system sees the development package and prompts the user with a transport request, forcing him or her to choose a transport number to assign the change.

Once assigned to that transport, the object is once again locked by that user for future change until the transport is deleted or released. Any new user who requires an additional change needs to either be added to the transport or have the original transport reassigned to that user.

This locking of objects helps to communicate and enforce all changes. For example, if I try to change an object that someone else is working with, I will get a prompt to join onto his or her transport. I should then find out why the other person is locking the object and the timing of the change. I can then decide if I want to join the other transport or wait until the transport is migrated and create another one for my change.

If an object has never been migrated, there is no locking. This is where developers can easily step on each other. The best way to avoid this is to set up a process that requires each developer to immediately add any new InfoCube, DSO, InfoObject, etc., to a transport immediately after it is created. This will force the developer to assign a development class and will minimize the conflicts of shared objects.

2.3.4 Transport Steward Process

Locking of the BW objects is not the sole strategy for resolving development conflicts. The most efficient BW development groups establish an individual or a group as the transport steward. This person keeps track of the transport and helps to determine potential conflict in development before it occurs. This requires organization and an understanding of the entire BW development group and its work. The steward process can help in seeing problems and setting the priority of transports. In the previous examples, the steward would recommend that one of the conflicted parties wait on his or her configuration until the first group is complete.

> **Example**
> I worked on a project that had such a complex environment that we did not allow developers to create their own transports. Every time new development was to occur, we had to go to the transport steward to get a new transport. Only he could create new transports. We then attached our new object to the transport and locked the object during development. This process made sure that the transport steward could track the transports and new development by all the developers in the group.

This is a rather extreme example of managing change; your situation might not be this complex. Your level of transport and change management depends completely on the complexity of your environment, the size of the team, and the amount of shared development that is occurring.

In smaller BW projects, this is simply handled by word of mouth or informal emails. The important thing is to be aware of others when doing shared development and to understand that if heavy shared development is expected, a process should be developed.

2.3.5 Keep Thorough Log of Transports

Transports in BW are much more complex than in R/3 or ECC environments. This is because BW transports typically generate multiple objects on the destination system. R/3 or ECC transports usually involve adding one entry to this table and replicating that entry in the same table in the destination system.

Because BW transports are performing so many tasks behind the scenes, there is a much greater possibility for transport failure. It is important to keep very good notes of each transport that has been created, released, and migrated.

Any special instructions or notes on the transports should be clearly documented. These notes will be used as the notes for the cutover process. To cutover to production, these instructions must be followed exactly.

This means that if a transport has been sent to the QA system and it failed because of missing objects, and a new transport was migrated following that transport, both transports need to be sent to production. The first transport should be sent, it should be expected to fail, the next transport should then be sent again.

The failed transport is sent because even though the transport failed overall, there may have been objects that were transported successfully. If we ignore the transport and only send the second transport, we risk some objects being missing in the destination system. By sending all transports to production in the exact order they were sent to the QA system, we keep the two systems in sync. When tracking the transports the following must be recorded:

- Transport number
- Requestor
- Creation date
- Transport date and time (to track order of transports)
- Comments on transport, failure, etc.

2.3.6 Develop a Process for Troubleshooting Failed Transports

There are many reasons a transport can fail, some of which are described here:

- **Objects Missing from Transport**
  If we try to migrate an InfoCube without first migrating all InfoObjects in the InfoCube, the transport will fail. This is the most common reason for BW transport failure.

2 | Defining an Implementation Strategy

- **Replication of DataSources Did not Occur**
  If there are dependent objects in the R/3 or ECC systems, a replication may be required before the transport can succeed.

- **No Logical Reason**
  There are times that transports fail without any clear explanation or logical reason.

A clear process should be developed to troubleshoot transports with clear roles and responsibilities. This can be a very time-consuming job involving both the Basis and development teams. Troubleshooting transports is a very technical and specialized job. In most projects, we centralize this job with one or two experienced consultants.

I have been on projects that have assumed that the basis group would do most of the troubleshooting of transports. This is typically not the case. Instead, the Basis group informs the applications group of a failed transport. The applications group researches the reason for the problem and suggests a solution. Quickly diagnosing and fixing failed transports is a very important, but not easily acquired, skill.

Troubleshooting transports is a project task that a very experienced hands-on consultant can fix in a few minutes what may take an inexperienced consultant several days to correct.

2.3.7 Some Objects Will be Changeable

To develop a sound transport strategy, it is important to understand and determine those objects that will not be transported at all. These objects are bypassed in the transport process.

> **Example**
>
> InfoPackages are used to kick off loading in BW. The InfoPackage contains information such as the file name and location, selection criteria, destination information, job name, etc. The InfoPackage settings can change each time the data load is run. Most projects require the flexibility to change the InfoPackage in production.

As a result, most projects do not transport InfoPackages. They set these objects to changeable in the production system. This allows the InfoPackages to be created and changed in the production system without the necessity of a transport.

The **Object Changeability** button on the **Transport Connection** screen, seen in Figure 2.7, allows for objects to be edited in a closed system. A closed system refers to those systems that do not allow configuration, like the QA or Production systems. This allows a subset of objects to be changed without transport. Typically, this involves a very small group of objects that require the ability for change in a closed system. This is found using Transaction RSA1 > Transport Connection.

Table 2.1 shows all objects that can be set as changeable. In most cases, there is a very limited list of those objects that should be set to changeable in a closed system. Thus, in most QA and Production systems a very limited list of these options should be set.

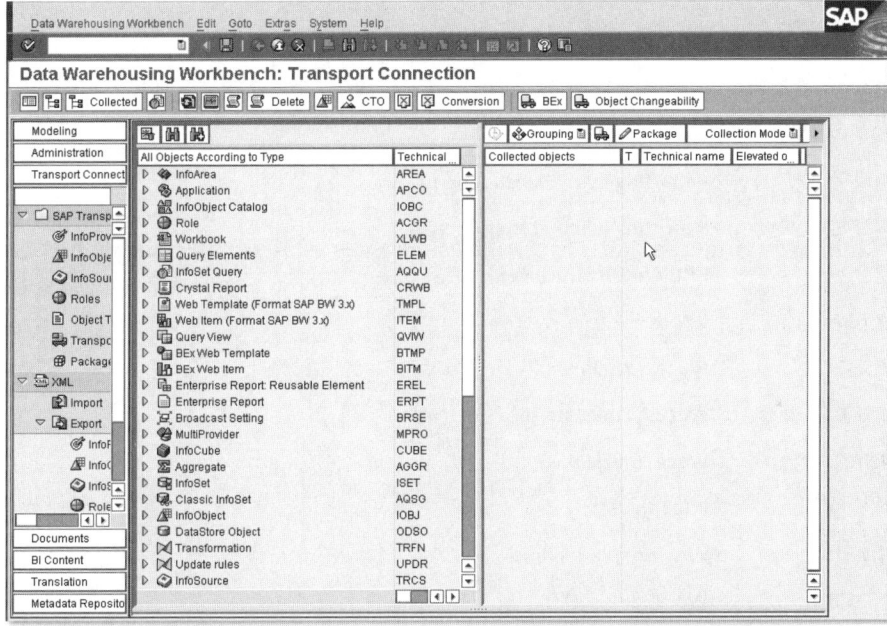

Figure 2.7 Object Changeability

Object	Desctription
AGGR	Aggregate
ANMO	Mining model
ANPR	Analysis process
ANSO	Model source

Table 2.1 Changeable Options in a Closed System

Object	Desctription
AQQU	Infoset query
BRSE	Broadcast setting
CRWB	Crystal report
CTRT	Currency translation type
DEST	Open hub destination
DMMO	Data-mining model
ELEM	Query element
EVEN	Event processing chain
ISIG	InfoPackage group
ISIP	InfoPackage
ITEM	Web item
QVIW	Query view
RAPA	Reporting agent scheduling package
RASE	Reporting agent setting
RRCA	RRI InfoCube receiver
RRQA	RRI query receiver
RSPC	Process chain
RSPT	Process chain starter
RSPV	Process variants
SPOK	InfoSpoke
TMPL	Web template name
XLWB	Workbook

Table 2.1 Changeable Options in a Closed System (cont.)

2.4 New Release Rollout Strategy Challenges

There are various challenges for rolling out BW, and the BW rollout strategy should clearly navigate these challenges. Let's examine these in the following subsections.

2.4.1 Timing of BW Rollout

A significant challenge exists when BW is being configured at the same time as the transactional system, such as R/3 or ECC. This is because decisions made in the transactional system configuration have a rather profound affect on the BW configuration.

BW must have a steady transactional system to determine mapping and analysis needs. If these keep changing, this places an extreme burden on the BW team to constantly adjust BW to match this changing environment.

It is also difficult to get the project teams to provide valid master and transactional data because they are constantly changing the configuration. When they finally have valid test data, it may be well after the BW team needs to have its data model completed.

Compounding the issue is that the transactional project teams typically do not want to devote a lot of time for reporting when they are trying to configure the process.

Most projects find that this burden is significant enough to delay the BW go-live several months after the R/3 or ECC go-live. This gives the BW team an opportunity to configure BW based on final R/3 or ECC configuration, which allows for a more sound BW system.

2.4.2 Rollout Scope

The scope of BW and the timing of this rollout is an important decision that is largely based on the analysis needs and availability of source data for extraction. A comprehensive rollout strategy should be developed, and this should be coordinated with each of the teams.

The process teams need to make sure that they can deliver the transactional data in a valid form to support the rollout data. The technical and Basis teams must make sure that the infrastructure and systems can support the rollouts both from sizing and system-build perspectives.

If possible, this strategy should be developed for as far into the future as possible. The most recent rollouts should have a more detailed plan. In the distant future, a multi-generational plan can be developed.

Rolling out a new system inevitably involves the rollout of an upgrade. In order to provide these upgrades to the end users, an upgrade rollout strategy must be developed. This strategy is used to plan and determine how the end

2.5 Upgrade Rollout Strategy

users will acquire the new upgraded system and how their jobs will be directly affected. These all become part of the upgrade rollout strategy.

There are several key decisions defining the upgrade strategy that are discussed in the following subsections.

2.5.1 Timing

The most common reason for upgrading in R/3 or BW is: "SAP made me." This is because there is always pain and cost in the upgrade process. Timing of the upgrade should reflect significant time to do a full regression test, and some contingency plan should be created for issues and rework that result from the upgrade. Typically, during the upgrade process, no new development can occur. This restriction needs to be built into the development schedule and timeline.

2.5.2 Features and Functionality

Most successful upgrade projects do not use new functionality right away. The goal is simply to get the system upgraded to the new release and regression-tested. New features and functionality can be rolled out later. Trying to implement new functionality while performing an upgrade can cause the complexity of the upgrade to be increased significantly, and thus, stretch the timeline.

2.5.3 Upgrade Testing Strategy

A regression-testing strategy makes sure that the existing functions and processes continue to function without issues following the upgrade. This should include plans for creating test scripts, executing tests, reporting issues, and issue resolution. The testing strategy should include volume and stress testing to ensure that adding a large amount of data or many users to the system will not cause new issues.

2.5.4 Upgrade Change Management Strategy

There are many new features in the new release of BW. The look and feel of the system differs, so a sound change-management strategy to communicate the changes and differences is very important to a successful upgrade. Another important area to understand in BW is the strategy for the database. There are many parts to the database strategy. Let's learn more about the database strategy now.

2.6 Database Strategy

BW is database independent. This allows for decision-making flexibility with respect to the underlying database system in the technical environment. Typically, the type of database used for BW does not matter. Database design comes into play only for various features, such as MOLAP aggregates, that are only available in specific database systems.

SAP as a company will always state that it will not influence a customer's database decision and will try not to steer a customer toward or away from any database system or company. This allows SAP to remain neutral in the database-selection process of a company.

Typically, the database system of BW mirrors that of the R/3 or ECC systems in the landscape. Rarely is BW of a different database system than that used in the rest of the landscape, simply because of the burden this would place on the database administration and Basis teams to maintain different database systems.

I have worked with organizations with many different database systems, and in my experience the organizations that have had the fewest database issues and most stable SAP BW environments own Oracle databases.

This is because Oracle is a very popular option for database designs in BW, and thus is tested by many users on a daily basis. Also, I have found that the overall design of the Oracle database seems to fit well with BW's design I have experienced fewer performance and database specific issues when using Oracle than with any other database system.

The issues that are common with other database platforms and not as common with Oracle involve the many dynamic joins that BW data uses when running a query. Oracle has a better data-access process than other database systems that I have used. This makes for better query performance and better load performance.

In my experience, some database platforms, especially DB2, perform very poorly if the database statistics are not pristine. Without warning, a load that took several minutes each day suddenly takes several hours to complete. To prevent these issues, we had to spend much of our batch-loading time in the evening running statistics to make sure that the loading windows were not affected by outdated statistics.

> **Note**
> Oracle is better at handling outdated database statistics, and a more stable environment occurs as a result. Even with new releases of other databases, Oracle continues to be ahead of the curve in this area.

In whatever database system you are using, seek out the other customers who are also using your database and keep in communication. I worked with several DB2 customers that participated in periodic conference calls to go over DB2 BW specific issues and their resolution.

They were able to help influence IBM to incorporate some of their suggestions into the DB2 patches and future design. Once the database strategy is complete, there are other decisions that have a global reach on the BW system. One of these involves an enterprise data warehouse strategy.

2.7 Enterprise Data Warehouse and Global Rollup Strategies

A BW enterprise data warehouse (EDW) is a system that gathers data from multiple sources and serves as a global reporting system. This can be quite complex, depending on how regionalized a company's culture and development functions are. This strategy takes into account any global data needs and regional aggregations and transformation of data into a global view. A global EDW project dramatically benefits the following departments of a company:

- **Marketing**
  An EDW brings visibility to sales and marketing program effectiveness and product line profitability across the entire organization.

- **Pricing and Contracts**
  These departments can better understand pricing and usage to optimize negotiation.

- **Forecasting**
  An EDW provides timely visibility of global demand.

- **Sales**
  The sales department can better determine sales profitability and productivity for all territories and regions. It can use results by geography, product, sales group, or individuals across the enterprise.

- **Financial**
  This department receives daily, weekly, or monthly results quickly, enhancing financial management throughout the organization.

- **Supply Chain**
  An EDW enables faster, thorough analysis of purchase quantities and prices.

- **Inventory Management**
  This department gains a holistic view, which helps identify ways to manage inventory more effectively.

- **Customer Service**
  Service staff can deliver consistent customer service metrics for all facilities.

- **Information Technology**
  This team can reduce it manual consolidation workload by providing each user with fast and easy access to regularly used queries, reports, or analyses.

An EDW project can be a difficult and sometimes painful process in many organizations because it combines many diverse groups. An EDW strategy should meet the following goals:

- Assessing of data from multiple source systems
- Extraction of data from these systems
- Aligning and cleansing the data as necessary
- Loading this data into a new EDW environment so data appears to come from a single source

The source systems may be multiple ECC systems, BW systems, other legacy systems, or a combination of these. Many different groups may own the transactional or master data, which increases the complexity. The overall challenges of a BW EDW surface in the following categories:

- **Cultural**
  The culture of the organization may not be ready for an EDW. Although management may feel that an EDW will bring great benefits, the organization may not agree and/or follow the EDW standards.

- **Political**
  Many organizations do not want to give up their local reporting flexibility to enter into global standards. The EDW might also reduce the number of reporting systems in an organization. The prospect of retiring formerly essential systems may cause anxiety among users.

- **Technical**
  Sometimes the technical infrastructure that supports an EDW is not robust enough to handle the data volume. An EDW may require a network upgrade or enhanced hardware to support global reporting. Technical problems may arise when trying to consolidate the disparate systems.

- **Fiscal**
  An EDW effort can cost a great deal of money because of the significant challenges with data integration, consolidation, and cleansing. This process is most successful if funded as its own project.

The global EDW strategy is important to determine from the beginning of the project because it dictates how data should be rolled into a global data view and affects harmonization of data across the enterprise. This can involve significant scope and challenges. The entire organization needs to have a clear and concise query delivery strategy to allow consistent access of data. In the next section, I will discuss some decisions about query development in BW.

2.8 Query Strategy

There has been an ongoing debate in BW that started from the earliest BW systems ever implemented. The issue: Where should queries be developed? There are two options:

- Create and develop queries in the development system, and require transport of all queries to the production environment
- Create queries directly in production

I did an informal poll to determine what option most customers with BW chose. What I have found is that this debate is almost split evenly between the two options. The option to develop queries in development and transporting is slightly more popular with the customers I contacted.

So what is the right answer for this question? As with most decisions in BW (and SAP overall), the answer is: "It depends." I will provide the advantages and disadvantages of each approach to help your decision-making process.

2.8.1 Pros and Cons of developing Queries Directly in Production

There are several pros discussed below:

- **Increased Speed and Flexiblity**
  This allows new queries and changes to be rolled out very quickly. No waiting for a transport to be created, approved, and migrated. Query development is not *owned* by the IT department.

- **Easier Development**
  All data needed for testing is available in the production enviornment. Therefore, the tasks of creating a query and testing the formula, filters, etc. much easier than in a development environment with limited data.

- **Reduced Transport Activity**
  Transports for queries would not be required if these are developed directly in production.

Now, let's take a look at the cons:

- **Auditing Effort**
  It is difficult to audit reports to make sure they conform to standards.

- **Data Quality Issues**
  Quality and consistency issues can arise. For example, a user creates a query with a key figure called *net sales*, and they forget to filter out the intercompany sales. This skews the net sales number.

- **Performance Issues**
  Performance problems can arise because power users are not always aware of the data and its volume. They can create queries that allow unfiltered access and thus create performance concerns.

- **Data Redundancy**
  Duplication of data is inevitable. After many years of using BW, this can become a rather significant burden.

2.8.2 How Do I Allow Development of Queries in Production?

Here, you set the object changeability using the functionality as previously described in Figure 2.7. To allow the development of queries in production, you must set the changeability flag of the following options in the production system. This will allow the changeability of these objects. See Table 2.2 for a look at some of these options.

Object	Desctription
AQQU	InfoSet query
ELEM	Query element
QVIW	Query view
XLWB	Workbook

Table 2.2 Object Changeability Options for Query Processing

Create Central Key Figure Matrix

The most successful projects have some central document that details all key figures or key performance indicators (KPIs) in the organization. This key figure matrix gives the name of the key figure value and the calculation used throughout the organization to arrive at the value. This makes sure that each time someone sees a particular name, such as days of supply, everyone understands how this is calculated.

The key figure matrix can either be published on the portal or a link can be established for each query, workbook, or web report. If this key figure matrix is properly maintained and adhered to, there is no confusion with different people or groups calculating data differently.

If a situation arises where the finance group calculates the same key figure differently than the sales group, we simply make a new name for one of the key figures. This keeps the consistency of the environment and makes it easier for users to understand the data they are viewing in a query.

Develop a Validation Process

To keep a clean and consistent production environment, the queries that are developed directly in production should be validated. This process starts with thorough training of the power users in the data and standards for development.

Once queries are created, these queries also go through a validation process either with the BW team or peer evaluation before they are rolled out to the end user community. This ensures that the query has been reviewed for standards, key figure consistency, and quality.

2.8.3 Developing Queries in Production vs. Development

I have seen projects that have been successful using both approaches. The projects that perform all development of queries in the development system and transport all queries are able to keep strict control on the number of queries and are able to verify and test all queries for data quality and consistency before they are transported to production. This reduces the redundancy and makes the environment much stronger because the queries have been validated.

However, these projects sacrifice the flexibility and speed that development in production allows. This can become a serious concern when a vice president calls the BW department and says: "I need analysis on the following values, and I need this quickly." The team is forced develop, test, create the transport, transport approval, migration, etc. This can be rather frustrating for the vice president who is waiting for his or her data (and quite stressful for the BW development team too!).

Those customer environments that have allowed production to be opened up for development can quickly spin out of control as the number of queries explode and the support of so many queries becomes crippling.

Those customers that are the most successful either do not develop queries in the production system or they allow only very limited development of queries in production. They limit the creation of queries in production to a certain naming convention and to a very, very small group of well-trained power users.

This allows them to quickly know the difference between those queries that are developed in production and those that have been migrated. The development and production support teams offer only limited support for those queries that are developed directly in production.

This approach reduces the redundancy because the small team can create a process to determine if a query has already been developed. This approach allows the flexible development of queries while also allowing the discipline needed for a consistent, high-quality, and efficient environment.

2.8.4 Visual Composer

Beginning in BW Version 3.5, SAP delivered the Visual Composer software. This was enhanced significantly for BW version 2004s. This enhancement changes the options significantly when reporting and querying data in BW.

Visual Composer is a web-based solution that allows the linking of objects by dragging and dropping the objects and establishing links between them. Visual composer generates code to establish the link and passing of data between applications. It is independent of any platform, technology, or language.

This greatly improves the analysis in BW because through Visual Composer you can link third-party or legacy systems views to BW queries. The goal of the tool is to reduce the effort involved in bringing this data into BW directly, harmonizing it, and presenting it. This allows the data to be visually reported and even some interaction of the data through Drag & Drop functionality.

This can be a good addition to the BW reporting strategy because it allows for a flexible view of data in outside systems together with data in BW. The user does not have to even be aware of the source of this data.

Part of any sound reporting strategy is to make sure that the data being accessed is done in the most efficient way. One way to make sure this occurs is by keeping the system up-to-date with support packages. These support packages allow for periodic fixes of software issues. Understanding and keeping a clear support-package strategy is important to keeping the system health.

In the next section, I will discuss this strategy.

2.9 Support Package Strategy

All BW teams must have a documented support-package strategy to document the process and timing of support package applications. SAP releases BW support packages periodically, and these need to be applied to fix various issues in BW.

The SAP BW support team prefers to release fixes only as part of a support package, not as an individual SAP Note fix. This ensures that they can test the quality of the fix with other fixes, and they aren't often forced into a situation where one notes fixes one thing but breaks several others. A team is then required to put in more notes to fix the old note.

Many times when I run into an issue in BW, the support group refuses to provide fixes in SAP Notes at all and directs me to the newest support package to fix my issue. This can be quite difficult because applying an SAP notes requires a full regression test of the BW environment.

Most organizations are not able to do a full regression test often. Thus, we often find ourselves working around issues until we can apply support packages. There are several different kinds of support packages in BW, which are discussed here.

- **BW Application Support Package**
  These are support packages released periodically by SAP to fix various issues in the BW system.

- **BW Front-End Support Package**
  These are support packages designed to fix issues in the query processing tool in BW. They are installed as a separate component, so the support packages are administered separately. The BW front-end support packages are backward compatible with previous releases of BW. They are loaded on each invidual PC that runs BW.

- **Plug-in Release**
  The plug-in release is not really a support package but rather the release of the DataSources (extractors) on the ECC system. It should be noted that prior to ECC Version 6.0, the plug-in release was independent of the release or ECC support packages. It is now included as part of the ECC release and will automatically have the lastest plug-in.

To see the most recent support package and plug-in compatibility go to: *service.sap.com/bi*.

2.9.1 Recommendation

The most successful companies using BW stay as up-to-date as possible on the support packages. These support packages differ in their quality and number of issues they fix (and new issues they cause). However to keep a system performing at its best, keeping current on support packages is vital.

> **Tip**
> The best way to roll out new support packages is with a new release of BW. Piggyback all BW support packages with each new release of functionality.

Thus, when you plan a new phase of development for your system, the first thing that you should do is to move the development environment to the newest support package and keep all development and testing on that support package. This allows for the support package to be regression-tested fully, as part of a project release strategy. Migrating to the support package can occur with minimal disruption to the business.

This strategy typically forces the BW system to lag several support packages behind. By the time a BW functionality release gets to production in a project, SAP has released at least one new support package. Thus, we usually accept that we cannot be using the newest support package at all times in production; we just stay as close as possible with minimal disruption.

> **Tip**
>
> A process should be developed for any support package that is needed to fix a critical issue.

Sometimes there are critical issues that are only fixed in support packages. SAP, on occasion, cannot provide these fixes as part of an SAP Support fix. Thus, an emergency support package upgrade is necessary. As part of the support- package strategy document, a strategy for this should be clearly defined.

2.9.2 Front-End Support Packages

The BW front-end support packages are the most difficult and cumbersome support packages to deploy. This is because, unlike the BW application packages, these are not deployed in one place. They must be deployed to each PC that is accessing BW. Rolling this patch out to the individual users can become quite a task.

Prior to the NW 2004s release of BW, the front-end patches were developed separately from the application support packages and thus were released independently. In the NW 2004s version, the front-end patches are in sync with the application-support package. Starting with NW 2004s, the front-end patches are renamed to *BI Front-End Add-On Support Packages*.

Any fix in between support packages will be released as a Hotfix. The Hotfixes that are released in between regularly scheduled support packages are now named *BI Front-End Add-On Patches*.

Most customers use a centralized software package to push the front-end patches to each user. They do this periodically to keep all users on the latest front-end patch.

2.10 Authorization Strategy

An authorization strategy involves making decisions about the BW environment and determining what parts, if any, need to be secured. This helps to keep sensitive data away from unauthorized parties, while still allowing analysis by those who need the data.

Developing an authorization strategy for BW is important to consider from the earliest stages of a project because many of the decisions regarding the implementation of BW can be guided based on these requirements. An authorization strategy in BW takes into account the security of the following areas:

- Functional security within the BW tool
- Data security
- Presentation security
- Profile and role strategy

In order to define an authorization strategy we must first look at the scope of data that will be loaded into BW. We need to know if there is data that will be loaded that will be sensitive and should not be viewed by some of the users of BW.

2.10.1 BW Security

BW security is based on a roles and authorization concept. Users are assigned to one or many roles. These roles contain authorizations. Authorization objects are assigned to the objects in BW. The system checks the authorization objects against the authorizations for the user.

This concept differs from ECC or R/3 because these systems are transaction based. The transaction-based systems secure values based on transactions or specific field values to determine what tasks a user can perform.

BW is based on analysis-based security. This is driven by InfoProviders, queries, and data. Basically, this means that we look at the analysis methods and determine which analysis is sensitive. We secure the sensitive data by user role.

To establish an authorization strategy, we do not need to know exactly how security is to be configured, we simply need to know what data needs to be secured and by whom. If this has been determined early in the project cycle, these needs can be incorporated into the data model design.

You should create an authorizations strategy document and revisit this document each time you roll out functionality in BW. This document should clearly state what data is to be secured and the roles that should be included and excluded from the data.

The document should also detail the authorization strategy within the BW tool itself. This would show what BW developers and production support users are allowed to do, and not allowed to do.

The strategy document also should reference what security is required on the raw data loaded into BW such as flat files and direct connection to legacy databases, XML, XI, etc. This needs to be a living document, because as new data and users come onto the system, new security needs evolve.

2.10.2 Authorizations for Upgrade to NW 2004s

There has been a significant redesign of the authorization concept in the NW 2004s release. SAP has converted from reporting authorizations to an analysis authorizations concept for BW data security. This redesign of authorizations allows for much more flexible data-security functionality.

No new development will be done to the BW 3.x authorization functionality in BW. SAP strongly encourages customers to move to the new security design. There are tools to migrate the security in the Version 3.5 reporting authorizations to the NW 2004S analysis authorization.

If you are using the 3.x security (any BW data security at all) you should plan to upgrade to the new security concept. However, the 3.x security will continue to function in the NW 2004s environment. Since no new development will be performed on this security method and it is somewhat limited in its flexibility, the new analysis method of authorizations is preferred.

Time should be allocated in the upgrade process to migrate the security to the new analysis authorization. The redesign only affects the data security in BW. There is still a transactional-based security to provide security for the BW administrator and developer activities within the BW system. For example, SAP still provides the ability to secure transactions in BW, such as RSA1 and SPRO. This is covered by the standard security and will remain unchanged in BW.

2.11 Conclusion

If the different strategies mentioned are planned, organized, and implemented, it allows for a much smoother project overall. Since many if not all of the areas will come up in any BW project, getting in front of the demand and planning for the decisions in each of the areas allows for a more efficient BW planning process, and thus a smoother implementation.

Now, let's proceed to Chapter 3, where we'll review the most common mistakes made when implementing BW.

History, despite its wrenching pain, cannot be unlived, however, if faced with courage, need not be lived again.
– Maya Angelou

3 Common BW Implementation Mistakes

When I began working with the BW product, I started assembling a notebook of BW *lessons-learned*. I had a unique opportunity as a Platinum Consultant with SAP America, Inc. to perform project reviews at many BW client sites. Based on these reviews and various spot consulting engagements, as well as working with other projects long-term, this folder has grown quite large. This chapter details the results of my findings.

3.1 Unclear Definition of Goals and Scope

Implementing BW, as with any project, you must start with clear goals and a clearly defined and documented scope. While it seems that any project manager would admit this is the most important task in BW project management, its absence is the most common reason that projects miss their scheduled go-live date or are cancelled altogether. How can we make sure that the goals of BW are clearly defined and communicated?

3.1.1 Develop Clear Project Scope Documentation

BW scope definition needs to be agreed to and signed off on by all parties before any development can begin. The more detailed the scope documentation, the better the understanding of the requirements, timing, and implementation of BW, and thus the more likelihood for success.

The scope document should be considered the most important document in the BW project. The BW scope should be first established as part of an initial scoping exercise, then refined through an interview process, and finally be subject to a scope document signoff. This scoping exercise is part of the very earliest phase of the project, the project-preparation phase.

There are multiple subsequent documents that will establish the scope in even greater detail. However, these documents will come in the analysis phase of the project, not in project preparation. The critical components of the scope document include:

- Information that will be included in BW
- Subject areas, with their priority status
- Scope of each subject area
- Summary of transformation needed
- Summary of the level of aggregation and summarization of data
- Description of the presentation tools

The initial scoping document should provide information on the following critical areas in the scope process.

- **Business Requirements**
  Business reasons for the project and business questions answered by the implementation
- **Stakeholders**
  Roles and responsibilities of those in the implementation process
- **Critical Success Factors**
  Determinants and measures for a successful project.
- **Source Systems**
  The source systems that are involved in the project and the sources of data in these systems.
- **Data Access**
  The intended audience of the BW project and their use of the information.
- **Transformation**
  Any transformation that is needed in order to provide the data in its desired format.
- **Security**
  The data-access security requirements to prevent unauthorized use of the infrormation.
- **Batch Window**
  The frequency of load and approximate timing of loads.
- **Archiving/History**
  How much historical data is needed, and how long will this information be kept in BW?

- **Testing Procedures**
  The basic process for testing and some testing and validation parameters.
- **Master Data Requirements**
  The master data tables and infromation that are needed to support the reporting in BW.
- **Change Management**
  Strategy for rolling out the process changes to the organization.
- **Timing**
  Project schedule and timeline.
- **Transition to Production Support**
  Some information on the go-live process and transition from development to production support.

3.1.2 Establish Milestones

Establishing milestones and measuring these milestones is one of the most important measures of a project's chances for success. Setting these milestones allows the BW team to understand and work to these goals. I call this process setting micro goals. The micro goal is a small, attainable goal that can be used to track a project week to week. Examples are setting up connectivity with a source system, doing a test pull of data, and transformation of data in one area.

If we measure to the micro goals, we can make sure that the project is on track. We can then quickly add resources to those areas where the micro goals are not being met. Often project teams find themselves simply measuring against a macro goal, such as completing the analysis phase. Often, projects that focus too highly on larger goals do not know they are behind schedule until it is too late to act.

By breaking up the BW project into smaller, more digestible chunks, it is much easier to see the whole picture, understand dependencies on other groups, and make sure that the BW project will make its scheduled go-live date.

3.1.3 Avoid Scope Creep

Scope creep can occur in a BW project just an easily as an R/3 or ECC project. The best way to prevent the scope creep in BW is to have a firmly established scope right from the beginning and require signoffs on the scope document.

3 | Common BW Implementation Mistakes

Adding more detailed governance, such as the functional model process, further establishes the intended scope.

Keeping to and tracking against the scope is one of the more difficult challenges facing a BW project, and there are no easy solutions to scope creep other than to clearly document all requirements.

A functional model is a document that clearly states the scope and delivery of the data in a BW functional area. Chapter 5 walks through the functional model process in detail. This process helps to establish the BW requirements, business questions, and needs. The functional model serves as the most important scope-management document, and a signed off functional model can help avert scope creep and keep the project on track.

3.1.4 Establish a Scope Change Control Process

As tightly as any BW project team would like to control scope, changes inevitably occur. These could be the result of missed scope areas, new opportunity, changing business environment, or newly discovered challenges. Thus, scope cannot be assumed to be unchanging. A scope review and management process to allow for changes is vital to communicating and accepting these changes. This should involve review, communication, and escalation.

Controlling scope helps to avoid another common issue, an over-ambitious scope. This can often be the result of simply trying to do too much, too fast. Let's find out more about over-ambitious scope now.

3.2 Over-Ambitious Scope

As with many R/3 or ECC projects, the failures that occur in BW projects are often the result of attempting to implement too much at one time. BW has the power to pull significant amounts of data from multiple source systems both in the SAP landscape and outside this landscape. This freedom to bring almost any data into BW tempts many organizations to become overly ambitious.

There are several things that need to be learned and accounted for in any BW implementation. A developer must understand the information requirements, the data, and the presentation and loading needs, and must reconcile all these needs with the BW tool itself. Thus, any overly ambitious scope forces the team to take short-cuts on the analysis and understanding of the data and information needs and thus can cause the BW project to stall.

3.2.1 Start Small

How can an overly ambitious scope be avoided? The only answer is to start the BW implementation plan with a small go-live scope and build from a small but well-designed base. This allows the process of implementing BW to be firmly established. The lessons-learned from the first implementation can be used to make each subsequent implementation that much stronger.

A good example of a small project is one that limits the data to one source system, typically and most often the R/3 or ECC transactional system. Within that transactional system, the scope should also be reduced to one subject area, such as sales tracking or general ledger (GL) postings.

The smaller the scope the more focused the team can be on understanding the requirements and delivering these as a quality deliverable on time. As previously stated, once the user loses confidence in the BW solution and the information provided from BW, it is extremely difficult to win the user back.

Thus, a small scope allows a very robust user signoff and testing process. This makes sure that any data anomalies that occur on the source systems are fixed in that source system and that BW is aggregating and reporting the data in the most effective manner.

Many organizations will opt to start with some small financial or sales reporting. They set up the extraction process to bring this data into BW and present it with a limited number of queries. The users can then look at these queries and formulate the requirements for the next phases of rollout.

Because BW is independent of the R/3 or ECC source system, in some cases new BW functionality can be created and rolled out to the end users without coordination or synchronization with the R/3 or ECC rollout schedules. In other words, if the source data is available, BW can allow the reporting on this data to go live without tying it to an overall project phase go-live involving the ECC or R/3 teams.

BW can have many mini project go-lives to stagger delivery of functionality, thereby preventing a big bang overly complex scope from crippling the BW team. Often, a small go-live provides the momentum (and funding) needed for subsequent go-lives.

3.2.2 Be Wary of Implementing BW at the Same Time as ECC or R/3

Projects that attempt to implement BW at the same time as the source ECC or R/3 system face especially big challenges. This can be compared to trying to climb a mountain whose summit is constantly moving. No sooner do you get a foothold and start to climb then the goal changes.

Having a constant and steady source system when implementing BW helps ensure consistent rules for the data. When the ECC or R/3 system is evolving at the same time as the BW system, this causes severe frustration and delays in the BW project.

For example, I worked with one large company that was implementing the Materials Management (MM) module of R/3 to enter and track its purchases. They set their transactional configuration and pricing for the purchase orders, and we began our first extractions of that data into BW. We configured the purchasing data into what we believed was a sound data model.

As we began to extract more and more data, the purchase order price fields became inconsistent. We had net price in one key figure value; later this same key figure value included the freight charges. It took a lot of testing to determine that the issue was a result of a last-minute pricing configuration change on the R/3 transactional system. A small decision in the source system can have huge ramifications for the BW system.

The problem is that few of the people configuring pricing were aware of the impact of their decisions. If we had waited until after their configuration was complete, we would have mapped the freight and net sales consistently and saved a great deal of time.

Many projects look to BW to become the place for reporting of data for an ECC or R/3 implementation. However, when developing BW at the same time as the source area in ECC or R/3, challenges are inevitable.

There are advantages to developing both systems at the same time. By developing both systems together, it is possible to have a clear integrated test process in conjunction with the R/3 or ECC systems.

Implementing BW with R/3 or ECC also eliminates some of what would be throwaway work on the transactional systems. This is because the reporting functionality is often needed on the source system. If BW is not there to provide this reporting, there must be some other system to provide this reporting.

In some cases, custom ABAP reports are created for temporary use on the transactional systems. Some, if not all of these could be eliminated if the BW system were there from the beginning to provide this type of reporting.

The biggest challenge is to try to implement BW on a changing source system platform. Good communication and change management are needed in order to coordinate the transactional team and the BW team.

In most BW implementations, the BW team usually lags the transactional team by four to six weeks. This allows the transactional team to be more firmly established and create some sample configuration and data in order to configure, load, and test the BW system.

> **Note**
> To assure that the BW project budget does not get exhausted waiting for R/3 or ECC configuration to finish, the BW project should not kick off until four to six weeks after the associated R/3 or ECC project.

Setting the timeline for a BW project in coordination with the ECC or R/3 teams often means adjusting the BW timeline if the transactional timeline shifts. It also means setting a realistic timeline that can be achieved. Issues often occur when projects have an unrealistic timeline.

3.3 Unrealistic Timeline

Some projects start with a timeline that is either unintentionally or intentionally unrealistic. There are several reasons for this strategy. To get management approval for a project, I have witnessed one project team provide what it knew was an unrealistic timeline. This got management on board, and then slowly the dates were moved into a more realistic timeline.

Naturally, we don't suggest this for long-term project management. Let's look at another example. In one case, I saw project management intentionally set unrealistic timelines in order to motivate the team to act. The project managers felt that if they didn't put a *stake in the ground* the team would never move forward. This strategy backfired because most of the team members knew that the timetable would never be met and therefore ignored the fact that their deliverables would be late.

A clear realistic timeline is the most honest way to ensure longer-term success and keep the team motivated toward the goal of a successful go-live, within budget and on time.

Once a clear timeline is established, this timeline needs to be clearly communicated to the team. This communication and other project related standards become part of the project governance. This governance helps ensure there are common standards for the project.

3.4 Governance

Governance in any project covers the various templates, tools, documents, and standards that keep the consistency and communication of the project sound. One can compare the governance of a project to the laws in society. Governance helps to make sure that there is a certain standard and uniform way of doing things to help everyone configure and communicate effectively.

In many ways, the governance of a project defines the culture of the project itself. I have worked on projects with extremely lax standards, with many of the BW developers doing their own thing and configuring BW in many different styles. I have also worked on projects that have very strict governance: so strict that making any changes required approval from many layers of management.

Striking a good balance between a clear and consistent governance document and stiflingly rigid standards allow the project to keep standards while also allowing for rapid change.

A clear set of governance standards are necessary to achieve project success. This governance is achieved through processes and clear documentation. There are several important documents that must exist in any BW implementation. These are discussed next:

- **Project Charter**
  The project charter states the reason for the project, main deliverables, sponsors, success measures, etc.
- **Stakeholder Document**
  This document lists all stakeholders and the roles the stakeholders have in the success of the project.

- **Project Plan**
  Two types of project plans are typically used in a BW implentation. There is the BW project plan and the overall project plan. Typically, the BW project plan is managed locally and is very detailed with detailed tasks, timelines, etc. The overall project plan integrates the BW plan with the Basis, transactional, and other system projects to ensure that the BW project goals and milestones can be met.

- **BW Organization Chart**
  This document shows the BW team and their roles.

- **BW Development Standards Document**
  This document spells out the methodology and strategy for the BW implementation. The development standards document states the master data and transactional data strategy and the different BW rules and conventions that are followed. These include, for example, how the Persistent Staging Area (PSA) is typically used, how transformation is performed, whether function modules are used to house Advanced Busienss Application Programming (ABAP) code, or whether mutli-level data store object (DSO) structures are used to store data.

- **Naming Standards Document**
  The naming standards document is used to define the convention used to name custom objects in the BW system. This document is very important to ensure some consistency in the design. This spells out how the naming will be used for InfoProviders, InfoObjects, Queries, etc.

- **Landscape Document**
  The landscape document details the different systems in the landscape and the transport path of those systems. For example, the landscape document shows the sandbox, development, QA, production, tranining, and production support systems in the BW landscape.

- **Transport strategy Document**
  This document shows the strategy and timing for transports and the documentation and procedure for transport approval.

- **Architecture Document**
  This document shows the different InfoProviders and the flow of data through the system. This document shows all source systems and all infoproviders and the flow of data from the source systems to the InfoProviders and to the presentation of data.

- **Disaster Recovery Document**
  This document details the disaster recovery standards, restore plan, etc.

This document is used by the project to plan to deal with issues that occur. For the Basis organization, this involves backup and recovery. For the BW applications team, this often means preparing to dump and reload data from the source, if needed.

- **System Copy—Refresh Document**
  The copy/refresh document shows the schedule and strategy for refreshing and copying systems from one system to another. For example, it shows when the sandbox system will be refreshed, and how often.

- **Review Checklist**
  This document is used as a checklist to review the design of a process in BW before transport occurs. This document shows all things that should be checked, implemented, and documented prior to transport.

- **Functional Model Document**
  The functional model document shows the requirements and scope of a subject area.

- **Functional/Technical Specifications**
  These documents define and detail the design of BW and the specific details of the implementation.

- **Security Standards Document**
  This document details the security standards and methodology.

- **Change Management Strategy Document**
  This document gives the strategy, roles, and templates for change management in the organization.

- **Glossary**
  A document with commonly used BW terminology, defined for both the project team and the business.

- **Cutover Plan**
  This document is prepared prior to the go-live to detail all steps needed for the cutover to production.

- **Go-Live Checklist**
  This documentation is a list of all things needed before go-live can occur.

- **Communications Documents**
  These are for various communications, such as status reports, issues lists, etc.

Having the documents is important, but even more important is making sure that these are living documents. It should be assumed that these documents will be modified and changed based on the needs of the project and the issues that arise.

This flexibility allows for the documents to be used to familiarize new developers and also to communicate to the business the different processes and methodologies of the project.

These can be used to prevent the most common communication issues that occur in a project. I will now explore some of these communication issues.

3.5 Communication Issues

Many BW projects face challenges in communication. These communication issues occur within the BW team itself and between the BW team and the various other transaction process teams in the project. The best way to minimize these issues is to have checkpoints throughout the project. These serve as milestones and also allow for people inside and outside the project to understand the progress and status.

3.5.1 Insist on Weekly Status Reports

Weekly status reports help the groups communicate what has been done. This practice allows the team to report on their status and also allows the organization to see what each other have been working on.

3.5.2 Encourage Informal Discussion

Sometimes after-hours or lunchroom discussions lead to the most innovative ideas for issue resolution. These should be encouraged whenever possible. Some of the strongest teams are able to solve issues when they are physically apart from the situation. This experience results in bonding that develops trust and helps build a stronger team.

3.5.3 Locate Centrally

I have learned about or was able to resolve many issues by simply overhearing someone speaking about something they were encountering. Locating a team close to one another allows this to happen and keeps communication more free and open, and thus allows for faster resolution of issues.

3.5.4 Centralize Issues List and Use It

The issues list should be considered a place where project challenges can be communicated and brought to the attention of all parties. Communicating of the issues through weekly or even daily issue meetings allows the BW issues to be understood.

I have worked on projects where the issues list either was not reviewed often enough by the project teams, or where individuals were unable or unwilling to add their issues to the central list, instead listing and managing their issues locally. This was the result of a culture where issues were seen as a weakness and process teams avoided making issues visible. Thus, many of the issues lingered on local lists for a long time awaiting resolution before they were centrally reported.

Many of these issues, if reported quickly, would have been resolved quickly. It is important that issues are managed centrally and tracked centrally. The project-management organization should encourage issues to be reported on the list and schedule meetings to resolve and escalate issues as necessary.

An important part of issue tracking is to clearly assign ownership of the issues to ensure that issues are addressed and escalated, if needed. The more clear the ownership of the issues, the better the action plan. Establishing clear ownership across the project also allows for a better action plan in the implementation. However, a lack of ownership can be one of the more common mistakes.

3.6 Ownership Issues

One of the quickest ways to keep a project successful is to spread the ownership of the project across the enterprise. The more involved the business users are in the project, the more the project reflects their needs. Some of the least cost effective and most tedious projects I have seen were staffed mainly with IT resources and had almost no user involvement.

I reviewed several projects that followed the same basic flawed methodology. The BW team would briefly meet with user representatives. These teams would present their requirements, and then the BW team would independently interpret those requirements and translate them into a BW data model. They would then deliver a prototype, and finally present it to the users. The users would look at the prototype, redesign it, and suggest many changes. The process would begin again.

In some cases, this iterative design works because the users are simply presenting their small changes to the model. However, in many cases, because there was little interaction between the BW team and the user representatives, the prototype was very far from what the users actually wanted. A lot of reworking of the prototype was needed in order to meet the requirements.

This extremely inefficient methodology was repeated again and again at different phases of the project. Rather than insisting that the development of the solution include active involvement of the users, the BW team simply involved them only at the beginning and the end.

Most of the time, the project managers agreed this was an inefficient use of resources. However, they found that getting the users' time to work with them on the design was not possible. This was mainly due to the perceptions of the user representatives. These individuals felt that minimal time was required from them in order to deliver the model. Once this perception was established, it was difficult to change.

The problem was in not getting the users to agree and sign off on a level of involvement from the beginning. Rather than allow this iterative development, the BW project manager must insist on time from the user community, and get this commitment before any scoping begins.

> **Tip**
> The more ownership business has in the BW solution, the more support they give when issues occur (and they will).

3.6.1 Insist on Signoff of Documents

In order to keep the involvement of the users and give them some stake in the project, I find that a simple signoff process on all requirement documents helps greatly to keep the scope and development clear to all parties involved. Typically, once stakeholders are forced to sign off on a document, their involvement increases.

3.6.2 Have the Power Users Develop the BW Queries

Another great way to keep the users responsible for business processes involved in the development process is to have them develop all queries. This gives them an understanding of the reporting tool, its advantages, and limitations and helps them to understand the data, filtering, etc.

There is nobody who knows the queries better than these business-process teams. The best way to start involving them is to identify those business users that are the most adept at understanding the requirements and learning new tools and groom them as the power users. The power user has three main roles, which are:

- Develop, test, and roll out queries to the end user community
- Aid in training the other users
- Act as the first level of support for issues

The business user community often responds well when trained by someone who understands their business and can speak to their requirements. These power users can help to answer some of the business questions that inevitably come up during the training process. They also reduce the load on the help desk after go-live because they can often assist their peers with issues.

More important, this work helps to make sure that they are part of the process and own some of the development, as well as the issues when they occur.

It is very important to make sure power users are acknowledged by management for their role on the project throughout the process. I have worked on several projects that simply would not have been successful without the extremely good power users testing and helping on issues. This is a very difficult role, so the proper recognition from management is imperative.

These power users help to address and solve some of the biggest issues on the project. Many times these issues are the result of problems with data quality. Understanding the issues that can occur as a result of data quality concerns cannot be overstated, as these often represent some of the biggest challenges in any BW project.

3.7 Data Quality Issues

Data quality refers to the fitness of the data for use by the end user. Data quality is a subjective measure, so it is not always easy to quantify. However, poor data quality is the quickest way of losing user confidence in BW. Many BW issues after go-live occur because of bad master data.

For example, a user runs a query to see the total sales by division. In this case, the user is running the report based on the division found as an attribute on the material master. In order to run the report, the system does not show the division from the transactional data, instead it looks to the master data attributes of the material reported. A small percentage of the master data division values are mistakenly left blank on the material master data. These values would not appear on the report by division, thus, to the user, the data in BW is incorrect. This user starts to lose faith in the BW system because the data is wrong.

Let's take another example. When a new material master record is created in BW, the configuration team has the option to set select fields as mandatory. However, there are no rules checking the validity of the fields, just that the values are filled.

There is also very little checking on the ECC or R/3 system for conflicting or illogical values. This would occur on fields that relate to one another. Such as making sure that any material master that is priced by weight has a net and gross weight populated in the material master. Rules to check for validity of various master data fields are often missed or not implemented in the ECC or R/3 system.

Since it is not easy to verify the master data and its validity, in most organizations there are huge mistakes and missing data in master data. This becomes a problem for BW because queries in BW are often based on this master data. Those queries that are not based on the master data itself are often referencing the transactional data that was filled from the master data in the transactional system.

This user starts to lose faith in the BW system because the data is wrong. The user is correct that the data in BW is indeed wrong. However, it is consistent with the values in the ECC or R/3 systems. If this master data is wrong, then BW will be wrong too.

Many of the BW issues are the result of this kind of error. In many projects, much of the time is spent screen-dumping the incorrect data values in the R/3 or ECC system to prove that BW matches the R/3 or ECC data. In many cases it is this source data that is incorrect. This issue is then passed onto those teams to correct.

Data quality is a very big topic; it helps to break the topic up into the following types of issues:

- **Data Integrity**
  Data must be of the proper level of granularity and must be extracted, transformed, and harmonized correctly with other data.

▶ **Data Completeness**
Data must be extracted at the right frequency at the right time for data availability with the proper level of history for analysis.

▶ **Data Timeliness**
Data extraction must include timely, fresh data with a response time that is acceptable to the user for analysis.

A good master data strategy takes into account all the possible errors and develops means to keep this data consistent.

3.7.1 Don't Completely Rely on the Source Systems to Ensure Data Quality

It is important to remember that the goal of configuring the various transactional systems is to make sure that a transaction can be entered completely, correctly, and quickly. Keeping the master data consistent is part of this job. However, even the best-configured systems end up with some bad master data.

Users do not always follow the rules and guidelines when entering master data or they inadvertently place incorrect values into the master data. To ensure that the BW system has the best data possible, it is often necessary to build some testing and checking tools in BW.

Create Transformation Rules to Check Master Data During Load

When data is loaded, it may be necessary to use rules to verify and check the data during the data loading process. The system provides many places to put transformation rules in order to determine the validity of the data. These allow for simple or complex checks of this data against established rules or against the data's source.

This is not always easy to do. However, if there are specific fields or rules that need to be applied to the master data, the master data can be checked during data loading for consistency. There are several different means and functions in BW to check this master data and determine its validity.

Create Reports to Manually Check Master Data and Spot Anomalies

All master-data InfoObjects can be turned on for reporting. This allows BW queries to be run against the master data. The queries allow checking of the master data for incorrect or inconsistent values. Although this governance is quite tedious, it does allow a more proactive checking of the master data in BW and a way to avoid some future issues with incorrect or incomplete master data.

3.7.2 Establish Active Governance of Data

Active governance refers to an active process to keep master data as accurate and complete as possible. Unfortunately, the R/3 and ECC systems have very few tools to ensure that the master data is kept consistent. There are some tools to make sure that mandatory master data values are filled, but it is very difficult to configure rules in R/3 or ECC to make sure that the various fields in master data are consistent with one another.

For instance, when a new material master record is created in BW, the configuration team has the option to set select fields as mandatory. However, there are no rules checking the validity of the fields, just that the values are filled.

There is also very little checking on the ECC or R/3 system for conflicting or illogical values. These would occur on fields that relate to one another. These include, making sure that any material master priced by weight has a net and gross weight populated in the material master. Rules to check for the validity of various master data fields are often missed or not implemented in the ECC or R/3 system.

Since it is not easy to verify the master data and its validity in most organizations, there are often mistakes and missing data in master data. This becomes a problem for BW because queries in BW are often based on this master data. Those queries not based on the master data itself often reference the transactional data that was filled from the master data in the transactional system.

This puts the BW team at an extreme disadvantage. The master data is an integral part of the success of BW, yet the master data rules and data are filled on the R/3 or ECC systems. The BW team has very little say on the configuration of that data. Thus, in most BW projects, much time is spent chasing missing or incorrect master data.

One way to do this is to work with the ECC or R/3 teams to develop active governance on their master data. This consists of running audit reports periodically on the master data to ensure its correctness.

3.7.3 Turn to a Third-Party to Help with Validation

I have worked with one third-party vendor, BackOffice Associates, that helped one project with active governance on its ECC system. Basically, its software sits on top of the ECC or R/3 system. Master data is entered into the BackOffice system, checked for rules, completeness, etc., and then BackOffice saves the master data into the ECC or R/3 system.

If data is incorrect or missing, the system does not allow the data to be entered. It also has a component to make sure that if there are several roles involved in establishing the master data, each user can perform his or her own role and notify the next role group. Thus, if a new product requires information from purchasing, finance, and the warehouse groups, each one can enter its part, and the data can be verified and passed onto the next group.

This process, whether handled manually using workflow in ECC or R/3 or handled via a third-party vendor, can safeguard the integrity of the master data and thus help the overall quality of the reporting solution that is built with this master data at its core.

If a third party system cannot be implemented, a significant effort should be planned before each new BW implementation to check and fix the master data to make sure that BW has the most complete and consistent master data for reporting.

Processes should also be put in place to ensure that data is checked periodically for completeness and consistency.

There is another third-party vendor that does provide a very good tool in order to validate data from the SAP source systems and the BW system. This is called Validata from Validata LLC. See the section in this chapter on third party tools for more information on this product, or visit this site: *www.validatabw.com*.

Once data has been validated and found to clearly match its source, the next step is to assimilate this data together into a clear and consistent BW data model. This process is often called harmonization of data or data alignment. The process of aligning data can be quite challenging, and is a frequent source of challenges.

3.8 Data Alignment Issues

Data alignment involves taking data from various source systems and harmonizing that data so that it is consistent and appears to have come from one source. It is very common to overlook the complexity of aligning data from different systems and performing the transformation to keep this data consistent.

3.8.1 Master Data Alignment

There are several strategies for combining master data in BW. We need to combine master data when there is more than one source system providing master data values for BW. For instance, a company may have two different purchasing systems, one for external orders and another for internal orders. The transactional data from each of the systems will be loaded into BW, so the associated master data also needs to be loaded into BW.

These two systems are independent of one another and the master data values are not in sync between the two systems. How can we make sure that the master data is loaded but also make sure that there are no collisions between the streams of data? A collision occurs when each system has the same master data key. If this occurs, the values would overwrite and cause inconsistent values in the master data.

Master data alignment refers to the process of removing duplicates and bringing data together with a common key. For example, in order to perform global reporting on Wal-Mart, a common Wal-Mart customer number needs to be determined, and all Wal-Mart locations must then reference that number. This is not always easy because of the many ways that each of the local systems has used to store customer data.

Often these differing systems do not use a common master data key. However, for a global BW project to be successful, the master data must use a common key. This would guarantee that reporting across the enterprise can occur with a common material number, customer number, etc. This effort requires taking existing master data, removing the duplicates, determining commonality, and centralizing this data into one structure. This effort is often a very difficult task.

Typically, most data alignment efforts must take place outside the BW system. This is because it is very difficult for BW to provide active governance and perform merging and matching of master data objects when these are loaded into BW from several source systems.

This alignment is vital to ensuring that data from different source systems do not overwrite each other. For example, without master data alignment, one R/3 system can have customer 1234 identified as Wal-Mart and another R/3 system could have customer 1234 as Target. If both R/3 systems load customer data into BW, these customer numbers need to be handled to ensure that there is no overwriting of master data in the enterprise data warehouse (EDW).

Master Data Maintenance (MDM)

The most popular tool for master data alignment in SAP is Master Data Maintenance (MDM). Although this tool is not related to BW, the results of common master-data governance with common master-data keys provide a great opportunity to allow for global reporting and global alignment of data. The MDM tool allows for this central monitoring and governance of master data. The goals of MDM are the following:

- Reduce the inaccuracies and redundancies of master data
- Allow a one-stop maintenance of data
- Provide a central master data repository

These goals fit in very well with the reporting goals of BW.

> **Tip**
> The more effort spent keeping master data aligned, correct, and less redundant, the better the resulting reporting is in BW.

Concatenated Keys or Compound Keys?

If data cannot be easily harmonized, many BW projects look for a way to make the data unique, even if it is not unique at its source. Since the data cannot be loaded verbatim without facing collisions of data with the same keys, a new approach is needed.

The most common approach to making the data unique is to use either a compound or concatenated key. Both of these processes change the key structure of the data to make each loaded value unique from its source. This allows data from two different sources that otherwise would collide to be harmonized into one master data table.

The compound master data key approach appends a key onto the master data values with a designator for the source system. The concatenated approach increases the size of the master data key and prefixes the value with a source-system identifier. Both approaches ensure that no data is duplicated when data is loaded into BW.

The differences in the two approaches center on establishing the data integrity and keeping the two sets of data separate. When using a compound master data key, the system is added to the master data key to make a new compound key. For example, Material A1 can be the same in two source systems. Thus, if the key is not just material number A1, but material A1 and a source-system designator, the two values remain unique.

Concatenating the data would simply change the existing key value by giving the value a prefix with the source system. In this case, material A1 would be SYS01_A1 and SYS02_A1. These ensure that the two values also remain unique.

The concatenation approach is much less invasive and allows more flexibility with the data model than the compounding approach, so in general terms it makes sense to favor the concatenation approach. A compound key is much more difficult to remove. The compound key value must always be shown in queries. Without it, a user can make an incorrect assumption because—without the source system being shown—the system can and will aggregate values based on the customer number. This can be a problem if the values are not consistent. This problem does not occur with the concatenation approach.

However, both approaches affect how the data is stored in BW. In many cases, the user is not presented with the compound values or concatenated values in their queries. Another field is added as an attribute of the master data and is used to show the value to the user independent of the concatenation. The filters in the query make sure the same material does not appear twice.

A better and more long-term approach would be to harmonize these values into one material code. This requires work to analyze the data, decide on a common value, and provide the change management to move to this common value. This can be difficult and time-consuming.

3.8.2 Transactional Data Alignment

Transactional data alignment can also prove to be a very difficult effort. For example, suppose a company has orders coming in from two different systems, one ECC and the other a legacy system. The company wants to be able to report these ordered together. This causes significant challenges.

The two systems may have radically different ways of treating and saving transactional data. They may also have different values for master data elements such as the customer or the material. Therefore, the effort to bring the data into BW involves creating complex transformation logic to bring the data into a common format. This often involves a series of cross-reference tables that must be read to convert this data.

The level of effort for this process can be easily overlooked. There is no easy way to perform the data harmonization other than to clearly understand both sources of data and map together the fields one by one. This is a tedious and lengthy process.

To make the process easier, I recommend that the original sources of data be first loaded unchanged into their own DSO structures. Thus, there are two DSO structures, one with the legacy data and one with the ECC data. This data can then be combined into a second level or subsequent DSO. The transformation rules are used to transform data into the second-level DSO.

This allows for a much easier reconciliation and reload of data because each source exists unchanged from the source in its own BW DSO. If there is an issue with the harmonization of the data, the second-level DSO can be purged and reloaded from the two sources of data once the transformation rule or cross-reference table is adjusted to fix the error.

Even the best efforts to align data can lead to incorrect results. When the data in BW is incorrect, it is usually not easy to fix. Most often, this means dumping out the data and reloading from the source. For obvious reasons, this needs to be avoided as much as possible in any BW project. Anticipating the realignment needs and avoiding realignment as much as possible helps to make the project more successful. In the next section I will describe some common issues with realignment and show how these can be avoided.

3.9 Data Realignment

Realignment is a nasty word in a BW project. Realignment refers to the process of taking data that has already been loaded into BW and changing some of the attributes of the data so that it can be presented differently to the end user. The problem with data realignments in BW is that many of these realignments require a full dump and reload of BW data. This can cause a severe interruption of the data warehouse.

In a typical realignment scenario, the InfoProviders need to be purged of all data, the rules for aligning data need to be adjusted, and the data needs to be reloaded. Often this means a shutdown of the transactional system while the data is reloaded. Downtime of the R/3 or ECC systems can be substantial, depending on the volume of data that needs to be reloaded.

The complexity and pressure of shutting out the users from the transactional system and effort to test and validate the data in BW make for an extremely difficult realignment process.

3.9.1 Realignment Without Reload—Is It Possible?

Many organizations handle realignments often without ever reloading master data. This is done by preparing the BW data model for the realignment in the design phase of the project. If a BW project team can find out where and on which fields the realignments typically take place, they can often make sure that the fields needed for realignment are part of the master data objects, thus making it possible to realign without performing a dump and reload of the transactional data values. Let's look at two possible realignment scenarios.

> **Scenario 1**
>
> Sales order data is loaded into BW by sales division, and the sales division is loaded into the transactional data from the master data. This data is stored directly into the InfoCube and used for reporting by the users.

> **Scenario 2**
>
> Sales order data is loaded into BW by sales division, but the sales division is not loaded directly into the InfoCube. The data is read dynamically in the query as an attribute of the material. The queries for reporting on the sales division use the attribute of the material master to reflect the division, thus the users always see the current material master data for the division in their queries.

The sales department now gets a new vice president and she decides to change the sales-division rollups for reporting. In Scenario 1, to realign the data, the transactional data must be purged and reloaded. This is because the values are loaded into the transaction data values with an *as-posted view*. This as-posted view hard-codes the value of the sales division into the transactional data of the InfoCube at the time it is saved. Thus, in order to change these values, the data must be reloaded.

In Scenario 2 a dump and reload of data is not required. In fact, during realignment in the second scenario there is nothing that needs to be done. The realignment occurs naturally because as the divisions change in the master data in the ECC or R/3 systems, the master data in BW would automatically change.

When this data changes, the resulting queries would then show the new values rather than the as-posted values in the transactional data. The two sample scenarios show that realignments in BW can be avoided if:

- We anticipate the fields that will be needed for realignment
- The users accept the restated field in their queries

The second bullet point can be a very complex and stir heated debate among users. The design of BW and the shared master data allow for both an as-posted view of data and a restated view of data. As the two scenarios show, the as-posted view hard-codes values into the InfoProvider, as the values existed at the time of the transaction. The restated view represents the values from the master data, as it currently exists.

It is important to make sure users understand that they have this option when viewing data in BW. When a query is created, both options are possible. You can use a display attribute to show a value, or the same value might also appear in the transactional data.

Using the display attribute from master data always ensures that the user is seeing the most current view of the data and will automatically realign the data via the normal master data changes. When an ECC or R/3 user changes the division, the new division will automatically appear in the associated BW reports.

There is a performance concern with the restated view. This view is typically much slower than the corresponding query on the transactional data because the system must access the master data table to provide the data. This can be offset by adding database indices or BW aggregates, if needed.

Any BW system with significant data loaded has the potential for performance issues. Understanding and avoiding these as much as possible can circumvent many common BW issues. In the next section, I will discuss some of the common performance issues and their impact on BW.

3.10 Performance Issues

Outside of data quality, performance is the most important concern in BW. What makes performance tuning in BW so challenging is that many of the decisions made early in the project affect the performance significantly.

> **Note**
>
> Unlike the R/3 or ECC systems, the majority of the performance problems in BW are not the result of the database or Basis system setup. They occur because of the data-modeling decisions made by the applications team.

In this respect, BW is unlike almost all other SAP modules. Usually there are few decisions that the applications team can do to affect the performance of a module in R/3 or ECC. When performance is slow, it is due to a network, database, or Basis issue. In BW, the performance tuning must be built into the application during the configuration.

Unfortunately this is not always done, or done well. One project manager I worked with described performance planning and data modeling in BW as a young man getting a tattoo: "Sometimes a decision that you make when you are young and new to the world is one that you may regret later, and they aren't always easy to change."

> **Tip**
>
> Data modeling is an area where good advice can make a data model performance optimal not only for the current needs but also for future growth. Invest in a good data architect for your BW project and hold onto that resource.

3.10.1 Establish Clear Goals for Performance

Performance is a very nebulous topic. One user could perceive a performance issue where another does not. The only way to understand and prioritize performance issues is to develop a method for tracking and measuring performance and, most important, goals for performance in the organization.

These goals should be established for both query-presentation and loading performance. This best statement of goals comes in the form of a service level agreement (SLA) with the end users. The SLA should state the average goal for query performance and uptime of BW. This sets the goal for measurement and tracking of the BW system.

An SLA at one organization set the overall query performance to stay under 30 seconds, on average. Because the implementation had large volumes of data, it was a challenge to maintain aggregates and queries so that they would bring back smaller amounts of data to the users in order to keep the overall performance of the system within the goal. The SLA in an organization depends on many factors, however, after the system has been stable for a few weeks, it is usually a good time to assess goals and reset the SLA, if needed.

Data Load Performance Goals

In most BW projects, the majority of data loading occurs each evening. The loads are usually designed to be complete by the next morning so the users can query the data. If the data loading performance is sub-standard, or runs late, the InfoCubes and DSO structures aren't loaded in time for the users to perform their reporting.

The data load performance goals should clearly state when data is supposed to be available for the end user's reporting.

Query Performance Goals

Query performance is one of the most important factors for users. They expect queries to return their desired data as quickly as possible. The problem is that many times the users are unaware of the data volume in BW and don't understand how the way they query this data can affect performance.

Part of any query-performance goal in BW is training the users to go after the data in the most efficient manner. Users who drill a report down to the most detailed level might feel that the report is performing poorly, when, in-fact, they might be better off looking that the data at a more aggregated level and only drilling into the data that is relevant for their analysis. This should be considered an important part of BW training.

3.10.2 Measure Against the Performance Goals via Statistics InfoCubes

BW has effective tools for monitoring performance. The most important of these tools are the statistics InfoCubes. These InfoCubes allow for reporting on load performance, query performance, and use of the BW system.

As part of my job, I do a lot of performance consulting and review of BW systems. As I look at many of their systems, I am amazed at how often projects either do not have the statistics InfoCubes activated at or are not using the statistics data in their production systems to monitor performance.

> **Tip**
>
> Monitoring of the statistics InfoCubes is the single best way to make sure that you can be proactive rather than reactive in your performance efforts.

There really is no other way to address, determine severity, and set the priorities of issues without the statistics InfoCubes.

3.10.3 Establish a Performance Sub-Team

Several project teams have created a performance sub-team to track performance issues in BW. This sub-team needs to be made up of representatives from the Basis team, the database team, the applications team, and business users. The team can work together to look at the statistics information to determine which queries and data loads are the most important and how to rank and discuss performance issues.

This would not be the full-time job of the performance sub-team members. The members act as a committee to solve performance problems and give some visibility to BW performance tracking and issue resolution. It is important to have representatives from Basis, database, applications, and the business operations to make sure that the issues are addressed together.

Sometimes, because these groups represent different parts of the organization, they don't formally work together on performance issues, and problems linger while one group points to another in defining the root of the issue.

By using the statistics InfoCubes for this analysis, the team can quantify a performance issue. If a query is running slowly but that query is only run a few times per month, there is very little payoff from tuning that query for performance. However, having the business as part of the performance team can help, especially if the business users determine that the few such queries run each month are for the CIO. Suddenly, this query becomes much more important to tune.

3.10.4 Keep Up-to-Date on Support Packages

One of the most important ways of keeping performance optimal in BW is to stay current with support packages. SAP adds significant performance-enhancement modifications to each support package and can minimize various bottlenecks in loading and query performance.

3.10.5 Data Model for Performance

Entire books have been written on data modeling, so this topic is quite vast. However, one of the very important factors in establishing a data model is to clearly understand how the decision-making in BW affects the overall performance of the data model. Poor performance can manifest itself in both load performance and query performance. Thus, understanding the effects of the data model on performance is crucial to making sure that the data model is optimal.

Data Granularity

One critical decision that is made very early in BW development is the granularity of the data stored in BW. The granularity of data refers to the lowest level of data that is stored in BW.

For example, when loading sales orders into BW, there are many choices of granularity. Data can be loaded at the most detailed sales-order schedule line level, showing each release of the sales order. It could also be loaded into BW and aggregated monthly without the document detail at all. The granularity of the data is determined based on the keys of data in the DSO structure or the combination of the characteristics in an InfoCube. The characteristics are the data fields used to analyze the key figure values in an InfoCube.

If I include the sales-order schedule line, line item, and header information in every sales order that I load into BW, I increase the volume exponentially over the same data that is aggregated monthly. This increase in volume typically leads to inferior performance in BW simply because the system must look through a larger data set in order to perform analysis.

In order to make sure that performance is considered when looking at data in BW, we must understand the granularity of the data and thus the size of the data that is being loaded into BW. When I am evaluating BW designs for a project, one of the first things I ask is: "What is the data volume that you expect in this InfoCube/DSO?"

Decreasing the granularity does not automatically improve the performance, but it goes a long way toward aiding the performance and flexibility of the data model.

Of course, there is a price to pay for decreasing the granularity. The flexibility of the analysis is also dictated by the granularity of the data. If the lowest level of granularity for my sales data is monthly, I cannot analyze sales by day or week. In BW, it is very difficult to serve both needs. You must take into account the needs of the users and balance this against the performance needs of the users.

The way most projects handle this concern is to pull the detailed data into the DSO in BW, and aggregate the data up into the InfoCubes. Whenever possible, the detailed data lies in the DSO and the less granular data is in the InfoCube.

Hybrid Approach to Granularity

There is also a hybrid approach that works rather well in many implementations. This is to have two or more InfoCubes with differing levels of granularity. For example, there may be many people in the organization that look at sales data at a monthly level. These people make up the majority of the user base.

However, there are a few users who require this same sales data at a lower level of granularity, weekly, or even daily. In order to satisfy the users with the lowest level of granularity you could create one sales InfoCube and have the time characteristic of 0CALDAY and/or 0CALWEEK. By adding and populating these time characteristics, the data is automatically at a daily or weekly level of granularity. This increases the volume of data exponentially, and load performance and query performance suffer as a result.

Why should the majority of the user base suffer the performance burdens for the few users who desire the data at a very granular level? The answer is that in many cases they shouldn't. How can we give them their data at a much summarized level while also providing the data at a granular level for the other users?

The answer is to create two InfoCubes and queries that are exactly the same except for the time characteristics. One InfoCube would include the time characteristics of 0CALDAY or 0CALWEEK. The other would only include the 0CALMONTH and neither 0CALDAY nor 0CALWEEK. This makes sure that the level of granularity in one InfoCube is at the day or week level and the other is at the monthly level.

The users who desire the monthly reporting could be pointed to the monthly query and thus would have significantly better performance because of the reduced volume of data queried.

Train the Query Developers Properly

Some of the worst query performance issues projects face are because of the design of the queries themselves. BW is designed to allow users to bring back a great deal of data in one pass. This flexibility allows users to take poor advantage of BW's query power.

Some users create queries that bring back huge volumes of data in the first pass. This happens because users are accustomed to working with several very long reports. Having acquired huge volumes of data, the user can then look at these multiple-page reports and find information on any issue or question that they have.

BW works best in an interactive, drill-down fashion. A query should take advantage of this approach. The first view of a sales query should not typically show the sales data by customer and material at a very detailed level that stretches on for many pages. Instead, the report should be structured to show that same data at a higher level, perhaps sales by sales organization. The users can then use the interactivity and slicing technique to hone the overall sales data to the specific data they desire.

They might first drill down by sales organization, eliminating the sales organizations that are not relevant, and then select by distribution channel, division, etc. This drilling down reduces the granularity at each selection. By the time the user gets down to a detailed level, the volume of data returned is limited, and thus performance is better.

Sometimes issues occur with BW projects that are outside the control of the users or development teams. These technical issues can not only slow a project, but depending on the level of understanding of the Basis team, can linger and cause many unnecessary delays. In the next session I will discuss these issues.

3.11 Technical and Infrastructure Issues

There are many technical and infrastructure issues that can cause BW implementations to fail or be delayed. For example, I worked on a large BW implementation that loaded large volumes of data into the system. When reporting on this data, the system occasionnally queried the data so slowly that it would take several minutes to bring up a query that previously took several minutes. I quickly reported the issue to the Basis and database teams.

This issue was not addressed quickly because the Basis team attributed the issue to the resource constrained development and QA systems. We continued to suffer through the issue through unit testing and integration testing. It was only when the issue surfaced in the production environment that the Basis team reacted to the issue.

This was very late in the implementation process, and what should have been a high priority issue early was left to fester until the issue became an emergency. These types of technical issues need to be recognized and addressed as soon as possible. Several of these issues are listed here:

- **Application Issues**
  These issues are common on a BW project. They are typically resolved either through an SAP Note application or a support package. A BW support package is an interim patch from SAP that contains numerous fixes for the BW system. These support packages are issued periodically by SAP and are listed in the SAP Service Marketplace.
  In between the support packages, SAP often issues SAP Notes to fix single issues. SAP does encourage BW applications fixes to be implemented through a support package. This is to ensure that the fixes coordinate with one another. Thus, if a fix is not critical, it may make sense to wait until a support pakkage is released in order to get the latest fix. If the fix is critical, the fix can be implemented via an SAP Note.

- **Database Issues**
  BW is a database-independent system. Thus, projects can choose any database system in order to use with BW. However, some databases work better with BW than others. This is because the more popular databases like

Oracle are used by more projects and thus issues are discovered more quickly and can be resolved quickly. Most database issues are fixed via a patch from the database provider.

- **Network Infrastructure Issues**
  Network issues can cause BW issues both during data loading and query presentation. Network stability and size are vital to BW's success. An improperly sized newtwork infrastructure can cause data transfer to slow or even stop altogether.

- **System Issues**
  These involve disk, memory, and similar aspects. Sizing of a BW system is very difficult because the sizing effort typically takes place before any BW data is loaded and before the true scope of the project has been determined. Thus, periodcally, the sizing effort should be reveiewed to determine if the size of the BW system is adequate for current demand and future growth.

- **Desktop Issues**
  Users with various desktop configurations will access BW. BW integrates with Microsoft Excel and with the user's Internet browser. Keeping the desktops at a standard release and patch level of these products help to minimize some of the technical issues that can arise from older and more unstable versions of these products.

The technical issues can be quickly resolved through a clear testing and escalation process when issues occur. However, as with any team, the deeper the knowledge of those on the team the more likely the team is to succeed. A stong team that understands the issues faced in BW and works together to solve them is an asset to any project. When this team strength fails to occur, the opposite is true.

In the next section, I will discuss some common BW team resource issues.

3.12 Resource Issues

Many potential resource issues can arise on a BW project. Resource issues involve team members and the interaction among the different roles and personalities on the project. Because any BW project requires a significant amount of communication between the various teams in the organization, the team dynamic of a BW team is crucial to its success.

3.12.1 Insist on the Best, Not Just the Most Available

For a BW project to be successful, it is imperative that the BW team has subject matter experts working on the project team from day to day. In the best projects, the organizations have dedicated these people 100 percent to the BW team and free them up from their other responsibilities.

It is through the constant interaction with the subject-matter experts that the BW data warehouse can clearly represent the needs of the business. A good subject-matter expert can see a potential problem very early in the process, allowing the project team to switch course in the design before too much time is wasted.

It is not always easy to get the most qualified subject-matter experts. Here is an example of a very common struggle on a BW project. There is an employee named Melanie who works as a sales department analyst. She is responsible for providing the various reports that the sales department needs to run their operation.

Melanie would be a perfect fit for the BW project because of her vast knowledge of the reporting parameters. However, the business unit does not want to give Melanie up because she is too valuable to its organization. The organizations with the best projects understand that they need to provide this level of resource to the BW team to make it successful.

3.12.2 The Consultant-Heavy Project

It is quite common for projects to fall into the trap of having the consultants do all the work, with very few employees involved. This happens because it is much easier in many projects to defer the work to the experts. In this case, the experts are the consultants.

I have provided reviews for projects where I could not find one employee on the BW project. A very political discussion ensues when the consulting partner is asked why there isn't employee participation on the project.

In one case, I was presented with an organization chart that showed that there were employees on the project team. It was clear that the day-to-day configuration and project development work was solely done by consultants. Make sure your day-to-day decision-making and configuration is provided, at least in part, by employees.

The quickest and easiest route is usually the one that is most often taken. In this case, the quickest and easiest is simply to have the consultants provide the configuration and completely lead and support the implementation.

In my experience, often the largest SAP consulting partners are most guilty of this practice. This is because of a conflict in goals. The consulting partner is measured by its ability to bring a project live, on-time, and within budget. How can you do this if you are spending time keeping the employees up-to-speed? It is much easier doing the configuration, and then planning a hand-off of the project configuration, after it is complete, in a knowledge-transfer process.

The consultants on the project must then be charged not only with implementing the project but also bringing the employees up to speed on the product and nuances of the BW product. Unless there is a serious mandate to do this, it rarely happens in a project. It is the employee BW project manager's responsibility to make sure this occurs. If this is left up only to the consultants or the management of the consulting partner, it rarely happens.

You should rely on your consultants to provide the product and BW configuration knowledge. However, make sure employees are in charge of each area of BW and are performing the configuration. The consultants are there for issue management and implementation advice.

3.12.3 Insist on Interviewing All Candidates

To ensure that a consultant fits into the culture of an organization and is competent to do the work, it is important that an interview process is conducted. Use the BW knowledgeable consultants to determine the product knowledge, and take time to assess the interpersonal fit.

3.12.4 Transition Out Bad Consultants

Every project, sooner or later, ends up with a consultant that is not a good fit. It is amazing to me how many projects let poor consultants continue working on the project. I feel that the reason you staff a project with consultants is so you can use their advice and later transition them off the project. Therefore, it is difficult to understand why an organization might be hesitant to remove a non-productive resource.

On larger BW projects, the staffing is done by the consulting partner. The situation can become quite political if you ask the consulting partner to provide you with resources, make the partner accountable for the project's success, and then tell their resources to go home. It is quite difficult for them to be successful if you do not allow them to staff with those they think would be a good fit.

However, if a consultant does not fit in with the organization culture, has communication issues, or does not have the skill set to complete the BW tasks, then transition this consultant off the project. Try to remember that a poor consultant not only does not help the process, but slows the process because the rest of the team must slow down to keep them up to speed.

3.12.5 Avoid Conflict Between Consulting Partners, SAP, and Others

I have also worked on BW projects that get rather political. This is because no matter how a project is staffed, there is a competition at the high level to secure the limited consulting spots.

> **Example**
> I worked on one project where the various consulting companies' project team members would not freely work together to resolve issues. They each felt the delays on the project were the result of the others' incompetence. This caused the project to be delayed even more as issues lingered longer than needed.

It is frustrating when the various consulting firms are trying to cover their own mistakes and emphasize the mistakes of others for political gain with the client.

Sometimes I see clients who lose track of the big-picture goal of consulting firms. There are two goals of a consulting firm. The first is to keep the client happy through successful project management and consulting advice; the second is to improve the consulting firm's position at the client site.

The second goal can be counterproductive to the first goal. Various consulting firms attempt to gather more consulting seats on a project, and there are only two ways to do this: grow the project, or take existing seats. Sometimes it seems easier for a consulting partner to spend his time casting doubt on various participants in the project in hopes he can gain more consulting seats than it would be to ensure quality work that could ultimately grow the business, which in turn would expand the BW project.

Thus, I have worked on projects where I was forced to spend a great deal of time justifying the various goals and methodology when that time could have been spent on the configuration and tuning of the BW system. Although a certain amount of verification is good to ensure the methodology is sound, this can get out of control if it severely interferes with accomplishing the goals of the project.

This problem is ultimately a result of the culture of the organization and cannot be tolerated. In the best-run projects, the consulting firm is irrelevant. The project goals are the ultimate goals. Watch for this in your project and make every effort to stop this counterproductive behavior.

3.12.6 R/3 or ECC Basis Experience is Not BW Experience

A Basis team refers to the technical team in any organization that performs the technical system operations such as installation, support package upgrades, or backup and recovery.

BW is a very different implementation than R/3 or ECC systems. The BW application team typically has much more interaction with the Basis team than does any other. Making sure the Basis resources are knowledgeable in the product helps to make sure that all teams function at their best.

Sometimes, in order to fill a Basis role, an ECC or R/3 Basis resource will be used to fill the BW Basis role. It should be understood that BW has many fundamental Basis tasks that are unique to its environment. Therefore, an ECC or R/3 Basis team member accustomed to dealing with transactional data in the relational database structure of ECC or R/3 often has an unexpected learning curve when dealing with the unique star schema design of BW and a data-warehouse environment. Thus, it is necessary that the Basis resources have sound Basis skills, in supporting and maintaining the *BW* environment.

3.12.7 Keep the Project Team Physically Together

It is amazing how many issues are solved by simply sitting in close proximity. Many times a seemingly insignificant, overheard conversation can evolve into a design session that solves some of the most challenging project issues. If the team members are physically separate in different buildings, or even separate countries, this dynamic thinking is much more difficult.

It also helps to try to avoid some of the political issues that can occur on any BW project. These issues often involve collaboration within the team and between the team and its management and other management in the business. In the next section I will discuss common political issues.

3.13 Political Issues

Any BW project has its political issues. Sometimes these are the result of the priorities of the BW project; other times they are a direct result of the project manager. For instance, I was bought into a company to help assess the BW project in order to pinpoint why the project was slow to achieve results. I was first introduced to the project manager, who gave me a background of the project and the timeline. After watching the interaction of the project manager and the business organization for a very short time, it was clear that there was animosity between the two teams.

The reason for the animosity involved two different personalities in BW project management and one area of the business. Because these two managers could not get along, they worked to make sure the other was not successful. This caused the BW project to suffer and eventually caused it to be cancelled.

Understanding and avoiding these kinds of political conflicts can help an otherwise doomed BW project succeed. It is a fact that BW projects have the potential to be quite political. This is the result of the flow of information in the organization. It is inevitable that in the process of setting priorities for the subject matter to implement and defining the implementation strategy the project will become quite political.

The best way to overcome most political issues is with open communication and a project management organization that is willing to step in and resolve political issues when they arise.

Another common issue that can occur is when a project team attempts to change the system very drastically via customization. In the next section, I will discuss some of the common issues with over-customization.

3.14 Over-Customization

It is very easy to fall into the trap of over-customization. Typically this occurs when, rather than changing the process, companies opt to change the software or look to a third-party vendor to provide functionality. This adds much more risk and complexity to a project.

These risks are very difficult to quantify because the customizations that are required have never been done, so there is no template for scope. Applications that are not customized can be benchmarked against like projects. The dangers of over-customization are as follows:

- The more customized a solution, the fewer people are *in the know* about the solution, making support more difficult
- Testing is more complex
- Integration with other products is more challenging
- Upgrades are more complex

How can we avoid the trap of over-customizing our BW solution? The next subsections give some insight on this issue.

3.14.1 Determine If the Customization Can Take Place Outside BW

There are many organizations that opt to severely customize BW and transform data. In my experience, this is usually to harmonize data from an outside source to an SAP source of data. For example, if there are internal orders that are processed in an external system, we might want to extract the data from the internal orders legacy system and combine these internal orders with the other orders existing in the R/3 or ECC system. How can we do that?

We need to perform some significant transformation of data to make sure that the material numbers, customer numbers, order types, etc., are populated with consistent values so the orders can be analyzed together.

To extract the order data from the legacy system, a program is usually written to extract the data. In many cases, you can eliminate a cumbersome transformation of data in BW and centralize the development and transformation issues if you make the transformation of the data part of the legacy extraction program. This provides a single point of failure with the extraction and allows for easier testing in BW.

This approach often is better for performance because BW simply loads the file directly rather than provide the transformation and loading. In most environments, changing and testing of the extraction program can be less cumbersome than changing and testing of the BW transformation. This is because BW requires transports, reloads, etc., while the transformation program would only require a change to the program.

3.14.2 Develop a "Why not SAP?" Approach

The next step to reduce customization in BW is to reduce or eliminate third-party software solutions in the landscape. The best way of doing this is to develop a "why not SAP?" approach to customization tools.

This philosophy is very simple. Any time that a non-SAP product is used, there are always complexities that arise. This occurs no matter how integrated the product appears to be. I have worked on many projects that employ a third-party system for use with BW. I have never seen a seamless integration between the tool and BW.

There are usually connection and integration issues. These issues can take a long time to resolve because there are typically few people who understand both the third-party system and BW.

The best way to avoid these kinds of issues is to push back very hard on any requirement that requires the use of any third-party solution. I am not saying that third-party systems should never be used with BW. However, I would recommend that these be avoided whenever possible. This simplifies the environment and centralizes the issues on one product.

> **Tip**
>
> In most projects, there are enough issues simply getting R/3 or ECC data cleanly into BW without the added complexity of a third-party tool. Say no to the third-party tools unless absolutely necessary.

3.14.3 Know Where Many BW Projects Use Third-Party Tools

There are some circumstances where the business process cannot be redesigned or the requirements that are needed are not possible in the SAP environment. The next sections describe the common third-party tools and the typical reasons for employing them.

Extracting, Transformation, and Loading (ETL) Tool

An Extraction, Transformation, and Loading (ETL) tool is used to centrally alter or change data that is loaded from one or many sources of data. This tool is usually required in companies that have multiple sources or external data and they need significant harmonization of this data prior to loading the data into BW. The ETL tool can analyze, synchronize, or homogenize the data. The tool makes sure that this analysis and transformation is done in one central place in the environment.

Figure 3.1 Typical ETL Architecture

Figure 3.1 shows a typical ETL environment. An ETL tool is needed because there are multiple legacy systems and the data needs to be transformed centrally. Although this data could be transformed directly in BW, if there are other destinations the data either would have to be fed out of BW or transformed again.

Some companies prefer that this transformation take place in a central place, with a central tool set. The ETL acts as a hub. All feeds come into the ETL tool, and then ETL sends the feeds to the various destination systems.

> **Tip**
>
> An ETL tool should not be used between the R/3 or ECC system and BW.

R/3 or ECC data should be loaded directly from those systems' DataSources into BW. You should not plan on having an ETL between R/3 or ECC and BW. An ETL would cause a significant level of complexity and managing deltas, tracking loads, etc., would be much more difficult, if not impossible.

This is because one of the major strengths of BW as an integrated tool is the delivered extractors (in BW these are called DataSources) that are part of the ECC or R/3 systems. The DataSources can be extracted from one table or a complex program that pulls data from many different source tables to provide data to BW. Typically, projects do not use an ETL tool between R/3 or ECC and BW because the ETL tool cannot take advantage of these DataSources and would require significant work before it could implement them.

This is also true of other SAP data. CRM, APO, ICH, etc. also have DataSources that are delivered or can be created via a function in the system. This allows for an easier extraction of data than would be required if the extractor programs needed to be created in these systems.

Thus, for most implementations, using an ETL tool only as part of the non-SAP data is the norm. This allows the ETL tool to provide benefits without the effort of recreating the DataSources on the SAP source system.

OLAP Tools

There are various OLAP tools on the market that can be used with BW. OLAP tools serve as a presentation layer for delivering BW data to the end user. Most projects use the SAP-provided Business Explorer (BEx) and web tools to present BW data. However, there are some projects that opt for a third-party (non-SAP) OLAP toolset.

To gather data, the OLAP tools take advantage of SAP's Business Application Programming Interfaces (BAPIs). These are standard interfaces used to access data in BW. Major OLAP vendors are Crystal Reports, Cognos, SAS, Microstrategy, and Business Objects. When project teams turn to an OLAP tool, it is usually because:

- Users are already familiar with an OLAP tool, so using it with BW leverages this knowledge.
- The OLAP tool provides some functionality that BW does not, typically formatted reporting.

> **Tip**
> As a general rule, I recommend that projects not use a third-party OLAP tool.

There are usually unexpected complexities with the tool. No matter how seamlessly vendors claim their products interact with the SAP data, I have found that this is typically not the case.

> **Example**
> I worked with a project that was implementing a third-party OLAP tool, and we continued to have performance support help desk and data access issues for many months. When these issues occurred, we were often stuck between the third-party OLAP support vendor, our database vendor, and SAP's support.
>
> When analyzing issues, it was extremely difficult to understand where the problem was occurring. The third-party OLAP support group would tell us that the SAP BW application was causing the issue. We would report this to SAP, they would claim that it is not an applications issue, and push the issue back to the third-party OLAP provider support. Sometimes the database application would also be blamed. We had trouble establishing who actually owned the issues, so they lingered in limbo.

The bright news is that SAP, in version NW 2004s, has added significant functionality for formatted reporting and enhanced reporting capabilities, with many more features planned in future releases. Thus, the functionality gap between the BEx and web reporting tools and third-party vendors is shrinking.

Projects sometimes fall into the trap of planning to use a third-party OLAP tool in the very early stages of the project. This is even before their users have seen and worked with the BEx tool. When implementing BW, I typically recommend that they hold off on any third-party OLAP tool decision until after they fully see the OLAP tools of BW. Although third-party OLAP tools do provide some features, the complexities of these tools usually make them much more difficult to implement and add significant time to the project timeline.

I recommend that projects plan their first rollout of BW with the tools provided in BW. This allows them to use these tools and get familiar with them. It is very common that pushing off the third-party OLAP tool for reporting to another phase of the project allows this requirement to be eliminated altogether, because project organizations are quite satisfied with the power of the BEx and web tools in BW.

Scheduling Tools

BW requires a significant effort in loading data. This typically occurs in the evening hours in batch. When BW is live, there is a process for getting the batch-loading schedule correct. This is because data typically is being extracted from multiple source systems at various times and loaded into BW. Issues can arise when data can only be loaded after a specific event has occurred in a legacy system.

> **Example**
>
> A company using a legacy system to track freight payments needs to load these payments into BW. However, BW should pull the day's freight payments only after the freight payment posting process is run on the legacy system. This is once each evening, but at different times depending on the activity of the day. How can we make sure that BW only pulls the data after the posting process is complete?

We do not want BW to pull the data too early, before the process is complete. We could build a long delay into the data loading process and not pull into very late in the evening to make sure we get the data. This might not be possible, though, if there is a very tight batch window with many dependent jobs on the freight payments load.

We need to make sure that BW can pull the data immediately after the posting process is complete. Because this process occurs outside of the BW and SAP environment, it can be difficult to raise an event when this occurs. Thus, a third-party scheduler outside of BW can be used to schedule the freight payments loading and then, once loading is successfully scheduled, kick off a process chain in BW to load this data.

This can also be used for any other non-SAP scheduling as well. If certain other legacy processes need to take place before data should be pulled, the scheduler can ensure that this occurs.

Some popular third-party schedulers are Maestro and Control M. SAP also has a partnership with Redwood software's Cronacle scheduling software. This product may be preferred over Maestro and Control M because SAP supports the product; any issues with the product can be handled through the normal SAP help desk process. This may prevent the project team from being caught between the third-party vendor and SAP when issues occur.

3.14.4 Validation Tools

BW does not provide validation tools out of the box to easily determine that the data from the SAP source systems matches the data that gets loaded into BW. SAP has done little to address needs in this area. In many cases the only way to validate the data in the BW system and match this with the related SAP system is to build an application.

There are few non-SAP vendors with solutions in this area. One solution in particular, ValiData from ValiData LLC, provides extremely good and through validation between SAP and BW. This helps to find issues quickly before the users find them . The interesting thing about the product is that it can be used in both the implementation and production support phases of development. It thus provides both the project team and the production support teams with tools to check their data against the source to make sure this data is consistent. Chapter 8 describes many of the common practices used for reconciling and validating data from its source.

3.15 Meeting and Decision Paralysis

Many projects fall into meeting and/or decision paralysis. This occurs when a decision is either too difficult or too politically dangerous to make. This can occur in any implementation project. However, because BW projects typically shadow the transactional system implementation, the BW team can often be victimized by the lack of decision-making elsewhere.

3.15.1 Slow Decision Making

One large multi-national company was in the process of determining how its product hierarchy should be structured in source systems. This involved a rather complex series of decisions and had a very wide-reaching effect on the organization because the grouping of products also defined departments and the organization as a whole.

This decision-making did not directly involve the members of the BW team. The decisions needed to be made by the organization as a whole. However, once decided upon, the BW team would be called on to make sure that the product structure that was determined could be reflected in the reporting.

As this decision process dragged on, the BW project was delayed while waiting for the crucial information to complete their design. Once the decision was made, the transactional systems design followed, and BW, as usual, followed that. The ECC and R/3 teams were able to make the needed changes and implement them in time for the scheduled go-live.

However, this did not allow enough time for the BW team to reflect these changes in their design and test with the transactional team. Thus, the BW team was not ready for their scheduled go-live. Frustration ensued because the project manager told the organization that the project was not ready to go live because the BW team was not ready.

The BW team was not the problem in this circumstance, but because the timeline of the entire project slipped and BW is at the end of that process, the BW team got the blame for not being ready with the rest of the teams.

3.15.2 The Lonely BW Team

Other projects face a different issue. Sometimes the BW team is not connected with the transactional teams. Thus, when critical decisions are made, the BW team is not aware of them. This occurs quite often on projects.

Simply put, the attitude of some on the project could be summed up in one sentence: "Lets not invite the BW team; they will just slow us down."

The transactional teams want to keep their meetings short and prevent their own meeting paralysis. Often the best way to do this is to keep the number of participants to very few. This can cause issues because the BW team is not informed of critical decisions.

For example, one project's implementation team changed the pricing structure in their R/3 system. This severely affected the way the pricing data appeared in the BW reports. Because the BW team was not told of these changes, they were not added to the design. The BW reports did not correspond with the R/3 reports.

Fixing the issue to make BW consistent with the R/3 system was so complex that the R/3 team ended up backing out all their changes and going back to their original approach. This cost the time and testing resources that would not have been needed if the BW team had been informed of the changes.

3.15.3 The Popular BW Team

There is a flip side to the problem stated above. I have worked on other BW projects where the BW team is the most popular team in the project. The attitude of the groups could be summed up as: "We never know when a reporting decision will come up; invite the BW team just in case."

This approach is just as counter-productive as the previous one. While the BW team needs to be aware of the transactional team's approach and changes to design, it is very easy to get so involved in meeting with the transactional groups that the BW team cannot get its own work done.

3.15.4 What Can be Done?

The BW team should plan meetings with the transactional process teams on a regular basis with very strict rules. These meetings should be done sparingly, with a clear agenda to go over the issues and design changes that have recently occurred.

Keeping the transactional and process teams in sync with the associated BW team is never an easy task on a project. Entire books have been written on collaborative teams and synergy, and these strategies can be employed to help the teams work together.

The most important thing to understand in a BW project is that the BW team can often take the blame for slow decision-making simply because their processes are at the end of the timeline. Any structures or plans that can be put in place can help the BW team meet its goals.

The other key lesson is that all teams understand that when BW is implemented in conjunction with the transactional system, the BW team is at the end of the project timeline. It is very tempting for any project manager to seize this seemingly large chunk of time at the end of a project dedicated to BW testing and use this as the project contingency time.

Thus, the upstream efforts that missed their planned dates are accommodated by simply collapsing the BW timeline, or by reducing or eliminating testing of BW. Unfortunately, I have seen this strategy at several projects, and all too often the BW production support team suffers while trying to solve issues post go-live that should have been caught in the pre-go-live testing.

Another challenge faced by many organizations is to clearly communicate the various change issues that come with implementation. The next section gives an overview of some frequent challenges.

3.16 Change-Control and Change-Management

Change control and change management are two different things and should be dealt with as such. Some BW project organizations believe these two efforts are interchangeable; however, a separate strategy should be planned for each.

Understanding clearly who can make changes and allowing these users the access to make the changes is necessary in keeping the BW project on track.

If there are severe obstacles in order to make necessary changes, the momentum of a BW project can be slowed.

It is also necessary to clearly understand how these changes are moved from one system to another. This knowledge ensures that the process is clear to all developers and changes can occur efficiently.

Communication of the change to the organization is the final step in the process, and a strategy must be developed for this to occur in a clear and efficient manner.

3.16.1 Change Control

Change control refers to the process of understanding how changes can occur in the system and the processes of an organization. A sound change-control process ensures that when BW changes occur, they are carried out by the right group, in the right fashion.

The BW change-control process involves transports, security, and documentation processes for the intended change. A clear change-control process is very important to a project because it makes sure the intended person or group can make the changes needed and the processes are in place for them to do so.

Change Control Security

Setting the process team change-control security in a BW project is not always an easy task. Project management is often torn between two extremes: giving too much access and allowing a lot of flexibility for the developers and thus a bigger potential for unintended changes, and locking down the system so tightly that each change takes an extreme effort to implement.

I have worked in both environments. Organizations with a very rigid security strategy slow development, and I found myself waiting while I secured a development key or access to a transaction. I have also been in projects where the system was so unsecured that people who were quite inexperienced (and quite unqualified) were making changes in various parts of the system.

Small global changes can have rather severe consequences, and troubleshooting these issues can be time-consuming. Thus, there needs to be a compromise between a system that allows very little change without authorization and a system that is wide open for anyone to make changes.

The correct strategy for most companies comes as the result of time. Once developers have been working for a while, it is quite easy to assess the access needed by each individual. To keep the development process going when a change process is needed but access is not granted, the most successful organizations usually allow someone in the BW team to have far-reaching access. This is usually given to the BW data architect role or a similar position. This person or group of people can make more severe changes to system settings.

Each developer is not able to make changes to such things as permitted characters, overall aggregate settings, packet size, load balancing, etc. At least one member of the BW team, however, is able to change these settings, thus allowing the change process to occur without severely slowing the project.

Change Control Documentation

Any change-control process needs clear governance on the change process and clear documentation of those changes. BW is no exception. However, there is a very fine line in an implementation between writing documentation for documentation's sake and writing documentation to truly track and record changes in the system.

In order to keep the documentation from severely slowing development, proper thought and refinement is needed to assess the documentation that is useful and the documentation that is not. Here is a simple rule that I follow for documentation in BW: The BW system has limited self-documentation through the metadata repository. Thus, any documentation that duplicates the system's documentation process is redundant and often unnecessary.

In other words, the BW metadata repository shows the structures of many elements of the system. This documentation area of the system shows the InfoCube, DSO, and the flow of data in and out of these InfoProviders. Thus, it should be assumed that documentation that repeats all the InfoObjects that are in an InfoCube or DSO is redundant.

I worked on a project where I was forced to painstakingly go to each InfoCube and DSO and copy each InfoObject to an InfoCube document. This served no purpose because the document was not used for any future questions on the InfoCubes or DSO. The metadata repository took care of this for us. The documents became redundant and slowed development without any added benefit.

However, documenting why a process occurred or where transformation of data occurs is vital to any BW implementation, and a majority of the effort in the documentation should go to these types of documents. Most implementations that need to reference a document are much more interested in why a change was needed, who requested the change, and how the change was implemented than in the makeup and setup of the InfoProvider structures of BW. For more information on the documentation of BW, refer to Chapter 4.

BW Transport Strategy

Another important area vital to any project is a clear transport strategy. This strategy is defined by determining how the changes flow from one system to another and the tracking and administration of these changes.

A transport is the process that any SAP system uses to move the changes across the landscape. Since all development is performed in the development system and the QA and production systems are not open for any development, the transport process moves the configuration to the QA and production systems from the development system.

> **Tip**
>
> BW transports are notoriously difficult, so plan for this to be a difficult process in any BW implementation.

Transports are difficult to manage in any project. BW transports are even more so because of the nature of BW; things in BW build on one another. For instance, in order to create an InfoCube, the first step is to create or reference multiple InfoObjects. These InfoObjects act as the fields of data in the InfoCube.

If the InfoObjects are not present in a system, the InfoCube cannot be present either. Thus, if an InfoCube is transported to a system before all InfoObjects in the InfoCube are transported, the transport will fail and must be performed again.

Projects often face challenges when they do not clearly document and track the transports. Thus a clear transport strategy must be developed before any transport is sent from the BW development environment. This will ensure that the transports, although challenging, are processed as cleanly as possible.

For more details on developing a BW transport and change control strategy, see Chapter 7.

Change Management

Change management refers to providing the user base with understanding of the changes that have occurred. The earlier that this process occurs and the more ownership the business takes in this change-management process, the more smooth this process typically occurs. There are several steps in creating a change management strategy, as seen below:

- **Establish Clear Communication Path**
  This can be done via lunch and learn sessions, websites, newsletters, etc. The goal is to make the end users aware of the changes that will be coming as soon as possible
- **Keep Commincation Consistent**
  As much as possible keep a common consistent message to the end users. Conflicting messages allow for confusion.
- **Develop Robust Training Material**
  Develop as good a traning program as possible. Have the training delivered by the power users with a clear understanding of the business goals and objectives, and not by the consultants, if possible.
- **Keep an Open-Door Policy**
  Allow the end users to ask questions and keep them informed whenever possible.
- **Have a Good Help Desk**
  Staff a well-equipped help desk with clearly informed power users to help resolve post go-live issues quickly.

3.17 Conclusion

Simply working with a BW project team that understands the key challenges can often allow a project to avoid many of the most common mistakes. This can pay dividends in quicker implementation time and a more sound BW strategy. Where possible, it helps to clearly watch for the common mistakes others have made, and use these mistakes as a learning tool for the project.

Let us now proceed to Chapter 4, where I will discuss project planning.

"If anything is certain, it is that change is certain. The world we are planning for today will not exist in this form tomorrow."
– Philip Crosby

4 Project Planning in BW

Understanding and planning a BW implementation involves many different challenges. Often the diverse nature of the audience for BW reports adds to this complexity. It is important to understand the typical lifecycle of a BW project, and some of the common challenges faced when planning a new BW project or upgrading to a new release of BW. This chapter will help in the overall planning and aid in understanding the typical makeup of the project team.

In order to begin either an upgrade project or a new implementation of SAP BW, there are several things to understand about its implementation cycle. In many cases, the lifecycle of BW is similar to implementation of a transactional system. However, because projects in BW typically bring data from many different source systems and subject areas, rather than one source as with transactional systems, BW requires additional design iterations.

In other words, BW projects typically require more prototyping and rebuilding based on the lessons-learned from harmonizing data from multiple sources. This iterative design should be considered a normal and vital part of the BW implementation process. There are two main types of BW projects: the new BW project or the upgrade BW project.

The new BW project typically follows the data-warehouse lifecycle shown in Figure 4.1. The upgrade lifecycle is quite different. It requires analysis of the new release and new features and their impact on the existing design. We will discuss both lifecycles in detail.

4   Project Planning in BW

Figure 4.1 Data Warehouse Lifecycle

4.1   The Data Warehouse Lifecycle

The first thing to consider about BW is that it is a data warehouse. Thus, many theoretical data warehouse implementation strategies apply very well to BW.

- **Design**
  This stage involves seeking out the various decision-makers in the organization and determining the information they need to make decisions. The BW system can be structured to match both current information needs, and to look to the future to make sure that the data warehouse takes into account those requirements in the upcoming months and even years.

- **Prototype**
  The prototype phase is needed to show a select group of users or super users the various design features and the overall scope and data model of the BW system prior to deployment. Prototyping a design allows the stakeholders to influence the deployment and suggest changes to make sure that the design reflects the true needs of the organization.

- **Deploy**
  This is the formal rollout of the BW system to the end users and the process of putting the BW system into regular use. It is during this phase of the implementation that the change-control process transitions the BW system to the end users and trains them in its use.

- **Operate**
  Operation is the day-to-day use of the BW system, including data loads, query processing, etc.

- **Enhance**
  Typically, the implementation of BW is an ongoing task. Based on the changing needs of the organization and the source system, the BW system should be constantly evaluated to determine if it is still meeting the needs of the users. This includes the information delivery, performance, and technical environment.

Because BW is an SAP data warehouse, its use and its scope often reflect the same overall goals as those of the SAP transactional systems; however, both systems retain their distinctive cycles of development.

It should be understood that BW will be constantly changing, and redesigns of the existing environment should not only be expected but also welcomed. BW is not like most transactional systems, which remain relatively constant to handle core transactional activities. The BW model and configuration should be expected to change with the mission and goals of the company. Thus, models that are quite useful today could be replaced by others tomorrow.

SAP periodically comes out with new releases of BW. These should not be confused with support packages and stacks that are fixes to the existing product. The new releases of BW have significant functionality changes to the software and require extensive regression testing in order to implement. There are some differences in the lifecycle of an upgrade that differs from a new implementation of BW. In the next section I highlight some of the features of this lifecycle.

4.2 The Upgrade Lifecycle

In the upgrade lifecycle, we you take the existing configuration and bring that configuration and software to the newest release of BW. This differs from a new implementation, which is focused on creating new functionality and models in the existing BW environment.

The upgrade lifecycle is similar to the data warehouse lifecycle but with clearly different goals. Most upgrade projects are planned to simply provide a technical upgrade. The technical upgrade is not designed to take advantage of any new features of the software, but is only designed to get the software up to the newest release as quickly as possible.

Most projects opt for a technical upgrade because this has the quickest lifecycle and also provides the best opportunity for success. No new features or functionality other than those required for the upgrade are used in the technical upgrade. Thus, in the example of an organization upgrading from BW Version 3.x to the version NW 2004s, an organization would simply take the software to the newest release but would not take advantage of the new features of NW 2004s such has the new transformation logic or unit of measure conversion. These features would be added later as separate releases.

Those organizations that do not opt for the technical upgrade may opt for a features upgrade. This upgrade involves taking the software to the newest release and using many new features during the initial rollout. This is typically done by companies that require new functionality to run their business or when a feature offers a large time or performance savings.

The fundamental reason that many opt for a technical upgrade rather than a features upgrade is simply to minimize the risk. It is much harder to fully regression-test an intact environment than an environment that now has changed and uses new functionality.

To perform a technical upgrade, the Basis or technical teams take the development system's software release and upgrade this development environment to the newest release so that unit testing can begin. This poses a problem in many organizations because most organizations have only one development system. If this is upgraded to the newest release, it is very difficult to also provide production support to existing users during the rollout and unit testing of the new release.

This problem arises because the development system is the root of all system changes. If no transports can occur from the development system, there can be no production support changes during the upgrade process because there is no root system to make the changes. SAP does not recommend transports between two unlike releases, and in most cases this is technically impossible. In most environments, the development system is upgraded first. Later the QA system is upgraded and tested, and finally the production system is upgraded.

4.2.1 Upgrading on the Existing BW Landscape

There are several options for upgrading the BW landscape. In a very stable and smaller BW environment, some project teams opt to upgrade the existing BW system landscape in place without adding new systems to the BW landscape. This involves halting all production support fixes during the time of upgrade.

Once development is upgraded, the development and QA systems are now running different releases of the software. Transports must now be halted between the development, QA, and production systems. This means no production support fixes can be sent from development to QA, and then into production, during the upgrade.

This is a risk, because any mission-critical fixes cannot be implemented during the upgrade unless the systems are opened up for direct configuration and the normal migration path is not used. This scenario works best for small BW implementations and those that are extremely mature with few production support risks.

In many cases, this is not realistic. The risk of halting all transports during the upgrade process presents too many complexities and opens the BW team up to too much risk. In this case, many organizations opt to create a new stand-alone development environment created to support the upgrade.

4.2.2 Dedicated Upgrade Landscape

Many companies prefer to use the model pictured in Figure 4.2. This is similar to the two-release landscape strategy described in Chapter 2. A new development system is created (in this case labeled **DEV2**).

Figure 4.2 Typical Upgrade Landscape

Prior to the upgrade, the applications development team should create clear test scripts for walking through the functionality in the existing environment. These test scripts should detail the transactional feeds into BW and the full functionality in the form of unit test scripts. These scripts will be used to prove out the new release.

The first step in performing this upgrade is to take the **DEV2** system and make a system copy of the production system. The Basis team takes this new development system (which is a copy of the production system) and upgrades it to the new release with the most recent SAP support- package levels. This now establishes a new development system that is identical to production but upgraded to the new release.

If the production system is too large to replicate on the smaller development system, the development system is upgraded in place without copying of the production system. If this is done, however, more care will be needed during the testing phase because the data needed for testing must come from a non-production environment. This may not mirror the data in the production system.

The upgraded system is now typically connected to the QA transactional systems or a copy of the productive transactional systems, in order to test batch loading of data. Most organizations do not opt to connect the upgraded BW development environment to the production transactional systems for fear of causing issues in those production systems.

The Basis team then *hands off* this system to the upgrade development team. The upgrade development team takes this system and uses it for unit testing on the newest release with the production or development data. The goal is to perform many tests reflecting the current system in production in order to determine how the new release affects the existing implementation.

Special attention should be paid to the custom transformation. This involves specific testing of all user exits, modifications, and transformations that involve Advanced Business Application Programming (ABAP) code. These are the features most prone to failure during upgrade, because some of the features and functionality needed to make the code work may have been changed by SAP.

Special attention should also be given to the batch loading of data. Because of the complexity of batch loading and the timing involved, process chains should be run as if in production. This allows the timing and loading to be checked against the benchmark of the production system to determine if any new issues arise based on the new release. Most organizations opt to start the production process chains immediately and keep them running each night to see how the process chains act after many iterations.

Queries should also be tested in detail. This can be a difficult task because of the large volume of queries that typically accumulate in a BW system. To make sure that the queries are taken in proper order, the BW statistics InfoCubes can be used to determine the queries that are the most popular, so that emphasis can be placed on these queries.

4.2.3 Production Support During Upgrade Testing

In order to perform production support during the upgrade testing, the DEV1 and QA1 systems are used, as we saw earlier, in Figure 4.2 Because the DEV1 and QA1 systems stay at the newest release, any production support fixes can be developed in the DEV1 system and migrated via transport to the QA1 system, then onto production. This ensures that any fix can be sent to production.

This approach does allow or ensure that this fix will be in the new upgraded environment. This must be analyzed and implemented manually in the new upgraded development environment (DEV2 and QA2) that we saw in Figure 4.2. The fix may not be relevant in the new environment or might need to be developed differently.

If these fixes to the production environment need to be put into the new upgraded environment, a manual process is used. The fix is checked and evaluated with the new environment and then implemented manually in the DEV1 system. This manual fix is necessary because no transports can be used to move the fix from the DEV1 to the DEV2 systems, given the differing releases.

Because the fix cannot be transported and the fix needs to be evaluated based on the new release, it is best to make sure the fixes that are done to the production support system during the upgrade phase are manually tracked and manually inputted into the upgraded environment. These would then be migrated through the environment from the DEV2 to the QA2, and then onto the productive system, when the cutover occurs.

4.2.4 Obsolete Queries

Many organizations also use the upgrade time to make an assessment of their queries in the production system. Projects that have been live for a long time can end up with hundreds and even thousands of queries. Many of these queries may be obsolete. Thus I recommend a periodic *housecleaning* of the queries. To identify these queries, the statistics InfoCubes can show those queries that have not been used in a long time. These provide a potential query-removal list.

This query list of potentially obsolete queries can be posted or distributed to users. If they do not act on the list, the queries can be removed from the end user roles. Because these queries might be needed again, it is important that the queries are not deleted; they should simply be placed in an obsolete query role for an extended period of time. This role would not be assigned to any end users.

Most organizations find it very rare that an old query is needed again, but if a query in the obsolete role is needed it can be placed back in the active role. Once the queries have been in the obsolete role for a period of time, these queries could be evaluated for purging from the system.

4.2.5 Upgrade Cutover

Once the testing is complete in the development system, the same testing should occur in the QA system. The QA testing allows the testing of the environment with a different set of data.

Figure 4.3 Typical Cutover Landscape

After the QA testing is complete, the upgraded system is ready for cutover, as shown in Figure 4.3. The **DEV1** and **QA1** systems are retired and the upgraded **DEV2** and **QA2** systems become the new development and production support systems, as you can see in Figure 4.3. The Basis team shuts the users off the production system for a period of time and performs the upgrade on the production system. The team makes sure that the production system gets the same support- pack level and SAP patches (i.e., SAP Notes) that the **DEV2** and **QA2** systems received and that the production system mirrors the **DEV2** and **QA2** systems.

In most cases, there are transports that have been created in the upgraded system that are needed in production. These could include the following:

- New functionality
- SAP Notes (SAP help desk fixes) to patch system issues
- Workarounds or changes to existing flows
- Production support fixes, originated in the DEV1 environment, and manually done in the DEV2 system

More testing should be performed at this time to make sure that the production system is ready for users. If possible, several nights should be used to completely test and watch the processchains loading into BW to ensure that the batch is still working properly.

Once the process chains have been run and testing is complete, the system is ready to be opened up for users.

4.2.6 How Long Will This Take?

The timing of an upgrade project is extremely difficult to estimate. This is because there are many factors that go into the upgrade project. The factors include but are not limited to the following:

- **Complexity of Release**
  The BW releases between 3.0 and 3.5 were quite minimal and took little time in the testing. This was because these two releases had few fundamental functionality changes, and there was less risk in the upgrade. The opposite is true of the NW 2004s upgrade that is quite a bit more complex.

- **Features Implemented**
  The more new features implemented, the more risky a project becomes and thus the more time is needed for testing of these features.

- **Size of System**
  Size can play a large role in the upgrade of systems. The bigger the size, the more time it takes to do the technical upgrades. More volume means more time dedicated to testing because of elevated performance concerns in query processing and data loading.

- **Quality and Maturity of Release**
  SAP, like all software, gets better as more people use it. The longer the wait for the upgrade, the more software issues that will be discovered by others and fixed by SAP. An upgrade to the software in the early stages of the release typically takes longer because of the software issues encountered.

- **Resources**
  It takes time for consultants to get up to speed on the features of new releases. To make matters more difficult, it can be hard to get organization resources to help on the testing needed for the upgrade project. This can add significantly to the timeline, as the consulting resources learn the new release and the testing resources are secured and deployed to perform the upgrade.

In the early phases of a new release, I believe the best way to estimate upgrades is to have SAP assess the environment, compare this project to other upgrade projects based on the above factors, and provide a timeline estimate. SAP is in a much better position to make such an estimate than many of the other software partners simply because it has worked with more organizations on upgrades and has better benchmarks.

Often partners (non-SAP consulting companies) will perform one or two upgrades and use these for benchmarking, while SAP will benchmark 10 times that number or more. This usually gives a more accurate estimate of the upgrade.

> **Tip**
> If an upgrade is being performed in the very early stages of its release, I highly recommend having at least one SAP consultant (a consultant employed by SAP, not a consulting partner) working on the project during the upgrade.

This is vital because the experience of the SAP consultant in the new software often makes him or her more proficient. This is due to the available resources and training within SAP and also because of the issues that often arise during an early stage upgrade. An SAP consultant can help to expedite and really prod the SAP Service Marketplace (formerly called OSS, for Online Support Service) to resolve issues quicker than non-SAP partners. This allows for a quicker resolution, and thus a more efficient upgrade.

However, once the product has been released and has been in general availability for more than six months, many other third-party vendors have performed upgrades. Some project teams might use non-SAP resources after doing their own research.

4.2.7 When Should I Upgrade?

SAP, unlike other software vendors, has a select group of users that work with the BW product in its early stages to work through the various issues and challenges of integrating a new release of such a large software package. SAP works very closely with these organizations to help them with their implementation issues.

In return for their efforts and inconvenience, the organizations get some added advantages. They get the new software first and some on-site expertise to help in the implementation process. They also have the power to influence the decision-making and features planning of the product in return for their efforts.

I have worked with some organizations that have gone through this process with SAP and others that have evaluated the process. I usually recommend that organizations avoid being part of the *first customer ship* or *ramp-up process* of the BW software. Organizations that do this typically spend a great deal of time chasing issues and working through various problems with the system. This can add quite a bit of time to the implementation and can frustrate even the most patient project managers.

Thus, unless there are features in the new release that are vital to the business or the timing does not allow an upgrade at a later phase, it does not make sense to be one of the first with new SAP BW software. It is best to wait until the software is much more mature. As a general rule, this usually happens six months after the software has been available for general release.

After about six months, the software is usually at a state where upgrade issues are fewer and the stability of the software makes it more acceptable to upgrade. I urge organizations never to rush to the new release. Instead, let others find the potential issues with the software; this allows for a quicker and cleaner upgrade path in the future.

Once the timing of the upgrade or new implementation has been planned, the next logical step is to determine and document the scope requirements.

4.3 Scope Documentation

There are several important documents that need to be part of every BW project. Each project has many internal and external parties or organizations. Understanding these stakeholders helps to ensure project success. Thus, after completing the scope document, the next vital document is the one that formally identifies the stakeholders in the BW project.

4.3.1 What Is a Stakeholder?

A stakeholder is an individual or group who has a vested interest in a project and can gather resources to affect its outcome. Project stakeholders usually include the project manager, business users, and team members on the project. However, there are other stakeholders in any BW project.

When thinking about stakeholders, you must include those stakeholders who can affect the attention and resources committed to the project, both now and in the future. These stakeholders typically have individual agendas that may differ from those of other stakeholders.

Failure to meet the needs of one powerful stakeholder at a critical time can have significant adverse affects on a project. Thus, proper documentation of stakeholders' interests and expectations is critical to understanding and communicating with these individuals or organizations.

4.3.2 Stakeholder Document

The stakeholder document should include all organizations and individuals expected to use BW, along with all those affected by its use. The challenge with the stakeholder document is to understand the influence and importance of each of the stakeholders and their individual impacts on the project.

Of course, it is important to recognize that stakeholders change, as do their interests and impact on the project. This is a living document and can be updated as the various roles in the organization change and evolve.

The stakeholder document serves as a vital input to the communication plan because the communication plan can be tailored to keep the various stakeholders informed of the project and its progress.

4.3.3 Communication Plan Document

Developing a strong communication plan is vital to any BW project. The communication plan should include all plans and steps to keep the various stakeholders informed of the project. Some common elements included in the communication plan are:

- Project website
- Issue tracking lists
- Meeting minutes template
- Position paper template
- Status report template
- Training plan and templates

4.3.4 Integrated Project Plan

All BW projects require a project plan to track the different tasks involved. A sample project plan provided by SAP can be used as a template for starting a project. This plan is part of the ASAP methodology and can be found on the SAP Service Marketplace website.

This sample plan is useful for tracking the tasks needed to complete a successful BW project. Remember, however, that because of the many project integration points between a BW project and other simultaneous implementations, an integrated project plan is necessary. This would include but is not limited to the following:

- Integration and timing with the technical group for the installation and delivery of systems
- Coordination with the process teams for completion of configuration and sample master and transactional data
- Coordination with any outside source system dependency
- Integrated testing plan in coordination with the transaction systems
- Integrated cutover planning

4.3.5 Naming Standards Document

Naming standards are vital to identifying custom objects and SAP-developed objects, and to ensure consistency in finding and recognizing objects in the BW system. When a project starts, it is very easy to do without a naming standards document. This is a mistake, because it is very hard to rename objects after go-live to get them in line with new standards.

Thus, the best approach for any BW project is to make sure that a sound naming-convention document is in place before any development occurs. These naming conventions are only necessary for objects that are created in the development system and intended for transport to the production system.

It is not necessary to use and enforce the naming standards on the sandbox system because this system is designed for ad-hoc testing. Any sandbox prototype should be redeveloped in the development system using the naming convention document. The use of standard naming conventions will provide key benefits:

- Enhancing the usability of the system by providing a logical grouping of objects
- Providing a framework to develop appropriate security and authorization models (if needed)
- Ensuring consistency for all the layers of BW instances, thus making future developments more consistent
- Adherence to these standards allows for tracking of modifications and transformations of data, which leads to faster troubleshooting of issues

The naming standards document addresses the following areas of BW:

- InfoAreas
- InfoCubes
- DataStore objects and DSOs
- InfoObjects
- InfoSources and DataSources
- InfoPackages
- Process chains
- BEx queries
- Other objects such as custom tables, variables, etc.

The naming structure for each BW object is based on a series of logical codes, which can have a number of permitted entries. SAP by default begins all delivered objects with the number 0. This quickly separates the SAP objects from the project-created objects. Projects cannot develop objects starting with 0.

The naming standards document is only intended for those objects that are custom developed. When SAP standard objects are used, the naming standards document does not apply, and the standard object names should be used.

The naming standards document should be considered a living document that can be changed as new object types are added or as different releases of BW are implemented. A sample naming document is found in Appendix E.

4.3.6 BW Development Standards Document

The development standards document is used to document the various strategies that will be used on a project regarding the BW implementation. This may be one document or a series of documents that can be used to help new project team members understand the implementation standards of the project. These contain many of the following standards:

- **Data Strategies**
  How should an ODS or InfoCube be used to provide reporting? What features and functionality should be used during the loading process?

- **Source System Strategies**
  How can we determine when an external source of data should be loaded into BW? What is the process for transforming that data? Should it occur in BW or in the external system?

- **Loading/ETL Strategies**
  When should transformation occur? At what level should this occur? Should data go into an ODS first or to an InfoCube?

- **Query Strategies**
  Should users plan to create queries in the production environment? Should there be many smaller queries or fewer large queries?

- **Performance Strategies**
  How should performance be evaluated and tested? What should be implemented in the data model to ensure that performance is optimal?

- **Transport Strategies**
  How will transports be collected and handled? What is the process to send transports?

Who will prepare all this documentation and who is responsible for the various tasks in the project? The next section describes the typical roles in a BW project.

4 | Project Planning in BW

4.4 Typical Roles Needed for a BW Project

There are several roles needed for a typical BW project. It should be noted that these roles are not always held by separate individuals. Often several of these roles can be performed by the same person. This section is designed as a guide to help understand the skill sets involved in a typical BW project.

4.4.1 BW Project Manager

The BW project manager has the ultimate decision-making power on the BW project. He or she is responsible for every aspect in the BW implementation. This includes development, testing, troubleshooting, implementing BW, and even the transition of the system to a production support environment. The project manager's responsibilities include the following:

- Coordinate and centralize responsibility and accountability for the design, development, release, and maintenance of the BW system
- Work closely with business users, sponsors, and other stakeholders to identify and maximize opportunities for BW
- Ensure cost-effective BW design, development, and integration with other systems.
- Oversee maintenance and coordination of the integrated BW project plan
- Oversee the BW implementation, testing, and maintenance in support of business and information objectives and requirements.
- Provide BW technical and financial direction, by developing controls, budgets, and measurements to monitor progress
- Approve resources and staff BW project internally, and, if required, with external resources
- Provide overall responsibility for the quality and performance of the BW system
- Coordinate communication between all key IT groups, the user community, and BW team members.
- Facilitate adoption and change management of the BW system
- Develop cutover plans and activities and coordinate resources for go-live
- Develop and maintain a production support strategy
- Provide support and transition the BW system from development to production support

- Coordinate and assign priorities for new development in the BW system with production support activities

The time commitment of the BW project manager is full time during all phases of the project. All decision making and responsibility for the implantation of BW ultimately falls to the BW project manager. Chapter 1 describes the qualities of a good BW project manager.

4.4.2 BW Business Subject Matter Expert

The business Subject Matter Expert (SME) acts as the conduit between the business organization and the BW development team. The main responsibilities of the SME are to understand the reporting requirements of the business and incorporate these requirements into the design for BW.

The SME provides a voice of the business in each of the decisions in BW. Typically, there are multiple SMEs on any BW project, providing expertise in different functional areas of the system. The typical responsibilities for this role include the following:

- Understand the needs of the business and future direction of the business analysis needs
- Coordinate communication between the BW project and the end user community
- Aid in generating functional specifications for matching the business requirements to the design of BW
- Provide escalation of business issues and facilitate decision making
- Aid in the testing of BW to ensure that it matches requirements
- Work with the training and change-management team to communicate the new business processes as a result of the BW implementation
- Act as first contact for aid in resolution of issues
- Aid in transition to BW and away from the current processes

In a best-case scenario, the SME role is a full-time position on the BW team. This makes sure that SMEs are always available to make the decisions needed to keep the project momentum going.

In many projects, it is quite difficult to secure qualified SMEs. To be useful, the SME must be very involved in the day-to-day business operation and must be able to understand and communicate the issues that arise in normal business operation. Such people are thus already very useful in their current positions.

To keep the SMEs focused on the BW project as their priority, I recommend that they leave their existing business role completely and become part of the BW implementation team full time. This allows them to focus on the project without the distraction and needs of the day-to-day business process.

4.4.3 BW Data Architect

The BW data architect is the most important person on the BW project, from the BW product standpoint. The BW data architect plays a critical role matching the business requirements to the BW implementation that will satisfy these requirements.

This person must be very experienced in the implementation of BW and works with the BW project manger to make implementation decisions on the design of BW. Because the data design and model must be strong in order for the project to succeed, this role is critical for current and future success of the project.

In larger projects, the BW data architect is either a single role or a role filled by a group of individuals. They map out the design of the BW project from a product standpoint to ensure that the data model and decision making reflect the best use of the BW system.

In smaller projects, this task is typically performed by the various application consultants who are implementing their specific areas of BW. Because consultants have differing levels of skills and experience, this can sometimes lead to conflict. A BW data architect helps to steer the project and sets an overall BW strategy. If application consultants who are focused on their own deliverables are asked to take on this role, often not enough thought is given to the overall strategy and future direction of BW.

I saw this at a company where I was implementing several years ago. The company did not have a data architect overseeing its BW design. One consultancy was implementing a finance InfoCube. These consultants had several reports that they were focused on delivering as part of their project. They worked diligently to make sure that these reports were delivered.

However, if those consultants had understood the overall direction of the company was toward more finance visibility and more detailed financial data, they would have adjusted the BW data model accordingly. Because they were unaware of the multi-generational plan for BW, they did not bring this level of detail into BW. Thus, once these new requirements were due, much of the finance work that was done had to be redesigned.

If the project had a data architect role from the start, this person could have helped steer the current requirements toward a future goal and accomplish both at the same time. The data architect's responsibilities include the following:

- Act as the main point of contact for all data model and system-design decisions
- Have a clear understanding of the BW product and functionality
- Be the primary contact for BW decision making and functionality decisions
- Ensure the development of corporate standards for data warehousing
- Assemble and coordinate the multi-generational data plan and steer the BW design to this plan
- Develop and provide a clear understanding of the BW data model and strategies for data modeling.
- Work to avoid rework, reload, and restatement of BW transactional data
- Help to incorporate performance standards into the design of BW
- Understand the end user requirements and the data that makes up these requirements.
- Recognize the integration points of the data in the various systems in the BW landscape and bring this data together in a logical fashion to deliver reporting needs
- Recommend a BW landscape strategy and coordinate transports across the landscape
- Aid in troubleshooting the BW system issues
- Possess excellent communication skills to understand and articulate the overall vision of BW to the project community
- Evaluate the timing and need for upgrades
- Coordinate and plan the system tasks for go-live

4.4.4 BW Applications Developer

The BW applications developer uses the implementation strategy and data modeling decisions of the data architect to implement the various business requirements in the BW system. This involves creating the various BW

InfoObjects, ODS or DataStore Objects, InfoCubes, etc. The applications developer's responsibilities are as follows:

- Use strong BW product skills to implement business requirements of BW
- Work with the user community to verify that the BW data model captures the BW requirements
- Take direction and work effectively in a team environment
- Use strong communication skills to communicate and understand scope and requirements
- Track, troubleshoot, and escalate product issues
- Offer knowledge transfer about the product and design
- Document design, both from a functional and a technical standpoint
- Determine the transformation of data needed and provide that transformation in the BW system
- Code or coordinate coding of ABAP to complete design where necessary
- Work with the other consultants and team members to establish a batch load strategy
- Verify data quality and ensure BW is in sync with source systems
- Unit-test BW system, and work with the various parties involved to achieve a sound integration test
- Aid in transports and cutover to production environment
- Transition to production support team

4.4.5 BW Presentation Developer

The BW presentation developer is responsible for creating the presentation layer of the BW system. This includes, but is not limited to, BW queries, workbooks, dashboards, formatted reports, web queries, etc. This role covers all portions of BW that the user sees. In many projects, this role is covered by the BW applications consultant. However, in larger projects this could be a separate role. The BW presentation developer's responsibilities include the following:

- Understand the presentation needs of the project
- Plan the presentation of the BW data in the most effective way to fulfill user needs
- Communicate with the applications developers to understand the sources of data

- Keep presentation of information in BW consistent using common templates, query strategies, etc.
- Work with the business users and business SMEs to refine the presentation of data
- Troubleshoot and track presentation issues
- Aid in transports and cutover to production environment
- Transition to production support team

4.4.6 BW Basis Developer

The Basis developer is responsible for all technical and system areas of BW. This includes the setup of the system, administration of transports, patch application, etc. The BW applications consultants, presentation developers, and BW architects typically work very closely with the BW Basis developer.

Because the BW environment is usually a very dynamic environment, the BW Basis developer is usually kept quite busy monitoring the BW system and troubleshooting issues. Because the BW system has many tables being loaded and reloaded, there are many opportunities for Basis support.

Many BW projects make the mistake of trying to have one Basis resource to cover BW and the same resource to cover the R/3 or ECC systems. This is a mistake. The Basis BW role is unique and has different tasks and expectations that are not the same as the R/3 or ECC systems. The BW Basis resource spends much of the time working on connecting systems, troubleshooting loads and query performance, etc. This is a very different role than the R/3 or ECC Basis resource.

Because the teams work so often together, it is important that the teams meet regularly to go over the various open issues and prioritize the open tasks. The Basis developer is responsible for the following:

- Plan and execute new installations, upgrades, and maintenance of the SAP BW system
- Perform initial testing of SAP maintenance applications and ongoing SAP BW log monitoring
- Aid SAP BW system performance monitoring and tuning in conjunction with the BW application teams
- Provide database-performance tuning and log monitoring and issue resolution

- Perform connection creation and maintenance between systems setup and monitoring
- Plan and execute BW copies between systems
- Implement BW system backups and disaster recovery contingency planning
- Perform transports between systems execution and aid in transport issue resolution
- Maintain and monitor security in the BW system
- Document basis procedures and policies

4.4.7 ABAP Developer

Most BW projects require some ABAP coding. ABAP is the source-code language of SAP and the source-code language of BW. When data needs to be transformed, ABAP coding is often needed to perform this transformation. For example, a legacy system's orders need to be loaded into the BW system. These need to be combined with the orders that have been entered into the SAP ECC or R/3 system. To make the different company numbers and material numbers match, transformation is needed to change the source data into a common customer and material number. This transformation is done using ABAP.

Many BW applications consultants code their own ABAP transformations, and for this reason this role can be avoided or reduced on many projects. However, if the applications consultants are not proficient in ABAP or there is very complex transformation of data, a separate ABAP developer may be needed, at least temporarily. This is typically not a full-time role in any BW project because the ABAP coding needed in most BW projects is usually quite limited. This ABAP developer's responsibilities include the following:

- Understand the transformation needs of the project
- Understand ABAP coding strategies and possess development language skills
- Plan the ABAP transformation of the BW data in the most effective way to fulfill user needs
- Communicate with the applications developers to understand the sources of data
- Keep ABAP coding consistent, using ABAP development strategies

- Troubleshoot and track coding issues
- Document technical design

4.4.8 SAP Portal Consultant

An SAP portal consultant is necessary in many BW projects, especially those that use Release NW 2004s and later. This is because the portal is a mandatory part of the landscape. The role of the portal consultant can be limited or quite intensive, depending on the planned use of the SAP portal. Thus, the various responsibilities vary. However, it is important to include some portal consulting in any BW project.

The goal of the SAP portal is to allow all users one place to enter the various SAP systems and give a common look and feel to all applications. Thus, BW queries would be housed on the portal, and the portal would be used to present these to the end user.

In most BW projects, the BW developers are responsible for gathering up of the data from the source system and creating the presentation of that data, usually in the form of BW queries. After the queries are complete these are passed to the portal consultant for inclusion in the portal. Typically, the BW team is not responsible for the portal itself.

In many projects, the portal consultant is not part of the BW organization. Because this role is used to create the launch pad for all applications, it is often part of a shared services group, reporting to the Basis organization.

How do we find all these individuals? Understanding the staffing models and needs helps in filling the roles.

4.5 Staffing a BW Project

Staffing a BW project can be a difficult task because historically the demand for BW resources has been much higher than the supply of strong resources. In addition, I have come across many candidates who have strong resumes but really do not possess the skills that their resumes would seem to indicate.

Several times, when asked about details on their resumes, these candidates are unable or unwilling to give details about past projects and the tasks they actually performed at those projects. This often indicates that they were not active participants in this part of the implementation, and thus do not have a clear understanding of the functionality.

> **Tip**
> The first step in staffing any BW project is to ensure that you have adequate internal resources.

I have worked on many projects that are staffed entirely or almost entirely by external resources. This is a mistake for many reasons. There simply is no incentive to transition the consultants out of the project, and the effort to transfer knowledge is much too great after the implementation has been ongoing for a long time.

The best projects are those where organizations make sure that there is adequate exposure of both internal and external resources. Each functional area of the project should have an internal resource that is responsible for the implementation. For example, a project that is implementing sales, purchasing, and financial reporting should have internal resources who are ultimately responsible for each of those functional areas. The resource would be charged with making the day-to-day decisions that affect this data model and the report delivery in that area.

4.5.1 The Small BW Project

A small BW project organizational chart often looks much like the one in Figure 4.4. A typical small BW project has the following:

- Very few sources of data (often just SAP R/3 or ECC) — often fewer than 10 specific sources
- Few queries needed — typically fewer than 40
- Few end users — often fewer than 100
- A low volume of data
- Little transformation or harmonization
- Few subject areas of data (often only one), such as sales reporting or financial analysis
- Many large BW projects start as small projects as a *proof of concept* to the organization or to determine the acceptance and viability of product as a whole
- Smaller projects are best staffed with many resources wearing *many hats* because of the work needed and the resources allocated to smaller projects.

Figure 4.4 Typical Organizational Chart of a Small BW Project

Roles in a Small Project

In a smaller BW project, as with any project, the project sponsor is the resource providing the requirements, scope, and budget. In many cases, this is one person or a small group in the organization with a business point of pain or area of risk that BW is being looked upon to resolve.

The project manager coordinates the implementation. In many smaller projects, the project manager is not only handling issues and coordinating resources, but also aiding on the configuration and implementation of the product. A dedicated BW Basis consultant is needed, even in a small project, to keep the BW system running from a technical standpoint.

> **Note**
>
> It should not be assumed that in a smaller project the BW Basis consultant can be a part-time resource primarily dedicated to the R/3 or ECC environment. Each BW project, no matter how small, needs to have a dedicated Basis or technical resource to handle the technical and security tasks.

A portal developer is also needed if SAP or another portal is within scope. This is typically not a full-time position in the BW project because the portal is simply used to house the BW queries and present them to the end user. The portal consultant or portal resource works with both the BW team and the transactional teams to provide the launch pad for transactional and reporting processes.

If the portals resource is part of a larger portal implementation, the resource should have some time dedicated to the BW team. If SAP's or another vendor's portal software is only being implemented to provide a portal for BW reporting, this resource can be staffed for a short time during the latter part of the query development to provide a way for the queries to be published and launched.

In small BW projects, it is important to have capable business representation in the form of business SMEs to communicate the business needs and requirements of the project. These resources may or may not work full time on the project, but they must be available to the team to help scope and refine the BW data model. These resources are the first point of contact to the business users. They help to roll the end result functionality out to the end user community.

The developers and/or data architect roles work with the business SME or SMEs to provide the solution. The number of data developers or data architects depends on the resources and amount of functionality needed. Often in smaller projects, a dedicated data architect is not needed because the developers perform the data-modeling tasks.

Roles in a Medium-Sized BW Project

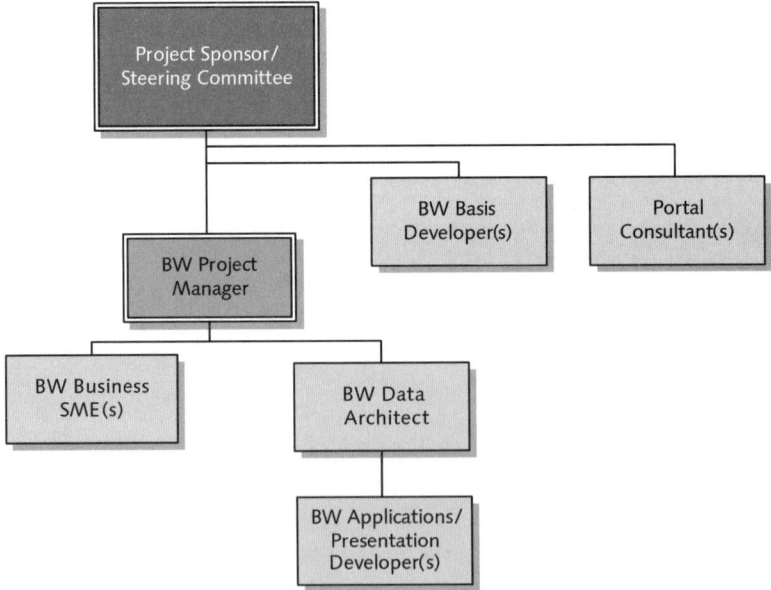

Figure 4.5 Typical Organizational Chart of a Medium-Sized BW Project

Figure 4.5 shows the organizational chart of a typical medium sized BW project. This would be a project that had moderate scope and some of the following characteristics:

- Several sources of data (often more than SAP R/3 or ECC)
- Several queries needed — typically 50–100
- Moderate number of end users — often 100–300
- Moderate volume of data
- Some transformation or harmonization of data
- Multiple subject areas of data such as sales reporting and financial analysis

In the medium-sized project, there is usually a dedicated BW data architect to oversee all development in the BW system. This person would make sure that all the data models are in sync and are following standards and work with the various developers on the common master data and data strategy. Typically, this architect is also doing some of the development. The developers work with the architect to deliver the requirements in BW.

In some cases, depending on the presentation complexity, there may be dedicated developers working on the presentation of the data. These are separate from the applications-development team and would work on extracting the data from the source, transforming and harmonizing the data and loading the data in the BW system. However, in many medium-sized projects, the presentation development is handled by the BW applications development team, and there is no separate resource to handle the presentation.

Depending on the source of external data there may also be another role: which is not shown in Figure 4.5. This role would be the extraction or ETL resource from the source system. This role is responsible for gathering the data from the external source system and presenting it in a format that can be read by BW.

For example, a project needs to report on data from a legacy transactional purchasing system. To be loaded into BW, data must first be extracted from the source system. If it cannot be extracted by existing extractors, appropriate views created in order to directly map BW via a database link such as SAP DBConnect or SAP UDConnect. These tools allow for a direct link between BW systems and eliminate the need for data to be extracted to a file and then loaded into BW.

To source this data, these systems must have the views or extraction programs written to gather the data. This role is usually considered outside the

BW team because it is done on the legacy system. This role is typically filled by someone familiar with the legacy system.

Roles in a Large BW Project

A large BW project typically has many of the following characteristics:

- Multiple sources of data, often in many subject areas with harmonization required between data
- Multiple presentation means, including dashboards, formatted reports, etc.
- Many end users, often more than 200
- Large or high volume of data
- Transformation or harmonization of data
- Multiple subject areas of data

Figure 4.6 Typical Organizational Chart of a Large BW Project

A large BW project typically has several distinct and separate subject areas with a complex scope, as seen in Figure 4.6. This requires dedicated BW business resources and dedicated subject-area developers. In small and medium projects, developers can work on multiple subject areas at one time, but in larger projects developers are focused on one subject area.

For example, one subject area might be purchase-order analysis. The developers in that area would work on the extraction of the purchase orders from one or many source systems, often including ECC or R/3 and external systems. They would then either develop the purchase order presentation queries, workbooks, etc., or work with presentation developers to develop the presentation of the purchasing data.

In a larger implementation, the large data volume and the higher complexity mean that more dedicated resources are needed to understand the data and make sure that the data is being transformed properly to meet the business requirements.

In a large project, the business SMEs are also dedicated project team members because understanding the reporting needs require a constant communication between the business and the development group. The developers work on prototypes that are refined by the business SMEs in a back-and-forth fashion until the data model is complete.

The data-architect role brings all the groups together to make sure that the design standards are followed and that the models make the most efficient use of the system.

As in any BW project, there are dedicated BW Basis developers to handle the technical and security tasks. In many larger projects, there are multiple Basis resources, and a dedicated database administrator to handle database-specific tasks.

Roles in a Large Global BW Project

A large global BW project typically has the following characteristics:

- Multiple sources of data
- Multiple presentation means
- Many end users
- Large or high volume of data
- Transformation or harmonization of data

- Multiple subject areas of data
- Global reach with one or many BW or data-warehouse environments
- One or many languages
- Regional requirements and global requirements

In global BW projects, there is much more complexity, and thus the organization is typically much larger than other non-global projects. Most global projects have one or many BW or other data-warehouse environments.

Global BW projects are typically quite complex because they usually have both regional and global requirements. These projects usually involve many different companies or affiliates, each working with some autonomy from the global parent. In this case, the parent company needs some data from the regional groups for global reporting. This may or may not be the same data requirement that the regional groups need for themselves.

In this case, a global template is typically built by a global organization or global Center of Excellence (COE). The COE is responsible for developing a global strategy for reporting across the organization and making sure that the regional groups follow the global strategy. This can be a difficult and often political task, because the regional groups also require flexibility to deliver regional reporting requirements in the same environment.

This global template spells out in detail the data that is needed from the regional groups and how the data is to be rolled up into a global view. The regional teams can utilize the global template in order to pass data to this global group, thus providing analysis across the regional groups.

This global template must allow for both flexibility of regional standards and needs and the rigor of enforced standards to make sure that the global reporting requirements can be met.

As seen in Figure 4.7, this involves separate BW groups. There are regional groups, each working on their specific regional subject matter. A global COE group with global BW developers help to gather data from the various groups and stage and transform this data as required for presentation to the global users.

In this environment, there may be multiple BW data architects and often multiple BW teams. Communication between the teams is vital to ensure that the data model is consistent and that the delivery of the data and implementation of the global and regional templates meet standards and can be aggregated successfully.

How can these needs be met? Many projects look to outsourcing to find resources, but with limited success.

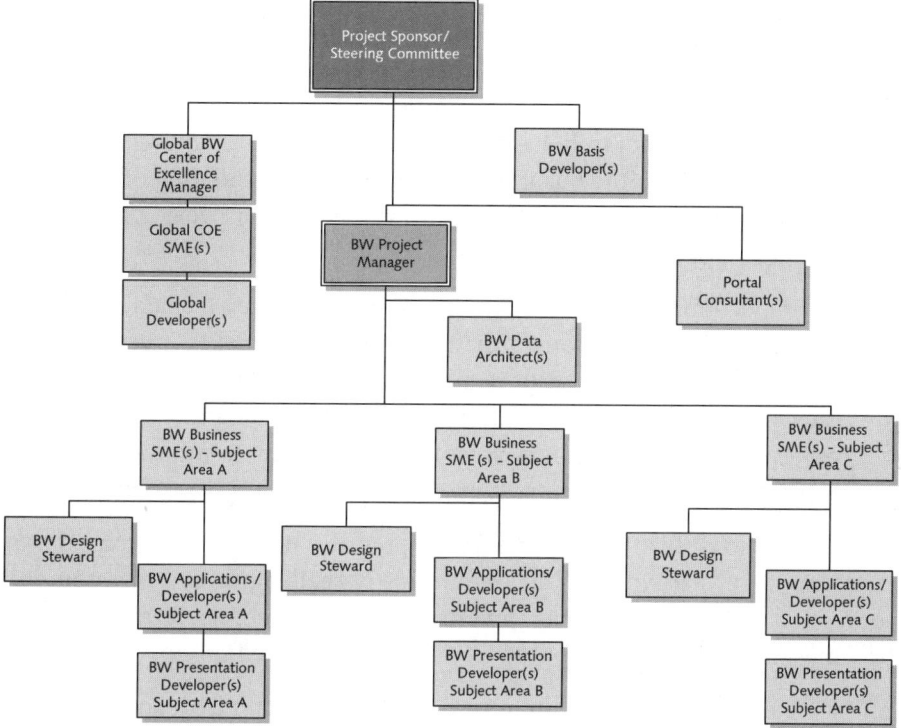

Figure 4.7 Typical Organizational Chart of a Large Global BW Project

4.6 Outsourcing and BW

Many project organizations that look to outsourcing as a quick answer to hasten development and ensure a less costly implementation. These projects typically gather the requirements and provide documentation to offshore resources that take the documentation and convert it into a data model and working BW system.

While this sounds like a tempting strategy, I have found that outsourcing the development of BW is of limited usefulness, in most instances and in most projects.

Outsourcing works well for clearly defined functionality with limited reach. This is because if there is a limited scope and the scope can be clearly documented, the process can be communicated, developed, tested, and transitioned. For example, many projects use outsourced resources to handle ABAP or coding work. This is because the work is of very limited scope, and once the specifications have been written, for the most part, there is limited interaction between the requirements and the delivery of the code.

Thus, if the specifications are clear, the project can save development costs by having outsourced resources to handle this custom coding work. However, BW development rarely has limited scope and often requires quite a bit of interaction between the business and the developer. Handing off a written set of instructions and waiting for the development to occur with limited interaction is usually quite challenging.

The BW environment usually requires multiple sources of data as well as many harmonization and transformation points. This makes it very difficult to troubleshoot without a lot of communication. Adding to the challenges are issues with data integrity. In addition, business users often have complex query-presentation needs; these are often difficult to communicate. These challenges can make for an extremely complex environment to outsource.

Often it is also difficult to enforce development standards to a group that is outsourced. In many cases, I have found it is challenging to get a non-outsourced group to obey development and data-modeling standards. This becomes complex, if not impossible with an outsourced group.

Many organizations find that in most cases it too difficult to document all the standards, requirements, and test cases, while also conveying an understanding of business needs and integrity issues in a small communication window.

Finding qualified outsourcing resources is also quite challenging. This is because BW has a steep learning curve and outsourcing firms are often competing for a small high-quality group of resources. Thus, turnover is often quite high and quality resources can be scarce.

4.6.1 When Does Outsourcing Work?

There are times that outsourcing BW work can be quite successful. If there is some very involved transformation of data requiring some complex ABAP, some organizations turn to outsourced resources.

For example, I worked with a company that needed to extract data from a legacy transactional system and transform much of this data to a SAP-friendly format. The coding became quite complex to check the data against existing source data tables and check various values for consistency.

This company looked to outside resources to deliver this functionality and was quite successful. This was because they could clearly communicate the tables needed for the transformation and validation and could provide clear test cases to check this data. This made the project easy to hand off to outsourced resources.

Outsourcing this kind of development work is often very successful. This is because the scope of the transformation can usually be limited to a small area; it has quite limited scope and can be communicated and tested quite easily.

Projects that look to outsourced resources to handle more localized requirements often find that the outsourced resources often succeed at delivering these types of application areas. The project saves some money over using internal or local resources to perform the development.

As previously stated, the interview process in BW is necessary to help select a qualified candidate, whether this candidate is part of an outsourcing group or in-house on the development team. Many times, when you are new to BW and BW consulting, having a few sample questions can help to choose the best candidate. The next section gives some common interview questions and some answers to expect.

4.7 BW Interview Process

It is often difficult to find the most qualified BW consultants and internal resources to staff a BW project. SAP does have a BW certification process. This is a test that is administered by SAP to determine some level of proficiency in the product.

In my experience, it is not helpful to use the certification process to determine the level of the consulting resource during the interview process. I have interviewed and worked with various consultants who have been certified (as am I).

I did not feel that the certification proves whether a consultant is any more qualified to implement BW. In some cases, the certified consultant resources were knowledgeable in the terminology but not in the processes and implementation strategies. Therefore, do not assume that a certified consultant is any more qualified than one that is not certified.

The lack of knowledge in the process and implementation during interviews is likely the result of the many test questions and books available to help people pass the test and become BW certified. Thus, I do not recommend that you look at these criteria alone when determining whether a consultant is qualified to implement BW. It does help to highlight those consultants with a basic understanding of the BW product, but not necessarily those who would be a great resource on your project.

I am most successful in finding the best resources when I conduct a detailed interview of the candidate. This allows me to understand not only their product knowledge but also their communication skills. Because both are equally important, I ask a lot of very open-ended questions to try to get the interviewee talking about his or her specific experiences in one area of BW implementation.

When I first started working in BW, the resumes seemed to match with the skill sets of the interviewees very well. However, in the last several years, I have seen many resumes that are embellished beyond what I would ever have imagined. A resume comes across my desk for someone that I worked with in a previous project. I knew their role on the BW team, and I'm frustrated when the resume lists many things that were not part of that role.

This trend seems to be a result of the many search tools that recruiters use to find consultants. Thus, consultants who were not closely working with CRM feel they need to list it on their resume to make sure that their resume comes up when CRM is searched in a job website. This is unfortunate, because I find myself asking consultants about things on their resumes that they cannot talk about with any degree of certainty.

This has made the interview process even more important. Of course, leaning on the other BW consultants I know has helped a great deal too. Because the world of BW is not that large, many times I can find someone who has worked with a particular resource and can give me some details about their background before I ever schedule an interview. This networking has allowed me to informally weed out those candidates who are less than qualified.

Interviewing BW candidates is not easy, especially if you are new to the product. I have included some interview questions that I like to use when I evaluate a BW consultant:

1. **What is the difference between an DSO (also called DataStore Objects) and InfoCubes and why is this difference important?**
   This question is intended to make sure the candidate understands the basic architecture of BW. This is a very basic question with quite serious rami-

fications if the candidate does not understand the use of each of the structures. The answer should clearly indicate that the InfoCube is the primary reporting repository for BW data, although the DSO can be used for reporting in some circumstances. The database structure of the InfoCube and DSO are completely different.

The DSO is a relational database structure with a user determined key and can have additive or overwrite capabilities. The InfoCube is a star schema design. The key is made up of a combination of the various characteristics in the dimension tables that establish dimension IDs used in the two central fact tables for reporting. The InfoCubes is only additive, there is no overwrite capability in the InfoCube.

2. **What kind of things can be used to determine query performance bottlenecks?**

   Performance management is one of the more difficult tasks in BW. This is because if you understand what performance issues can occur, you clearly understand the underlying design of the BW system. I have found that the more a candidate understands performance in BW, the more he or she seems to understand the product and its interworkings, and thus the stronger applicant he or she is. Thus, I like to ask many different performance related questions to determine if the interviewee understands performance management in BW.

   This also makes sure if candidates understand it, they will incorporate this into their data structures in BW, which is clearly an important overall goal of any implementation. In this answer, the candidate should mention something about BW statistics and an ongoing process to monitor these statistics. There are also some various other performance tools, such as transaction RSRV. But for the most part, determining performance bottlenecks should come from the statistics InfoCubes.

3. **What are some things that can be used to fix query bottlenecks?**

   This question is trying to get to the root of the performance questions to see how the candidates would actually apply their knowledge to a performance issue. Because there are many reasons for performance issues, I do not let a candidate give just one answer. I look for several of the following answers:

   ▹ Adjust the query, adding filter values to reduce the data retrieved
   ▹ Check the query to see if the filter logic is using exclusive logic
   ▹ Check the data model. If the query is going after an InfoProvider with massive amounts of datam reduce the volume by segregating the Info-

Providers into smaller individual ones, and use a multi-provider or adjust the data model appropriately

- Check to see if the query is running from an ODS/DSO. This is not the preferred InfoProvider for query performance; switch to an InfoCube. This is because queries typically run faster from InfoCubes, and more performance enhancing tools are available on InfoCubes. If the query is running from an ODS/DSO, the candidate should mention adding indices to the ODS/DSO.
- Check to see if the query is coming from a virtual InfoProvider
- Implement BW Aggregates
- Turn on/adjust OLAP Cache settings
- Implement the BI Accelerator (available only in NW 2004s and above)
- Implement partitioning
- Implement compression

4. **What is a navigational attribute and why would one use this in the BW design?**

This question is posed to ensure that the interviewee knows about the concept of data being read from either the transactional data or the attributes of master data. A navigational attribute is a master data field that is an related field of master data that can be used for reporting. For example, transactional data is loaded into BW with the customer and a net sales value. The customer master data record has an attribute "country" that is populated on the customer master data, but not in the transactional data. Although the transactional data does not have the country field, the data can be reported by country because the master data table for the customer does have the country.

This allows the BW report to show net sales by country without having this field in the transactional data. They need to fully understand that data read and accessed from the navigational attributes is stored in the master data and is dynamic. It changes with the master data itself. This provides an automatic restatement of the data each time the master data is reloaded. In this question, I am trying to make sure that they understand the concept of using master data in their design. There are several ways of delivering reports in BW. If all the data comes from the InfoCube directly, this means that all reports are sourced in the transactional data. This can be fine if the users are only concerned about a snapshot of the transactional data at the time that the transaction occurred.

However, understanding that the user can also view the data as a reflection of the current master data attributes gives them a more dynamic approach to the data, allowing transactional data to be restated based on the current view of the master data attributes. A navigational attribute is a master data field that is an related field of master data that can be used for reporting. For example, transactional data is loaded into BW with the customer and a net sales value.

The customer master data record has an attribute "country" that is populated on the customer master data, but not in the transactional data. Although the transactional data does not have the country field, the data can be reported by country because the master data table for the customer does have the country. This allows the BW report to show net sales by country without having this field in the transactional data.

5. **What is the delta initialization process and why is it important? Is there a way to resend a failed delta? How?**

    This question is intended to make sure that the candidate has actually loaded data into BW on an ongoing basis. Sooner or later a delta will fail for various reasons including data issues, space issues, etc. The interviewee should understand that the initialization of the delta process establishes the delta queue in the source system. This delta queue is used to store and track the changing delta records.

    If a delta fails, it is possible to resend this delta by simply backing out the failed delta on the BW system and using the delta-processing transactions in the source system, including Transaction RSA7, to resend a failed delta.

6. **What is the change run? (It is also called the *apply hierarchy change*)**

    Understanding the change-run job shows that the interviewee has done some work managing the batch processes of BW. Master data comes into BW in an inactive state. Changes to master data are not immediately reflected in the master data values. This job simply takes the new master data values and moves them to the active status. This allows the changes in master data to be reflected.

    The job also has one other important role. It adjusts any BW aggregates that have navigational attributes to the new master data value. Simply put, it does for the aggregates the same thing that it does for the master data. I have found that consultants who understand both of these parts of the change run have usually worked hands-on with aggregates, batch, and master data. This is a good sign that they understand the most important aspects of the BW design.

7. **Explain the methodology you have used for transitioning a project from the development stage to the production support phase.**
   This question is especially telling. Many candidates list multiple go-lives on their resume but cannot explain how the project was transitioned to the production support phase. Understanding this transition means understanding how knowledge was passed onto that group, how the help desk was staffed and transitioned, etc. This process is usually not clearly understood or articulated without being a large part of the process. Usually, if candidates cannot answer this question, they were part of a small piece of a project but were not there through the go-live and into the production support phase. If possible, I prefer those consultants that have been through this transition process. They usually understand what needs to be done to bring a project live.

The next step after choosing a team is to make sure the team is fully educated on the BW product. Understanding the typical training requirements help to make sure that the project plan reflects the typical training time needed.

4.8 Training Requirements

Product training is quite important for BW project managers and BW applications or presentation developers. However, typical SAP classes take several weeks and are quite popular. Thus, it can be difficult to book a class at the time and location required. It is important to make sure that the training be planned as early as possible to ensure that the training is completed in time for the design and build processes.

R/3 or ECC skills are not easily transferable to BW skills. BW has its own skill sets and one should not expect someone from an R/3 or ECC background to easily understand BW. BW takes some hands-on time to understand.

Most BW project scope includes bringing data from various parts of the ECC or R/3 system. For example, in order to successfully bring in sales orders into BW, one should understand the sales-order process. It helps even more if the BW developer can enter and change their sales orders in the development system.

It is likely to be necessary that the BW team either complete some training in the core area that they will be extracting or schedule time with that process team to educate the BW team on the basic workings and scope of that area. What works well in many projects is for the various process teams to schedule lunch and learn activities. This means each of the process teams, once a week or more, give a very informal presentation on the functionality and plans for their area of expertise.

For example, in a project that is bringing in data from ECC for APO and planning information from APO for reporting, the APO team could give a presentation on the entire planning process at a high level. This allows the BW team to ask questions and clearly understand the various part of that process so they can effectively ask the right questions during the implementation process. The more the BW team is aware of the scope and needs of the process teams, the better the implementation meets those needs.

These sessions should be planned to take advantage of the various process teams' expertise. Typically, during the early phases of the project, the resources on site are most aware and can devote more time to educating the BW team because they are not yet under extreme deadlines. This is the time to make sure the BW team is on their calendars for training.

4.9 Conclusion

Understanding the scoping and process lifecycle can enable a project team to have the right expectations when delivering BW. As with any team, selecting the right team members is vital to success. Using the typical team structure noted in this chapter helps to plan for all roles in the project and to help staff the project.

In Chapter 5, I will explore the process needed to gather requirements from the end users. This process involves working with them to understand their vision and analysis needs and help them articulate these into a clear document with which to begin work.

"To see what is in front of one's nose is a constant struggle"
– George Orwell

5 Gathering and Analyzing BW Requirements

In the most efficiently run BW projects, team members work to clearly understand in as much detail as possible the end user requirements for analysis. These requirements not only include the information needed, but other aspects such as the format and security requirements. Gathering these requirements in the detail required in order to implement in BW can be a challenge.

For example, I worked at one company that wanted to provide purchasing analysis. This involved taking data from two outside source systems and analyzing that data with the existing SAP ECC purchasing data. The requirements that we were given appeared to be detailed. We clearly understood which data that needed to be extracted. We understood the SAP data that was needed. We even had mock-ups of the queries that were expected.

The business users agreed with our approach and our intended data model in BW, so we started to build the solution. Only then did we understand that the external data was at many different levels of granularly and detail. It also did not always contain key fields that we needed for comparison.

In order to match the data, extensive transformations of data were needed in order to compare values and determine measurement values. It took us a lot of time analyzing the data and prototyping new solutions.

Since we spent a great deal of time trying to work around the source data, we were late delivering the solution. However, if we had understood the issues and challenges with this data and the difficulty of harmonizing the data with other data, we would have allowed ourselves more time to analyze and implement.

In order for the business requirements to be clearly understood by all involved, we need a clear methodology for gathering and understanding the

5 | Gathering and Analyzing BW Requirements

BW requirements. In the next section, I will discuss some methods for gathering these requirements.

5.1 Requirements Gathering

Analyzing BW data and requirements can be a difficult task. It requires not only an understanding of the BW software but also some level of understanding of the source systems and their functionality. This allows the data to be extracted and combined in a meaningful way in order to provide the necessary reporting.

The first stages of BW requirement-gathering are typically performed by the overall project-management organization, the BW project management, the BW data architect(s), and the business SMEs. Usually, the business SMEs present and fully communicate their business analysis needs and help determine where BW might help to meet these needs.

Once the overall project management organization and the BW project managers agree that requirements should be included in the BW scope, the BW data architect and BW project management then make a high-level assessment of the level of effort and timeline needed to implement those requirements in BW.

Figure 5.1 Important Document Deliverables During the BW Project

Figure 5.1 shows some of the documents that are needed at each stage in the BW project. It is through the completion of these documents that the scope of the BW project is established, agreed upon, implemented, and documented for handoff to the production support organization for post-implementation support. Samples of several of these documents are found in Appendix C.

In order to begin to start understanding the end user requirements, the most logical place to begin is with these end users themselves. The most common way to begin to gather requirements is through the interview process.

5.1.1 Interviews

The first step in any BW requirement gathering and analysis is to recognize the various stakeholders and interview these stakeholders to determine the reporting requirements and sources of data. The next step is to establish ongoing communication between the shareholders and the BW team to articulate the needs and business analysis pain in the organization.

The interview process allows the BW functional team and the business process teams to review their requirements and set the scope for the project. These interviews allow the BW team to ask focused questions of the process team members to determine where their analysis pains are felt.

The main goals of the interview process are to gain agreement with the stakeholders on the definition of the business questions and the causes of analysis issues. The interview should identify constraints to current analysis and create a clear mission for the BW project.

It may be helpful to have a business-modeling session to articulate more complex business problems and allow both parties to clearly understand the business issues. The next step in the process is to analyze the business requirements that have surfaced and determine how the requirement should be realized. This requires knowledge in where BW excels, and what BW does not do as well. This is a good time to determine whether the reporting requirement should be met in BW at all.

Once the business owners and intended users are interviewed, the requirements for analysis become clearer. This is a very important time in the BW lifecycle. This is where you are confronted with the basic question: BW or not BW? Often, the BW team assumes that because the analysis requirement was initially slated to become a BW requirement its ultimate delivery must be in BW.

This should not be assumed. After the interview process, when the requirements are fairly well known, the BW team should assess the requirements to determine where the analysis is best delivered. Sometimes BW is the best solution. At other times the analysis requirement is best fulfilled in another area of the system, or even outside of the system.

Some BW projects fail for the simple reason that they attempt to use BW for something that it is not intended to do. So, in the early stages of the requirement-gathering, a scoping session should be planned. This often occurs after the interview sessions but before any functional specifications are written. The goal of these sessions is to determine if BW is the right tool to deliver the analysis requirements that are needed.

It is best to do this early in requirements gathering because then you will not waste a lot of time writing specifications that are intended to be in BW scope but that are better served in another SAP application or even outside the system itself. The following subsections tackle the basic questions that should be asked:

5.1.2 Is All Data in SAP ECC or R/3 or in Multiple Systems?

If *all* data is coming from the SAP ECC or R/3 system, the source data should be evaluated to determine if there are standard reports or standard list functions in the ECC system to provide the analysis needed. This analysis is typically done by the process team that is implementing or has implemented the affected area of the system.

> **Example**
>
> An analysis report is requested that will show all customers with open credit balances in accounts receivable. There are several standard reports that can show this information in the SAP ECC or R/3 system. Thus, a representative from the finance team should evaluate the reporting requirement to see if there are already reports in this area that satisfy the reporting need. Although this seems a rather obvious step, I visited several SAP projects where companies spent a great deal of time implementing reporting that already exists on the transactional system.

5.1.3 Is Intra-Day or Real-Time Reporting Needed?

BW is not primarily designed to provide real-time data. Although there is functionality to provide some real-time reporting, this is not something that is often implemented in BW. Thus, intra-day reporting, or analysis reports that require data to be loaded multiple times per day, can become a challenge in BW. This type of reporting requirement is typically a red flag that the reporting requirement *might* be better served in the transactional system.

It is important to note that BW can provide intra-day reporting; data can be loaded multiple times a day into BW. I have worked with several project teams that do have this requirement and successfully provide this type of reporting to their end users. However, often when reporting requirements need to have the most up-to-date data as part of their analysis, this is a sign that you need to learn more about the requirement.

After analyzing these types of requirements, it is often found that either the most up-to-date information is not needed, or that the report needs to truly be real-time and the analysis might be better achieved in the source system.

Once data is loaded multiple times per day into BW or even set up to provide real-time reporting in BW, this often causes more issues. This is because users do to have a single point in time that the data is static for analysis. This can make analysis much more difficult, as data is constantly being updated in the BW environment.

5.1.4 What Else Do You Know About the Requirement?

There are several questions that should be asked to determine more about the requirement. It helps if you know the answers to these questions:

1. **Is the data analysis using high volumes of data?**
   This question is important because BW does handle high-volume reporting well. On the contrary, ECC and R/3 typically do not. When reports require analysis on a higher-volume data set, this is often a flag that the reporting should take place in BW and not the ECC or R/3 source system.

2. **Does the analysis need to serve many users?**
   The number of users is important because often BW can be quickly rolled out to a large user base with less effort than can a solution on the ECC or R/3 system. This is because the ECC or R/3 reports usually require a graphical user interface client to be loaded on the user's machine and training on the transactions in ECC to find and run the report.
   In BW, adding more users is often easier because the reports can run as a web link or iView on a portal. This basically means that many reports can be rolled out to users more quickly because the link, login, and security access only need to be established for analysis to begin.

3. **Is the analysis interactive? Does the user need to drill down in order to provide the information required?**
Often this is a red flag that a reporting requirement might be a good match for BW. Since BW is designed to provide interactivity and drilling down, often the reporting requirements that require this should be developed in BW. Drilling down is often very limited in ECC or R/3-developed reports.

4. **Is the data integrated from multiple sources?**
BW excels at integrating data from multiple sources, where the ECC system usually reports data from one functional area. Once data needs to be integrated or harmonized from several source systems or several modules of ECC or R/3 the report often is best in the BW system.

These types of questions are used to determine if the analysis requirements that are needed play to BW's strengths. If the questions are answered affirmatively, this typically means that the reporting requirements are often best in the BW system rather than the associated transactional systems.

Some project organizations opt to create a report-determination matrix to allow some of the evaluation of the reporting method to be performed by process team members rather than the BW team. For example, as the organization starts to grow and the analysis needs become more mature, new reporting requirements often surface. Sometimes each of these reporting requirements end up in a rather long list that is evaluated by the BW team for inclusion in the BW scope.

Many times, in order to keep the process of determining new BW scope more efficient, the process teams that are supporting or implementing the various modules of ECC can help with this effort. For example, if a finance report is requested, the finance team should first evaluate and prioritize these requests and then provide them to the BW team, rather than having the list of these requests given to the BW team immediately

In order for the finance team to help in this evaluation, they often need a report-determination matrix to allow the finance team members to look that the requested inventory of reports and triage them into the area that they are best suited. Figure 5.2 shows an example of a report-determination matrix that could be used by the process teams to help determine which reporting system should be used in order to provide the analysis to the end users.

Typically a dialog is needed between the BW team and the process teams to complete the BW scope. This allows the process teams to begin questioning the business users requesting the new reporting functionality to make sure that this can be evaluated most efficiently.

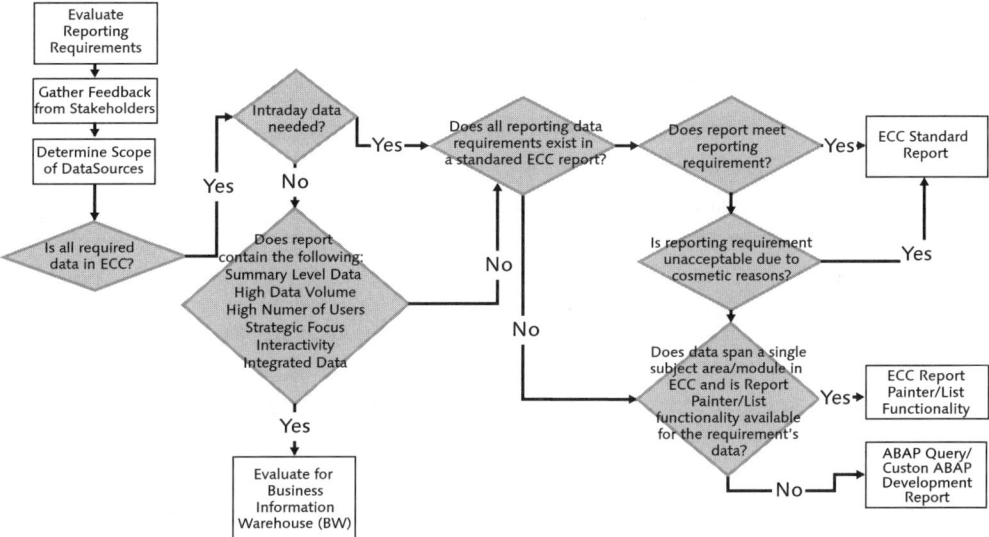

Figure 5.2 Report Determination Matrix

Often, the next step in any project is to gather up all the existing reports and proceed to plan how these can be duplicated in the BW system. Projects frequently create a full report inventory to track the current reports and map them to new BW reports. Let's look at this approach now.

5.2 Gathering a Report Inventory

While determining reporting requirements in new implementation of a subject area in BW, process teams often spend a great deal of time gathering up existing report inventories. For example, a company that is replacing a legacy system with the R/3 or ECC equivalent gets a large binder of sample reports from the legacy system. This is supposed to be used to track existing reports so they can eventually be mapped into the BW system.

In most cases, this effort does not yield many useful results. This is because typically there cannot be a one-to-one correspondence between the legacy reporting system and the new BW system. Typically, the new system and the legacy system track and record data in very different ways, so the data analysis needs are quite different.

Trying to map the legacy reports to new BW reports often leaves the process teams frustrated. Sometimes it keeps them thinking in the legacy system's terms and analysis needs. For example, suppose a company is moving its inventory distribution functions from a legacy system to a new ECC system. The analysis from the ECC system will be performed in the BW system.

The legacy system measured inventory obsolescence by determining orders and stock movements on inventory. If the user of this legacy system is to measure the same obsolescence in BW from a new SAP ECC transactional source, he or she might look to the same formula to determine obsolete items.

Thus, the business SME might ask for an obsolescence report with the same formula. This would not take into account some of the new functionality in SAP to track missed sales and other functions for planning, and inventory analysis. Because ECC has other tools for measuring and tracking obsolescence, the old factors may no longer be valid, or may be enhanced with new features from ECC. Many times, if a report inventory is used, the business limits its thinking on those reports to an exact or very close match of the reports without proper analysis of the functionality of ECC.

In some cases this works fine, while in others it may not be as effective. Many times it is more advantageous to track the analysis requirements and not match these requirements one-for-one with the report inventory. This allows the analysis needs to be driven by the reporting requirements and not the reporting inventory. This can yield new thinking on the new transactional data and often gives more meaningful reporting requirements than trying to map to existing reports.

Once these requirements have been established, the next step is to get more detail behind each of these requirements. It is not always easy to get all the answers needed to begin developing in BW. A document is needed that gathers all the requirements from the end user and matches them with some expertise from the BW team to develop and agree on the scope of each subject area that will be analyzed.

The best way I have found to get more details about the scope and to come to agreement on what needs to be delivered is via a functional model document. Let's explore this document and how it can be used to help gather and organized the requirements.

5.3 Functional Model Document

Once the business needs have been clearly established during the interview process, and the reporting functionality is determined to be in scope for BW, the next step in developing an understanding and agreement of scope is to develop a *functional model document*. This document serves as a template of the initial scope of what will be delivered in BW. A sample of this document can be found in Appendix C.

> **Note**
>
> The functional model document is a vital step in the BW requirements-gathering process. The better the effort up front getting this document as robust as possible, the better and more efficient the implantation process.

In most cases, there are two groups that need to agree on scope. One is the business process teams that are providing the business needs and asking that these business needs be represented in BW. The other party involved is the actual BW team that would provide and implement the need in the BW product. Getting clear agreement between these two teams is vital to a successful project.

> **Note**
>
> The most common reason for a BW project to fail is lack of agreement on the scope and lack of understanding of the requirements between the BW team and the process teams providing the requirements.

There are several reasons why the process of getting the scope agreement is difficult. Usually there is a combination of the following factors:

- Process teams have not completely decided on their own needs
- Communicating needs of the process team is difficult
- The process teams do not understand the BW tool
- BW team does not understand the process team's analysis or transactional needs
- Neither team understands one or many legacy systems needed to provide the analysis

From my experience, the best way to get the business process teams to help the BW teams and business process teams to agree on their scope is to work together to develop a functional model document. Basically, this document acts as a template for the process teams to communicate their needs and the BW team to ask questions to refine those needs. This functional model document process works no matter what subject matter data is being bought into BW and regardless of source.

> **Tip**
> The functional model document should be considered the responsibility of the process teams to complete.

This document should be listed and tracked as a deliverable of the process team. The reason this is considered a process-team deliverable and not a BW team deliverable is because we want to shift the analysis gathering and ownership to the process teams. This gives them the incentive to gather and own the functional model document, because without a completed functional model document, no development can take place in the BW system. This gives the process teams some ownership of the requirement.

In one of my projects, the project manager referred to the functional model document as the process team's ante. Like a player *ante-ing up* in a poker game, the process teams are forced to bring something to the table before anything other than preliminary analysis is done on the requirements.

Often the process teams will scrutinize their analysis needs and set priorities better if they are forced to write a functional model document for the reporting requirements that are needed.

Without this ante, the process teams often gather up reporting requirements in a spreadsheet list and present this to the BW team and ask the BW team to fill in the details of the scope. This is not only an inefficient use of the BW team's time, it often leads to conflict later as the needs are not clearly understood and therefore not clearly met in the design.

Even though the functional model document is primarily owned by the process teams, it should not be considered a document that is solely developed by the process teams. The document requires a lot of back and forth from the BW team in order to complete all the sections.

Understanding the security requirements and functionality of BW is often a complex task. The functional model document needs to clearly state the security requirements, but the BW team should help to steer the security requirements dialog to represent what eventually will be possible in the BW system.

The functional model document is designed to be a blueprint to begin creating a BW physical data model. However, during the process of creating, refining, and completing the functional model document, there should be no talk of InfoCubes, DSO structures, or any physical BW tables.

Once the functional model document is complete and the needs are better known, the BW team takes it and uses it to create a physical model, including InfoCubes, DSOs etc.

5.3.1 How Many Functional Model Documents are Needed?

In most BW projects, multiple functional model documents need to be developed. One functional model document should be implemented for each *subject area*. A subject area can include many different interpretations. The subject area is not always designed only to reflect one actual business area, such as sales and distribution, or purchasing. This is because there are many BW teams who track their scope at a more granular level than simply by business area.

To determine the subject areas in a BW project, the scope should be examined to determine where different sub-groups of the BW team would be used to implement the functionality needed.

For example, in some BW teams, procurement would be considered a subject area. The BW team would scope, staff, and deliver the procurement needs as a group deliverable. In this case, the procurement area would be one subject area, and one functional model document would be produced for purchasing.

In other projects, procurement is much more complex and would be delivered as more than one sub-group. For example, there may be one sub-group that delivers the purchasing; another that does vendor performance, and another that might deliver the receipt tracking.

If these sub-groups require significant work, involve significant scope, and answer very different business questions, they require individual functional model documents to track and deliver their scope.

The functional model document can be very time-consuming to create if there are many sections that need to be completed. Too many subject areas require a great deal of time from the process teams. This should be weighed against the business needs. If multiple business needs can be clearly captured in one functional model document, it is fine to combine the business needs into one document; however, each need should be clearly understood and documented.

5.3.2 Sections of the Functional Model Document

There are several sections to the functional model document. Each section needs collaboration between the BW team and the process teams to complete. Each section is designed to allow as many of the requirements to be understood and documented. This is the template for all future development.

Subject Area

Each functional model should cover one subject area. The definition of subject area can vary by project and scope, but the subject area represents one area of BW implementation that can be tracked and staffed as one unit of work.

Business Questions Asked and Answered

This section of the functional model document is designed to give an overall understanding of the business pains and the questions that this functional model should answer once implemented. Although this appears to be a very easy section to complete, it is often the one that process teams have trouble completing fully. The business questions detailed in this section are used for several things, which include the following:

- To help to make sure that the BW team understands the business pain and the business analysis needs.
- To allow the physical BW model to be developed with specific needs in mind.
- To help when questions arise that there is a foundation for the business analysis needs.

These business questions will also be used as a foundation for the test cases in the future, to make sure that the physical model, once implemented, answers the questions posed in this section.

These questions should be in bullet format, be listed with specific measurements, and include time horizons. In most cases there are several of these questions posed for each functional model. Examples include:

- To measure and track vendor performance to determine on-time delivery based on purchase-order expected dates and actual receipt dates across months
- To track inventory turns based on stock items across fiscal periods to determine stock availability levels
- To manage and track the voluntary turnover of a division in the calendar year based on the employee headcount

History Requirements of Information

The history requirements help to define the information and source of data for the solution. If history is required, it is important to understand what history and how much history are required in order to complete the model. This is most important to understand when there are legacy systems involved.

> **Example**
>
> A new SAP ECC implementation with sales and distribution data requires some reporting from the BW system. To provide that, the assumption is that the data needed for the reporting would come out of ECC as its sole DataSource. However, unless history is being loaded into ECC and converted to ECC SD orders, there will be very little meaningful data to support reporting.

Many projects need to have the legacy data loaded into the BW system and require that this data be harmonized with the ECC data so they can compare and provide analysis. It can be very time-consuming to map the legacy fields, master data, etc. to the ECC data. Understanding these requirements early helps to define and understand the scope of the reporting needs.

DataSources Required to Complete Model

DataSources are the places where data is stored currently and the scope of data to be loaded into the model. This section of the functional model typically requires input from the BW team. The goal of this section is to see what data is needed to satisfy the reporting requirements and where it is found. This section should concentrate on the transactional DataSources. It may require, in some cases to analyze the specific fields of data. You will probably need to compare the fields to the existing standard content DataSources.

For example, this section should state if data is to come from an external system, ECC or R/3 systems, Advanced Planning and Optimization (APO), etc. It

5 | Gathering and Analyzing BW Requirements

should clearly state the specific area of the system from which data is to be extracted. If the data is to come from a legacy purchasing system, this section should clearly state the system name, the tables, or files that are needed to load this data into BW, and some information about this data.

If the data is to come from the ECC or R/3 system, the BW team should work with the process team to analyze standard delivered business-content Data-Source extractors to determine which of these matches the data that is to be extracted. This helps to establish the scope and number of DataSources that will be needed to satisfy the reporting requirements.

Volume, System, Frequency

Understanding the volume of data that is required helps to set the eventual data model. If data volume is substantial the data needs to be partitioned into multiple ODS/DSO structures or multiple InfoCubes when eventually loading the data into BW. Understanding this volume helps plan and scope out any potential performance issues that could bottleneck loading or query processing.

It is also helpful to know the frequency with which data is required for analysis. This helps to spot possible needs for intra-day loads or real time analysis. Typically, if real-time analysis of data is needed, this involves a much more significant effort during the BW implementation. Often real-time analysis is better handled in the source system. The functional model can help to show these requirements so they can be managed.

> **Example**
> If sales-order data is to be extracted from a legacy system, this section might state that the sales orders will be extracted on a daily basis once a day, after midnight, with the approximate volume of 2,000 orders a day with approximately five lines on each order.

Dependencies, Constraints, Assumptions

Sometimes, data cannot be loaded until after a certain procedure or load is run on either the ECC or legacy system. It is helpful to know about any constraints or dependencies so that you can plan the data model accordingly. It also helps to spell out the assumptions regarding the data at an early phase to make sure these assumptions are shared by the BW and the process teams.

> **Tip**
> A billing document should only be extracted after the billing run is complete. It should be noted when the billing run typically completes and what other dependencies are needed as a result. This allows for the BW team to plan the data loads around these constraints.

This section is also good to clarify any assumptions that have been made on the BW data. If the data needs to be verified or checked against other tables to ensure that the data is valid, this can be stated in this section.

Transformation of Data Required

Often some type of transformation of data is required to meet a business need. This transformation can often require significant time from the BW development team. It is very difficult to determine all transformations of data until the data is loaded. However, those transformations of data that are recognized early should be clearly spelled out in the functional model document.

For instance, legacy data often needs to have its master data objects transformed into SAP objects. If legacy sales data is being extracted and will be compared with the R/3 or ECC data, this data must be shown to the user using a common customer and material. Often the legacy system has its own master data values.

In order to get the data harmonized, the data needs to be transformed in BW into the SAP master data objects. The customer data would need to read a cross-reference table, and the SAP customer would replace the legacy customer number. The same process would be needed for material, vendor, etc.

The transformation needs that are identified early can then be planned as part of the BW project plan. In the previous example, the BW team would need to make sure that they are also populated the cross-reference tables to map the legacy customer to the SAP customer. This data would need to be tracked and stored in a logical format and a methodology created in order to keep these tables up-to-date. A process would also have to be designed to determine what would happen if a customer is in the legacy extract and there is no entry in the cross-reference table.

Understanding the transformations needed enables us to properly plan and organize the data needs so as to ensure that a process is in place to develop the transformations and deliver the infrastructure needed.

Functional Model Diagram to Show Flow and Data Model

Often, a diagram of the functional model is helpful to see all the data and the sources feeding this data. This diagram can be used later when the model is being evaluated to determine if it meets the needs of the organization.

This diagram represents the different dependencies and the flow of the data into the BW system. This is often helpful in understanding that the feed of the data might come from SAP, but that the data may have originated in a legacy system first, and then was fed to SAP ECC and then onto BW. Understanding the flow of the data through the organization allows for a clearer understanding of the dependencies involved.

Presentation Requirements

The presentation requirements refer to the actual queries, dashboards, etc that will be used to show the data in BW to the end users.

When the functional model document is being developed, the presentation needs should be understood, but the main focus of the functional model document should be on understanding the information that is needed to deliver the model.

This section should spell out the presentation needs, but it is typically not necessary to list all queries or analysis needs in detail. There is a basic understanding that as long as the DataSources are clearly spelled out, that data is being loaded into BW. The presentation needs can be flexible and based on the needs of the organization. Thus, in this section, only the most vital presentation needs should be listed, with an understanding that the presentation layer of BW can be flexible to provide many different forms of analysis, as long as the source of data for the analysis is in BW.

This section should also list the audience and the form of distribution for the presentation. It is helpful to understand the roles of the BW users and how they will be accessing the presentation in order to understand and plan its delivery. This section should state whether web or portal access is required and if Microsoft Excel functionality will be used in reporting.

Security Requirements

Understanding and implementing security requirements are often left until the very end of the BW build process. This can be a mistake. If the security requirements are known from the beginning, the model can be planned and presentation of data developed using the security requirements. If the security needs to be retrofitted into an existing complete model, some rework may be needed in order to complete the security requirements.

This section should state if the security is not needed at all. If it is needed, how should the security be implemented? Is the security by query? Are there certain key figure values in the data that are sensitive and thus should be protected? Are there certain characteristics that should be secured? For example, if several divisions of sales data are being loaded into BW, should all divisions be allowed to see each other's sales? Is there a restriction on any other characteristic of the data?

This section should be filled out and verified before any modeling can begin. However, often this section should also be reviewed multiple times during the implementation.

I worked on one finance BW project where the idea of security needs was repeatedly rejected. The process teams clearly stated that all data could be seen by anyone who could access any of the finance queries. We built the model based on these requirements.

Later, as the implementation was getting ready for integration testing, the testers saw that there were research divisions whose queries should not be shown to other finance users. Otherwise, users could see budgets and planning of research that was considered confidential in the company.

The finance team was unaware of this restriction, and we were forced to retrofit the security in a design that was already complete. Had we known about this requirement, we may have designed the data model to exclude queries to exclude this data. We were forced to add the security after the fact, and it challenged our timeline for implementation and rollout.

Sign-Off

To make sure that all groups are in agreement on the functional model document, a signoff process should be established. This way, any changes to the functional model can be discussed as a scope-change process. No development or planning on the BW physical model should commence until the functional model document receives signoff.

Once the functional model has been completed, the next step is to get more detail and uniformity around some of the measures that are requested in the functional model document(s). The best method to provide some uniformity and structure is with a Key Figure Matrix or KPI Matrix. Let's look at this document next.

5.4 BW Key Figure or KPI Matrix

After the functional model document is complete, many project teams find that there are several key figure or key performance indicator (KPI) values that are used universally in the organization. Often these are used so commonly in the organization that few stop to ask what calculation was used to arrive at the value.

Common KPI values are Mean Absolute Deviation (MAD) and Mean Absolute Percentage Error (MAPE). These totals need to be universal in the organization in order to provide meaningful measurement of and tracking.

Many times while implementing a BW project it becomes clear that different organization might calculate the MAD or MAPE differently. This can lead to conflict when trying to implement BW. Unless the business organizations settle on one measurement for the KPI values, the BW team cannot implement these KPIs.

In order to proactively manage and encourage decision-making based on these values, it is helpful to make sure the organization has one common list of their KPIs, with the calculations of these values clearly spelled out. This can often become a political discussion, as the organization settles on national and even global standards. However, it is vital before implementation to make sure that these discussions do not affect the BW timeline. If a KPI matrix is developed and signed off by the organization, the BW team can work from this document to make sure that all KPIs reflect the calculations agreements of the organization.

5.5 Budgeting or Estimating BW Timelines

It is challenging in any project to estimate the timeline and therefore the budget needed for the project. There are many factors involved the calculation, and many of these factors are unknown or outside of the control of the project. This is typically the reason that estimates can be inaccurate.

However, in order to set an initial budget, a timeline needs to be determined. The only way to determine the number of days for a project is to break down the days into the primary tasks that need to be completed and assign a level of effort and number of days for each. The aggregate of the days, multiplied by the complexity becomes the estimated number of days. These days can be then multiplied by a rate per day to determine the budget.

There are several steps to budgeting and estimating the BW timeline, which are examined here:

- **Size BW Effort Based on Scope Presented**
  This allows a clear understanding of what is requested for implementation. This is typically done as part of the functional model document
- **Prioritize**
  Set priorities based on the functional models to determine the timelines needed for each.
- **Plan Delivery**
  Often there are organizational constraints on when functionality can be rolled out. These factors need to be weighed in budgeting steps.
- **Plan Resources**
  Based on the effort, scope, and delivery schedule, the resource plan can be developed.

Developing a clear formula in order to estimate timelines and budgets is very difficult in any project. This becomes even more difficult in BW projects as so many factors are involved in the calculation. We will describe factors that are used and a basic formula that can be used to determine the timeline needed for the BW implementation. This can then be applied to the resource plan to determine the budget and cost of the project.

The following subsections explain the factors involved in estimating the time and therefore the budget needed to deliver the BW solution. A time estimate should be given to each factor based upon the resource plan. Let's look at these now.

Complexity Factor (1–5)

The first step in estimating the timeline for a BW project is to understand the complexity factor involved in the project. This complexity factor is used in the timeline calculation as a multiplier, as seen here:

- **Complexity Factor One**
  A project complexity factor of one is the least complex project. These projects typically involve all business content and are usually straightfor-

ward in design. Most of the project time is spent evaluating the business content and ensuring that the content matches the requirements. There is usually some development work on the queries; however, very little development work is required getting the data extracted from the source and getting this data loaded into BW. These projects always involve only one source, SAP R/3 or ECC.

- **Complexity Factor Two**
  These projects usually involve a small amount of development effort on the loading of BW and some simple transformations of data into the BW system. There is usually some query development, and the data is typically coming from only one source.

- **Complexity Factor Three**
  These projects often involve more than one source system but the source data is not very complex. The source data often resides in legacy systems that do not require a significant amount of transformation. This is then harmonized with the SAP or ECC data to provide reporting to the end user. These projects often involve some significant query design.

- **Complexity Factor Four**
  These projects often involve multiple modules of R/3 or ECC or multiple source systems. The data requires some transformation in many areas. These projects also require some significant query design efforts.

- **Complexity Factor Five**
  These are the most complex projects and usually involve multiple source systems and multiple subject areas to be loaded into BW. Very little standard business content is to be used in order to realize the solution, other than the standard DataSources in the ECC or R/3 system. Often these projects involve significant transformation and harmonization efforts to bring the data from multiple source systems into one system and report the data as if it came from one source.
  Often, projects that are implementing the SAP APO system fall into complexity factor five. These types of projects typically bring data from multiple source systems, and then pass this data over to the APO system. They often also bring date from the APO system into BW for reporting of planning vs. actual data.

Once the complexity factor is established, the next step is to establish a time estimate on the most time-consuming tasks of the project. These tasks will later be multiplied by the complexity factor to come up with a project time estimate.

Project Management Time

This is the time dedicated to the early analysis of the solution, gathering the resources needed to understand the solution and set the infrastructure needed to implement the BW system. If this is a new implementation, allow much more time to establish review standards, naming standards, etc.

Education

This time estimate depends on the knowledge level of the people who will be implementing the product. The time needed should not only include the time in training to understand and grasp the BW product but also some ramp-up time to build on the knowledge in the BW solution. If an upgrade is planned, some time should be allowed for understanding the new upgrade and the new features in that release.

The education day estimate should also include the number of days that will be used understanding and getting any developers or consultants to understand the business aspects of the solution being implemented. This often involves several workshops or interview sessions to understand the business environment.

Interviews

The interview time estimate is a prediction of the time needed for conducting interviews with the process teams and the business SMEs to understand the business analysis needs and solutions requested. These interview sessions estimates should not only include the actual interview time but also the time needed to prepare for the interviews and the time needed to document the results and follow-up from the interviews.

Modeling Workshops

The modeling workshop time approximation represents the time needed to meet with the SMEs and business process representatives to understand their business issues and needs for analysis. This is typically not a great deal of time, but should be provided for in the overall time estimate.

Functional Model Development

The functional model development usually takes most of the time of the analysis phase. The time to complete this is often one of the longest time allocations of the project, other than the realization and the testing. This time estimate needs to take into account the time it takes to understand the business needs and fill out the entire functional model document. This also should include some time to review and ask for revisions to the document.

Business Content Review

This often takes a few days to review the content and understand how the content can match the business requirements. There is almost always some of this time in any project because almost all projects that extract data from the ECC or R/3 system use business content DataSources to extract data from the ECC or R/3 system.

Physical Design

The physical design estimate is the time it takes to fully design the solution on paper. This involves reading over the functional model document, reviewing the business content to make sure that the design can be realized in the BW system, and understanding how the design will be implemented. This often takes less than half the time that it takes to develop the functional model document.

Design Realization (Build)

The design realization phase is often the second-longest time allocation in the project (the longest is typically the testing phase). This phase expands with new releases and new functionality.

Tuning

The tuning phase occurs at varying stages of the project and involves Basis tuning, database tuning, and tuning of the application. This time estimate should be much higher if you are implementing a new release of BW in the earlier stages of release. There is often much time spent applying SAP Notes and working through software issues.

Testing

Testing is often one of the most significant time estimates in the project because it not only involves several phases of unit, string, and integration testing but also involves issue tracking and resolution. This should be given the largest time estimate in the project.

Security

Security is dependent on the complexity of the authorization strategy and the amount of roles required in order to implement the solution. This should also include the time for setting up the users in the various systems.

Transports

Transports in BW are much more complex than in the ECC or R/3 environments, and thus significantly more time should be allowed for this process. It can often take four days to move a solution up to another environment. This time is dependent on the number of transports that are associated with the design. If a design is kept in the development environment longer, the number of transports decreases, and the time for transporting decreases as well.

Rollout

The rollout timeline involves turning on the solution to the various users and the training of the power users on the solution. This depends on the logistics of the power users, their ability, and the timing of the training. This should also include time for training development.

Change Management

Change-management timing involves the time it takes to make the solution available to the end users. This often involves end user training, job aids, website development, deployment plans, etc. The change-management effort can vary widely depending on the new job functions created as a result of the implementation.

Post Implementation

The post-implementation time estimate should include the time it takes to transition the solution to the production support organization. It should also allow time for a post-implementation review of the solution and a lessons learned session. This time can significantly be reduced based on the quality of the documentation and the knowledge of the production support organization of the BW product.

> **Note: Formula**
> BW Implementation Timeline = (Project Management Time + Interview Time + Modeling Workshops + Functional Model Development Business Content Review + Physical Design + Design Realization + Tuning + Testing + Security + Transports + Rollout + Change Management + Post Implementation) * Complexity Factor)

Although this formula seems rather complex, it can be broken down into estimates in a spreadsheet and used for preliminary budgeting and timeline purposes. Because the formula takes into account many of the most time-consuming tasks and also allows for a complexity factor, it provides a basic estimate of the timeline of the project. In many cases, this estimate is not too far off what is eventually realized.

In most cases where the formula result differs from the actual timeline, this is because the complexity factor is set too low. Often a model that is assumed to be easy turns out to be more complex as more is known, this pushes all the pieces of the calculation off, and the entire project estimate is not valid.

Once the functional model, KPI or Key Figure Matrix, and budget/time Estimate is complete, it is now time to begin to take the requirements and begin to determine how this model should exist in the BW system. This becomes the BW physical model. Let's explore this next.

5.6 BW Physical Model

Once the functional model is complete, the next step is to create a BW physical model document. This document shows the various datasources, InfoCubes, DSOs, etc. It should clearly flow out all the data being loaded into the model and should clearly state the volume of data that will be loaded from each source.

Creating the physical model requires understanding of the functionality and development process of the BW system. This task is typically performed by a group familiar with the BW system and also someone well versed in the business requirements and analysis needs of the organization. In most projects, this is the data architect.

The first step in developing the physical model is to gather the requirements from the functional model document and break the requirements down to into data requirements. This allows the team to understand where the data is to come from and how this data is to be presented to the end user. Understanding this helps to know what data needs to be transformed and what data needs to be harmonized with other data.

In understanding the harmonizing needs of the organization the physical model can be established to make sure that the data that needs to be combined together is linked properly. For example, if the organization needs to track vendor performance, it may need to track purchases, good receipts, and even accounts payable information. In order to develop a physical model, these different areas must have a common link at least with the vendor that links the data.

The various InfoCubes and DSO structures can be planned based on the analysis needs. In many cases, the data volume also is a very big factor in determining the physical data model. As a general rule, it is far better to have many smaller InfoCubes or DSO structures with different slices of the data than it is to have one very large structure. This is because performance during loading and query analysis typically suffers if one large structure is used.

In my experience, the best way to start this process it to look at all the requirements and begin to *whiteboard* the model and flow of data through the BW system. This allows the requirements to be seen by the interested members of the BW team and also allows them to measure the BW physical model against the requirements that have been established in the functional model document.

This whiteboard physical model is then used as a template for refinements and eventually the model that is realized in the BW system. These whiteboard sessions allow a starting point and avoid paralysis in analyzing and re-analyzing the requirements. It gives the team something to build from. This task is usually performed by the data architect in the presence of various BW team members.

The data architect and BW team members should use best practices when developing the physical model. In order to make sure that the standards are known and that all parties are using the same set of standards, let's explore some common standards.

Many organizations have documented physical-modeling standards to make sure that any data model that is developed is consistent and can work with other data models that are developed.

The following are some common data-modeling standards. It should be noted that these are common standards and are not absolute rules. There are many legitimate cases where the standards are not valid based on the needs of the organization or implantation or system constraints:

- All BW structures built should follow clear standards developed by the BW data architect. These include best practices on development, naming standards, security, presentation, etc.
- All data should first load into an DSO structure and not directly into an InfoCube. This allows for the raw data to be available in BW without aggregation to other DSO or InfoCubes.
- All data should be loaded to the first level DSO with minimal or no transformation. This allows for this data to be used elsewhere in BW without having to un-transform the data. It also allows for easier reconciliation reporting.
- A consolidation layer DSO should be established whenever possible to allow for data from various sources to be harmonized and reported together.
- Very few changes should be made to standard InfoObjects in BW. For example, changing the standard customer InfoObject 0CUSTOMER to ZCUSTOMER precludes this from being combined and reported with any future analysis that includes 0CUSTOMER.
- Appending new fields onto existing master data or transactional InfoObjects, InfoCubes, DSO structures should be encouraged. For example, a new field that has been added to the customer table in ECC can easily be appended to the BW master data 0CUSTOMER object and mapped via a change to the DataSource on the ECC system. This is the preferred method for modifying existing structures.
- Think globally when developing the model. If the existing physical model is not designed for global reporting, it should allow for extraction to other sources that can consolidate the data into a global model.
- The model should be constantly checked to prevent future reloads and restatements of data. This can be prevented by leveraging master data or making sure re-stateable fields are read from navigational or display

attributes of existing master data values rather than write the values into the transactional data.

- All ABAP code transformations should be reviewed for consistency and to make sure they are following good coding standards.

In order to make sure that the physical model is sound, it is best to analyze the volume, presentation, and harmonization needs to make sure that the physical model can deliver the analysis to the end user.

Often, the best place to start with the physical data model is with the business content. This allows a clear flow and understanding of a pre-delivered solution as a springboard to help the development process. Let's look at the business content next.

5.7 Business Content Evaluation

SAP Business content is a series of pre-delivered DataSource extractors, Info-Cubes, ODS or DataStore Objects, InfoObjects, queries, and workbooks, etc. These can be either used exactly as they are delivered or may be modified to allow these objects to be tailored to individual company requirements.

SAP developed the business content by analyzing the business needs of customers who have used BW in the past and tracking future trends for analysis in industry. The goal of business content is to allow a company to use some of SAP's expertise and other customer's analysis needs to structure its own analysis environment.

The main goal of the business content is speed. It can be activated and filled rather quickly, often in a matter of days. This allows the BW system to have some productive analysis without a lot of time configuring and analyzing the BW and R/3 or ECC environments. Simply put, the BW Business Content allows BW to be implemented much more quickly than a project that had to be completely developed.

Business content can be very powerful for several reasons. If the business content fits well with the business requirements, it can be activated, transported, and used in a production environment. It can even be combined with existing structures in a data model, so a BW system can exist with business content as well as with custom objects in the same environment.

5.7.1 Business Content as a Learning Tool

One very popular use of the business content is as a learning tool. One of the analogies that I often use is this: It is very difficult to build a house if you have never seen one. This is often the case with BW Projects. Customers that are ready to start a BW project often have a difficult time explaining the use of the BW tool.

The business content allows them to quickly activate and fill the business content DSOs and Cubes and run the pre-delivered BW queries based on any existing data from the ECC or R/3 systems. This allows the project team and the business users a place to see some queries of *real* data to help them understand the use of the BW tool.

Although this practice can lead to these business content structures being used in the production environment, it can just as easily be used as a springboard for a discussion of the existing environment and the various ways that BW can store and present data.

> **Tip**
> Although the business content is a useful tool, it is not recommended that all business content be activated.

Activating a large amount of business content takes a great deal of time and would cause many needless InfoCubes, DSO structures, and queries to be activated without the corresponding transactional data to fill them. Thus, only the business content that is relevant should be activated to ensure that there is a manageable amount of the content in BW at one time.

Content Benefits

There are many benefits to business content; some of which are:

- Quick access to extracted information
- Ready-to-use reports, data models, extractors and transformations
- Significant reduction of implementation time and costs
- Easily extendable to allow modification
- Validated and comparable information
- Rich set of standard key-performance indicators (KPIs)

Business Content

Business content can be used as the following:

- A complete or partial solution for data analysis needs
- A repository of standard requirements and modeling ideas (examples and templates)
- A guideline during the implementation of a solution
- Powerful learning tool

5.7.2 Evaluating Business Content for Your Needs

The process of evaluating the business requirements involves looking at the reporting inventory, KPI matrix, and any other reporting requirements documentation to determine exactly what reporting demands exist in the organization. To quickly provide value and to leverage what has already been analyzed by SAP, we can look to the business content to determine if there is any opportunity to leverage the content datasources, InfoCubes, DSO structures, queries, or workbooks.

The DataSource represents the extraction method on the R/3 source system. In almost every case, we will look to leverage the DataSource because this will allow us to use the standard extractors in the R/3 system. Almost all standard transaction and master data have existing DataSouces with which to extract data. The following are contained in business content:

- Global views, and workbooks
- Queries, and web templates
- InfoProviders
- Extractors and InfoSources

The following steps are used to evaluate the business content and determine its usefulness for meeting the reporting requirements:

1. **Gather reporting requirements**
   Use the documents from the process teams such as their KPI templates, report templates, and other reporting requirements to determine what the process teams require for reporting. This allows you to understand what business content is relevant for activation.

2. **Group reporting requirements**
   Group the reporting requirements so you can determine what requirements are similar, both from a role standpoint and from a data-require-

ments standpoint. This lets you make sure you know what organizational roles of those running the reports and what information they are seeking. One way the business content is organized is by role, so it helps to know the role of the users running the reports.

3. **Walk through business content to determine leveraging opportunities**
There are various ways to search the business content. All business content is listed in the help area of BW. The metadata repository is also used to store and present all available and activated business content. It is best to search this content either by the DataSource on the ECC or R/3 system or by user role. The role will show those InfoCubes, queries, and/or DSO objects that are used as part of the role. You can then determine that all or some of the relevant content should be activated.

4. **Activate BW content as necessary**
If you have determined that the business content is relevant for training and/or possible productive use you must activate the content. Business content is activated in the business content area of BW.

5. **Activate R/3 or ECC DataSources, if necessary**
If there are associated DataSources from the R/3 or ECC system that are needed to load the business content you must also activate these in the transactional system. To determine which datasources are necessary from R/3 you can look at the sources used to feed the needed business content. For example, the InfoSource used to load the purchasing data line information is 2LIS_02_SCL. This DataSource would need to be activated in R/3 to load the purchase line item data from R/3 into BW.

6. **Replicate DataSources**
Replication of the DataSouces matches the DataSources from the R/3 or ECC system with the BW system. This must be done after activation of new DataSources on the R/3 or ECC system in order to use the DataSource in the BW system. To replicate DataSources, choose transaction RSA1 — Administration Workbench. Choose the **Source Systems** tab and go to the R/3 or ECC system and right click, select the option Replicate DataSources.

7. **Load data**
Use the InfoSource(s) in BW to load the data into the newly activated DSO, InfoCube, or master data records. This process involves following the data flows established as part of the overall BW business content design and loading data from the project ECC or R/3 systems into BW to see what the business content model looks like with *real* data. This assumes that the data exists on the ECC or R/3 source systems. If the data has not been cre-

ated, typically this means that the BW team needs to urge the process teams to configure and load the source data.

8. **Analyze business content for gaps**
   Evaluate the business content to determine how it fits with the requirements. This process includes looking at the various parts of a business-content section and at the existing requirements to see where the gaps exist. Usually, the best place to start this evaluation is with the delivered queries in the activated business content. Once you attempt to match the queries to the business requirements, it is easier to eliminate or include some of the underlying data in the overall assessment to see if it matches the user requirements.

9. **Supplement as necessary**
   If there is a gap between the activated business content and the requirements, this content can either be altered directly or can be copied and the new objects changed. If it is a standard master data object such as 0MATERIAL, changes should be made in the standard master data InfoObject. If there are changes needed to DSO or InfoCube structures, these should be copied to new custom InfoCubes or DSO structures using the naming standard document and changes performed directly in the new DSO or InfoCube.

There are two different versions of business content, which are:

- Content version
- Active version

The content version refers to the delivered content InfoCubes, Queries, etc of the standard content from SAP. So, this version of the business content is configured by SAP and cannot be changed. The active version represents the version that has been activated on a BW system. After activation, the content can be loaded and customized to fit business needs.

When business content is activated, it is moved from the content version to the active version. This allows the content version to be upgraded. An upgrade of the business content does not affect the active objects used in production. This is because BW only updates the content version of the business content and not the active version. If there is new functionality in the content version that is needed, the business content must be reactivated to use it.

Thus, modification of SAP BW business content does not influence the ability to update in the future. After analyzing the business content requirements, the next steps are as follows:

1. **Demo/Present to process teams**
   Once the business content is loaded, this can be demonstrated to the process teams to determine the fit with the business requirements.

2. **Perform custom development**
   For those requirements that do not match to the business content or are radically different from the existing content, custom objects must be created. These could include custom InfoObjects, InfoCubes, or DSO structures.

5.7.3 Using a Subset of the Business Content

In most projects, all of the business content is not used. Often a subset of the content is used. Most projects take advantage of the ECC or R/3 datasources in order to extract data from the ECC or R/3 systems. However, as the business content data proceeds through its model, less and less of the business content is used in organizations.

> **Example**
>
> Suppose that sales order data is loaded from the 2LIS_02_ITM DataSource into a business-content DSO, then into a business-content InfoCube. Queries can be activated to present data from the InfoCube. Many customers use the DataSource, fewer use the DSO, even fewer the InfoCube, and even fewer than that the queries.

The reason for the scenario taken in this example is that as the model gets more specific, the less chance there is that it matches the needs of the organization, and thus fewer customers choose to use it. This is expected when leveraging the business content.

Once the BW design is complete, whether using the business content, a completely custom design, or a combination, the design needs to be checked to ensure that it follows project standards. In the next section I will walk through the design-review process.

5.8 Design Reviews

In order to complete the design, several design reviews should be anticipated as part of the overall project plan. These design reviews should be considered mandatory and allow for the overall BW data architect and BW project manager to go over the planned designs to make sure that they are logical and conform to the standards established as part of the project.

Normally, the design reviews are conducted at specific stages of the design. The project manager and the BW data architect lead the discussions with the developer and BW process leaders representing the design in their various areas. For example, in a functional design review of the procurement area, the BW project manager, BW data architect, the BW process owner for procurement, and/or any BW developers should be present.

The project management should develop a checklist for each of the following reviews to make sure that at each stage the review it is clear what is expected and how the review is to be conducted. The review process needs to be non-confrontational and should act as a learning tool for all parties involved. This process helps the project manager and data architect to understand all aspects of the design and to speak about each one in a formal setting that allows comment from the developers

Figure 5.3 shows the most common design reviews recommended as part of the BW implementation strategy. These occur at different stages of the project and allow for a formal check of the process and design. A signoff document and results document should be published after each review to make sure that the results of the review are formally communicated.

Figure 5.3 BW Design Review Process

5.8.1 Functional Model Review

The functional model review is designed to make sure that the functional model document has all sections filled out clearly and that the functional requirements are clearly understood by the BW team. This review takes place during the analysis phase after the functional model document is complete but before signoff has taken place.

This review allows the BW team to make sure that the scope of the design is clearly understood and that all information is known in order to make a sound BW physical model from the functional model document.

After signoff of the functional model review, the BW team can begin to develop the physical model. This is simply a BW model on paper, and no system configuration can take place. The physical model document is a representation of what will be delivered in the BW system as a result of the functional model.

5.8.2 Conceptual and Physical Model Review

The conceptual model review is designed to cover the physical model documents and design to make sure that the model appears to match the requirements that were laid out in the functional model document. It also ensures that the physical model adheres to sound data-modeling design standards.

This review takes place after the physical design is complete on paper but before any building has occurred in the system on that model (other than some prototyping). The goal of the conceptual model is to catch any issues with the design before the full amount of time is invested in building a solution that might not be sound or may not provide the answers to the business questions raised in the functional model document.

After signoff of the conceptual model review, the configuration of the solution can begin. This configuration takes place in the development environment, using the development data.

5.8.3 Data Model and System Review

The data model and system review allows the data architect and the BW project manager to look over the design in the system to make sure that all BW design standards have been followed and that all documentation is complete. This review checks naming standards, design standards, data standards, etc.

This review takes place after the build but before any transports from the development system. The goal is to make sure that any design deficiencies are caught by the BW team before the design is released to the QA environment and the solution is formally tested. This design typically takes place after the unit test of the design is complete, but this is not mandatory.

Some project organizations opt to perform this review after configuration but before the unit test is complete. That way, any changes that are recommended as a result of the review can be incorporated into the design and formally tested during the unit test in the development environment.

After signoff of the data model and system review, the configuration can be transported to the QA system and string and integration testing can then be performed on the model in that environment.

5.8.4 Final Check

The final check occurs in the QA environment and allows the BW team one more review of the solution before the solution is moved to the production environment. Many project teams opt for several of these checks, one after each phase of the integration testing. For example, if there are to be three rounds of integration testing, they would perform a review at the end of each round to determine what issues occurred, why, what adjustments are needed in the BW data model, or what has been done to prevent the issue from occurring again.

After the final check, the solution is ready to move to the production environment. After transport and loading in the production environment, there typically is another final check to make sure that the data is sound and the solution is ready for users. This is more a validation check against the data than a check of the design, because the design should by then be complete.

5.9 Conclusion

Developing sound requirements is vital to any project. However, finding a method that can generate the requirements and have them agreed upon by the various parties involved is not an easy task. By using the functional model document and Key Figure or KPI Matrix, you should be able to get some scope agreement with which to begin making decisions. These will allow you to either develop the reporting requirement outside or in BW.

It is very easy to take short cuts on the functional model document and some of the other documents listed. If these documents are not fully filled out with a significant level of detail, it is very likely that the end product will not completely match the user expectations. This can cause delays in the project as different areas are re-done to fill the requirements.

It is much better to spend more time from the beginning working on getting these requirements to a significant level of detail than it is to re-do the work in BW. As a general rule, if you feel that the functional model document has any unanswered questions, this document should not be signed off, and no physical modeling in BW should commence. This will allow the issues to get the visibility the need and encourage all parties to agree on the scope and analysis requirements.

In Chapter 6, I will discuss how these requirements are developed in the BW system. I will point out some common pitfalls and things to be aware of when developing in BW.

"Had I been present at the creation, I would have given some useful hints for the better ordering of the universe."
– Alfonso the Wise

6 Sound BW Development Strategies

The actual configuration and build of the BW solution is typically performed by the BW development team under guidance from the BW data architect and the BW project manager. In most projects, the BW data architect helps to make sure that the design remains sound and the project manager helps to refine and enforce scope, while also helping to escalate and solve business and technical issues.

The development of BW can become complex, depending on the scope and nature of the various analysis requirements that are presented to the team. Explaining all aspects of the BW build process is much too lengthy a task for one chapter; but we will be able to gain some understanding of the flow of data in the BW solution.

Once the flow of data is understood, we can then explore some of the most common issues that might arise during implementation. Understanding these challenges will help ensure that the project manager can be more proactive in solving them and thus avoid unnecessary delays on the project.

Understanding all aspects of the development cycle and typical issues presented by any BW project takes a great deal of hands-on experience with the product. However, a clear understanding of the product and its typical challenges will help to prepare your project management for usual challenges.

During the build phase, all of the decisions and planning during the design phase are realized in a physical BW data model. This data model is the combination of the various DataSources operational data store and DataStore object (ODS/DSO) structures, InfoCubes, and the transformation of the data between these objects. The build phase also includes the presentation of the data to the end user.

6 | Sound BW Development Strategies

There is no replacement for actual product experience, and each project presents many different issues with the product. Still, reading chapter will help you to understand for the main functionality of the BW product, challenges that are typically faced, and ways to meet these challenges using the BW product.

One of the first things to examine in the development process is the extraction of the data from its source. This requires a thoughtful analysis of the source system data, its quality, and some of the common methods for extracting data. Let's explore this topic further.

6.1 Extracting and Loading Data from SAP Source Systems

The best place to start on the development cycle is with the extraction of data from the various source systems and the methods of gathering the data from these systems. The better the methods are understood, the better able the project team can be at choosing the best method to extract this data, and therefore can provide the most efficient path of this data into BW.

There are many different ways to extract data from source systems to be loaded into the BW system, as seen in Figure 6.1. This data could be sourced from either SAP systems or externally, from other legacy or third-party systems. In most cases, the key to choosing a method to extract the data lies in the source system itself.

Figure 6.1 Different Methods of Loading Data into BW

Because most BW implementations gather data from multiple source systems, each system should be evaluated individually to determine the best method of loading this data into BW. In choosing the method of loading, consider the following factors:

- **Source of Data**
  This could be R/3 or ECC or an external source. SAP Data being loaded from SAP systems typically follows and uses the standard delivered Service API DataSources (see below for details).

- **Volume of Data**
  The more data that is being loaded into BW, the more this data becomes a concern during the load process. There are several load methods that work fine when the data volume is low, but are not efficient at higher volumes of data. The volume is only relevant with non-SAP data, given that the Service API DataSources should be used with data extracted from SAP sources.

- **Transformation of Data Required**
  Often, data being loaded into BW requires some level of transformation. If possible, the loading should require minimal transformation. This increases the load speed and reduces the points of failure on loads. Thus, it is often recommended that any transformation of data from a non-SAP source occur on the source system prior to extraction.
  This allows for faster and less complicated data loads but enables faster and easier reconciliation of data from the external source system to BW. As an example, consider a project that is loading data from an external freight tracking system into BW. If possible, this data should be transformed into a BW-friendly flat file prior to extracting this data, to make the loading process less complicated.

6.1.1 Service API DataSources

Service Application Programming Interfaces (Service API) DataSource is a term that refers to the multitude of pre-delivered extractors provided by SAP. In R/3 and ECC Version 5.0, these were delivered as part of a software plug-in that is loaded onto the ECC or R/3 systems. The plug-in contains all of the DataSources that are available for that system. In ECC 6.0, the plug-in was included as part of the software release, and any changes to the DataSources are planned so as to be delivered via software patches.

If data is being delivered from any SAP system, including R/3, ECC, APO, CRM, or SEM, the system has some Service API DataSources, so these should be the first place to look in order to extract data from these systems. In many cases, these DataSources may deliver much more data than required. This is expected. Often, one DataSource is used to pull large data sets so that DataSource can be used for many tasks.

To see the list of the available DataSources, Transaction SBIW can be used. They are also shown in table ROOSOURCE. Transaction SE16 can be used to look at all DataSources in this table. When a DataSource is delivered in a system, it is delivered inactive. To use the DataSource, it must first be activated. This is done in Transaction RSA5. Once the business content DataSources are activated, the system then makes them available for use.

When extracting data from the ECC or R/3 system, the best way to determine which DataSources to activate in Transaction RSA5 is to look at the business content. The business content in BW shows the various delivered InfoCubes, ODS/DSO, queries, and DataSources that can be activated, if needed.

In order to see the available content, go to the BW help page at *www.help.sap.com*. Once in the help page, you will fine the *BI Content* area within the BW section. Typically, the best way to determine which business content to activate is to look the content and determine which InfoCubes, DSO/ODS, or queries match the business needs most thoroughly, and then activate the DataSources that correspond with that area.

After the DataSources have been activated on the SAP source system, BW needs to be aware of the newly activated content. In order to make sure that BW knows about these new DataSources, a *replicate DataSources* or *replicate metadata* step should be performed to allow BW to use the new DataSources.

The advantages of the standard business content API DataSources are described here:

▸ There are vast numbers of these DataSources and many more come with each release of the software. These DataSources represent a very large percentage of the data in SAP. Almost every standard transactional data table and master data table already has a standard DataSource that can be activated and used.

▸ These cover both transactional and master data, thus preventing the BW developer from needing to develop a DataSource. This lowers the development costs of the BW system.

- Most are delta-ready. This means that SAP has determined how to flag those records that are changed to ensure that only the changed or added records are loaded to BW, not the entire table.
- They are ready to be used immediately. The only thing that is required is to activate the DataSource and replicate the DataSource or replicate metadata to the BW system.

6.1.2 Generated DataSources

Some R/3 and ECC applications do not use fixed data structures for extraction but rather generated ones. This occurs when an application has a very open-ended mechanism for configuring and generating data. For example, the CO-PA module in ECC allows for an open-ended configuration based on cost and profitability analysis. SAP cannot pre-deliver an extractor for this module because each project team can configure its CO-PA differently, based on business-analysis needs.

Because organizations need to be able to gather this data and extract it to BW, SAP delivers programs that can be run to generate the DataSources to extract this data. These programs can be found in Transaction SBIW. Other examples of programs to generate DataSources deal with operating concerns, classifications master data, Special Ledger, and the Logistics Information System (LIS).

6.1.3 Generic DataSources

The generic extractor is intended to generate extractions specifically for data not covered by Business Content DataSources. Generic extractors can capture data from a database views, database tables, ABAP reports, ABAP queries, or ABAP Function Modules. Typically, the generic extractor is used to capture custom "Z" tables that have been customized in the SAP transactional system but are also commonly used for those standard ECC tables that are not covered by business content DataSources.

The generic extraction tool can be accessed via Transaction RSO2. It should only be used in the absence of a standard DataSource. This is because the standard API DataSources delivered by SAP typically are more efficient than a generic DataSource.

A generic DataSource is best used when there are custom-created tables on the transactional system that need to be loaded to BW. For example, a custom table might be created on the ECC system to house some custom cross-reference values. This is a custom "Z" table on the ECC system; there would be no standard extractor in order to gather this data to load to BW. The generic DataSource can be generated from this table and, in turn, loaded into BW.

In some cases, it is even possible to use delta functionality to bring over custom data. The system needs a date field in order to determine delta values. Thus, it is recommended that whenever there is a custom table with a large number of records, that a *last created date* be added to the table to be used for a generic DataSource delta. In the absence of this field, the entire table must be loaded on each extraction.

6.1.4 Custom ABAP DataSources

It is possible to write a custom ABAP report, extracting data from some dictionary tables and downloading those to a file, which then could be uploaded as a flat file feed into BW.

This would be considered the absolute last resort for extraction from an integration and administration point of view. This is only recommended in extreme cases where the data cannot be extracted via the service API DataSources or via generic extractors.

This is because understanding the complex table structure and extracting data from a combination of the transactional tables can be quite time consuming, given that we have to make sure that all fields and tables are being accessed and extracted properly.

I have never had to create a custom ABAP DataSource to a flat file at any project, I have heard of projects and implementations that do require this method, but it is very rare because of the maintenance and overhead of managing the program and flat file interface.

Any changes to the source systems via support packages or upgrades would require full regression testing of the custom ABAP DataSource. It is because of this type of overhead that this always should be the last option when considering how data should be extracted from the ECC or R/3 source system.

6.1.5 Testing the DataSources

There is a very handy tool used to test the DataSources to make sure that they are providing the needed fields. Transaction RSA3 allows for a test extraction to be performed in the transactional data system. This allows for data to be extracted without actually sending the data to the BW system. It can help test and troubleshoot the DataSources and ensure that all fields that are needed are coming through the DataSource.

This transaction can also be used to help troubleshoot any user exits that are used on the R/3 or ECC system, in order to populate fields that are missing on the DataSource.

6.1.6 Filling In Missing Data in Extractions

In many cases, projects run into issues because a SAP-delivered DataSource has most of the fields that are needed, but some are missing. For example, a DataSource might have all the sales-related fields that are shown on the ECC system except for some custom fields that have been appended onto the sales order-entry screen and tables by the project teams implementing the sales and distribution area of ECC. These missing fields will not automatically show in the DataSources.

If a DataSource provides most but not all data needed for extraction, it is possible to append fields to the extractor and fill these fields via ABAP code. This is a very popular way to enhance the existing extractors that might provide most but not all data needed for a requirement. This method also can be used to provide some custom data fields that have been configured and included in the transactional system design, but that are not in the delivered DataSources.

For example, a new field is needed to track and store the material color code. The transactional implementation could not find a field to store the color code and thus appended a custom field to the existing master data fields to store the color code. If the color code is needed in BW, this field will not automatically be extracted when loading the material data.

To get this data into BW, several steps are needed. First, the new field must be added to the extractor, this is done in Transaction SBIW or Transaction RSA6. In some cases, the system can automatically map the new custom field to the appended field in the extractor.

If the field that is appended to the DataSource has the same fieldname as in the stored custom master-data table, the system can sometimes map the field automatically to the new DataSource. This means that simply appending the new field to the DataSource will allow the field to be filled.

In other cases, the newly added field is not automatically filled by the system. It is also possible that some logic is needed to determine the value of the field, perhaps reading from multiple tables to fill the new field in the DataSources. In these cases, this field must then be filled via the extractor customization performed in the Transaction CMOD. The extractor customization functionality and capability is detailed in Transaction SBIW.

Customization of the extractor can range from mapping a simple field to performing a calculation from multiple table sources. Because ABAP is used in this method, the flexibility to fill any added field is virtually limitless.

This code is considered a user exit, not a modification to the core code of SAP. Thus, this code is not affected directly by upgrades to the system. The code does need to be checked to make sure the code still functions properly after any upgrade or patch, but the code will not be replaced by an upgrade or patch. This code is written into a reserved area of SAP designed specifically for user exits. Be aware that because this custom coding occurs on the source system, not on the BW system, the code is added to the ECC or R/3 system, not to the BW system.

Additional fields can be added to DataSources for transaction data, master data, text, and hierarchies. For more information on adding custom fields to DataSources and filling them via these userexits, Transaction SBIW has detailed instructions along with sample code that can be implemented.

As with any custom code, this code must be tested thoroughly. This often means testing with full loads, delta loads, and also testing for performance to ensure that the code added does not significantly affect the performance of the DataSource.

The user exit is designed to fill appended fields; I do not recommend that this user exit be used to attempt to change values in an extractor. For example, suppose that a sales organization on a sales order is showing as "1000." The process teams have determined that a selected number of sales orders have incorrect sales organization data.

Rather than fix the source, the BW team has been asked to change selected sales orders from "1000" to the correct sales organization "2000." In cases like this, it is not recommended that the user exit be used to fix values in the extractor. This user exit should be used mainly to fill appended fields that are not included in the extractor.

A common issue with this user exit is that a newly added field is not automatically flagged for deltas, and this should be tested in detail. For example, the material master data table noted above is being extracted in delta mode and only the custom field *material color code* is changed. Because this is a custom field, the system does not flag this as a delta change and the change could be lost. More custom coding or configuration might be needed to make sure that a delta record is generated when only a custom field is changed. This can also be avoided by bringing in full loads of the master data upon each extraction, but this might not be possible in some cases depending on the volume of the data.

Because many BW projects gather data from non-SAP sources, it is also important to understand and develop ways to extract and load data from non-SAP sources. These are listed and explained in the next section.

6.2 Loading Data from Non-SAP Source Systems

There are several common formats and methods for loading data for later processing and loading into the BW solution. The most common are listed below in the order of popularity. It should be understood that these are common methods for loading non-SAP data.

These methods are employed where there is external or outside data that needs to be loaded into BW. These methods would not typically by employed when SAP data is being loaded into BW because the SAP data typically has standard API DataSources that can be used to extract and load data into BW.

6.2.1 Flat File Interfaces

SAP BW supports the transfer of data from flat files. A flat file consists of data that is saved into a file with either a fixed record length or with separators or delimiters between the various fields in the file. This file can then be loaded directly into the BW system.

BW can accept files in ASCII fixed-length format or CSV format with a predefined delimiter to separate the data fields. The CSV format simply refers to the extension of the file typically added. A CSV file is a file with a specific delimiter between the records. The flat file interface is the most common way of loading external data into BW. This is because it is the easiest to set up and the quickest to implement.

Generation of the flat file must take place on the third-party or legacy source system, and the file must be saved to a location that can be read by the BW system. If the data file is sensitive in nature I recommend limiting the authorization to the file location.

BW must be configured for the file to be loaded. One benefit of BW is the ability to preview the data and available metadata to allow for a test of the load into BW. From the preview, you can then run a simulation of the data-loading process.

In most cases, some transformation of the external data is needed to combine this non-SAP data with SAP data. This can be done via transformation logic when loading into the ODS or InfoCubes in BW.

> **Note**
>
> The more transformation that can occur in the source system the better. Thus, if possible, the flat file should be generated in a format that is ready to be loaded into BW with minimal transformation on the BW system.

There are several reasons for keeping transformation in the source system. By allowing the source system to generate the flat file in format already friendly to BW, the performance of the flat file load is increased because the overhead of transformation is reduced. This also reduces the points of failure. The more frequently the data is transformed, the harder the troubleshooting of the loads.

In my experience, if the flat files can be loaded with minimal transformation, troubleshooting of the loads in minimized because the data simply needs to be reconciled back to the flat file. Otherwise, the data needs to be reconciled back to the flat file and the transformation logic applied manually in order to reconcile. This is much more labor intensive.

Because the flat file interface of BW allows for both a CSV (comma-delimited file) and a fixed file length, you must decide which of the two approaches should be used when generating the flat file for loading into the BW system. A comparison of these different file formats follows.

CSV Files

CSV files are commonly referred to as comma-delimited files. This means that between each field in the file, the data is separated by a separator (or delimiter), typically a comma. At the end of each record, there is also a designator to show the end of the record. Please note that any data delimiter can be used with flat files. Many projects opt for a delimiter other than a comma because a comma can come in many data feeds normally. This can cause the file to fail because the comma is read as a delimiter, not as the data set. For example, if a data feed has text values and the text contains a comma, the system would think that the comma represents the end of the text. This typically causes the load to fail because the data does not load properly.

Fixed Length Files

Fixed-length files are flat files where each field represents a full record length. For example, if there are five fields in a file, each set for 20 characters, the file will be padded with spaces to fill each of the fields, even those that are less than 20 characters long. This preserves the fixed length of the records. Thus, in the example above, each full record in the file would have a total length of 100 characters, comprising the five 20-character fields. These fixed length files are typically processed much faster than CSV files when loading higher volumes of data into BW. This is because the system does not need to look for the data separator to differentiate the fields and records. As a general rule, higher volumes of data should be loaded using fixed-length files if performance is an important factor, as when there is limited time to load the files.

6.2.2 DBConnect

BW allows extraction of data from non-SAP systems through a tool known as DBConnect. This tool allows you to create and keep *live* automated connections to these non-SAP systems that regularly feed data into your BW data warehouse. Although flat files are the most common method of loading source data into BW, DBConnect is a distant second.

In essence BW creates DataSources in the source system(s). DBConnect reads and references the views and tables on the external database system. BW calls these tables and views and allows the BW developer to extract these tables and views via a DataSource in BW.

This approach allows for the reduction of overhead generating, storing, and loading flat file data. The DataSource in BW reads directly from the database views and database tables on the source system through a live connection. This connection does require some set-up work in BW and in the source system. The source system requires a login for the BW system to gather the data. Proper authorizations must be granted to the user, and the views and tables must be maintained to house the data needed for BW.

There are many white papers and help resources on setting up and maintaining DBConnect for BW. These can be found in the SAP Service MarketPlace. DBConnect can be set up between two like or even unlike database platforms. If your BW system is built on Oracle and the data you wish to load into BW is housed in a SQL Server database, these can be connected and data can be loaded directly between the two different database platforms.

The advantage of DBConnect over a flat file interface is that DBConnect allows for a live connection into BW and less latency with gathering the data, saving the data, and loading into BW than would occur with a flat file interface. However, DBConnect does require maintenance keeping the connection active and maintaining the database tables and views on the source system side.

Often the source system's transactional and master data tables and views can be used for extraction, but in some cases these tables require filtering or transformation. For this reason, custom tables and views are sometimes needed on the source system to pull this data into BW.

Because there is some overhead establishing connections and setting up the source system in BW to gather data, we recommend that DBConnect be used for ongoing interfaces of data into BW. It is not recommended that DBConnect be used for one-time loads because of the overhead establishing the connections. In the case of one-time loads of data into BW, the flat file interface should be used.

6.2.3 UDConnect

UDConnect is similar to DBConnect but it uses Java connectors for different drivers, providers, and protocols (JDBC, OLE DB for OLAP). Thus it offers connectivity to a wide range of relational (MS SQL Server, Oracle, etc.) and multi-dimensional sources.

Some customers have had success with UDConnect and virtual InfoProviders. These are InfoProviders in BW that do not physically store data but instead map to an external system. For example, it is possible to connect to an external system via UDConnect and create a virtual InfoProvider to gather this data. The query runs off the InfoProvider, and the data is stored outside the BW system. This allows the BW system to be free of this data but also allows the data to be reported on within the BW queries.

In my experience, UDConnect does not support higher-volume data loads without severe performance degradation. Thus, if we can set up a connection using DBConnect, this usually is far preferable to UDConnect. UDConnect can and should be used with smaller data sets that cannot be set up using DBConnect.

6.2.4 XML Interfaces

Third-party or legacy systems that can provide data in XML format can be loaded directly into BW using the Simple Application Object Protocol (SOAP) service.

> **Note**
> The SOAP service is not automatically activated (although delivered) in your BW; it must be activated manually. Activation is a one-time process. Once complete, the service is available, and XML data can be loaded using it.

The transfer of XML files into BW is suitable for regular BW services with limited amounts of data for each call. An example would be the transfer of small amounts of transactional data. XML is currently not suited for large transfers of data because of the performance overhead associated with this type of loading. If large volumes of data need to be loaded into BW, the XML interface is not recommended, and either the flat file interface or the DBConnect functionality should be used.

6.2.5 ETL Interfaces

There are some Extraction, Transformation, and Loading (ETL) systems that connect directly into BW. These systems can be used to connect to one or many legacy systems and then are provided as a one-stop system for loading data into BW. The ETL system acts as a hub for the data, providing an intermediate staging and transformation area for BW data.

6.3 Extracting Data From the BW System

It is sometimes necessary to extract data from the BW system and move it to an external outside system. This might be an external data mart, data warehouse, or even a transactional or analytical system.

The Open Hub Service enables you to distribute data from an SAP BW system into external systems. In essence, this creates a DataSource in BW and this DataSource is used to feed the external systems.

When data is staged for an external system using the Open Hub Service, the data is extracted and the resulting data set is stored in a CSV table or a relational database table in the BW database system. This table can then be used for reading or extraction to the external system, as seen in Figure 6.2.

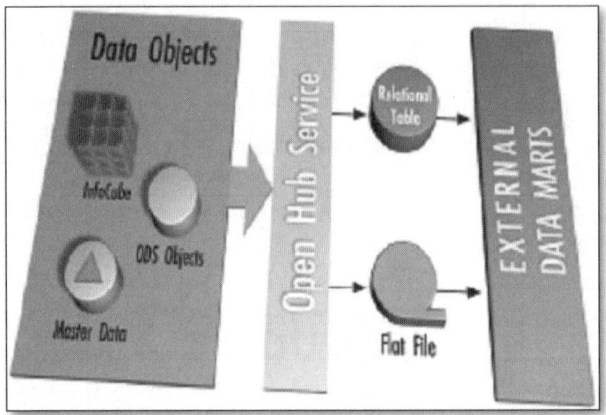

Figure 6.2 Open Hub Transformation

The Open Hub Service also allows for customization and transformation. Data from BW often fills input requirements of a third-party system. For example, BW data is needed to feed a third-party shipping transactional system. This system is used to track and maintain manifests of orders on a monthly basis. This third-party package has very specific requirements for data storage.

In order to extract the desired data out of BW into this third-party shipping system, the Open Hub Service may be used. However, the service will extract data in its current form. In other words, it uses structures and values of the data that is stored in BW.

Suppose the third-party system needs the material converted to another material number, or the division preceded by leading zeroes. This could be converted using the Open Hub transformation to change the data coming out of BW.

The ABAP code in the Open Hub transformation user exit allows for a flexible ABAP solution to meet these specific data needs of the third-party package while allowing the data to be unchanged in the BW system. The data is simply altered as it is extracted out of BW via the Open Hub transformation. Open Hub transformation is not mandatory, it is only needed if the data coming out of an external source into BW requires data to be changed or transformed.

In my experience, the Open Hub Service is not a very robust tool and does not provide extreme flexibility in the output files. Thus, when I have tried to generate flat files with a predefined format, it was a difficult to make sure that the file was generated properly. If this is a requirement, make sure that ample time is given to implementing the Open Hub functionality and also that sufficient time is devoted to the testing phase to make sure that the Open Hub file meets your specific requirements.

The next step is to understand the method and process for loading data into the BW system. Let's explore the methods for loading and the common ways to transform the data once it is loaded into BW.

6.4 Loading and Transforming Data into BW

It is very rare that data is extracted from a source system and loaded unchanged into the BW system. Thus, in most projects the majority of the build time is spent understanding the data that is being extracted and using the transformation tools of BW to ensure that the data that is being extracted can be harmonized with other data in the BW system.

In most projects, the data architect and the BW developers demonstrate their value through the quality and consistency of the transformations of data into their BW ODS/DSO structures or InfoCubes. Simply put, the more experienced developers and data architects are able to provide the best tools and methods to extract data consistently and accurately. They understand the interdependency of the data, and thus can help to make sure the solution is consistent for the end users.

Understanding the different ways that data is loaded and extracted is vital to managing a BW project. Many of the most complex and far-reaching decisions about the project deal with what data should get transformed in BW and what method should be used for this transformation.

There are many ways that data can be transformed once it has been loaded into the BW system. SAP radically changed the transformation logic between the releases 3.x and NW 2004s.

6 | Sound BW Development Strategies

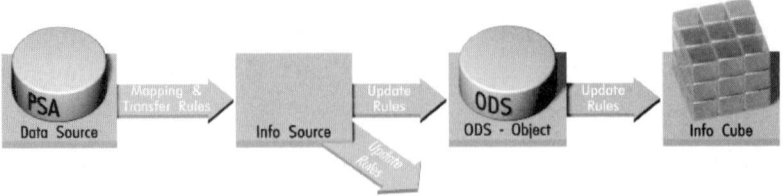

Figure 6.3 Version 3.x Data Loading

Figure 6.3 and Figure 6.4 show the different methods of transformation in the two releases.

Figure 6.4 Typical Flow of Data in the 3.x Version of BW

6.4.1 Transformation and Mapping of Data in BW Version 3.x

In the BW Versions 3.0 through 3.5, SAP provided two main places to transform data. These are:

- Transfer rules
- Update rules

The transfer rules and update rules are mandatory for transactional data being loaded into BW InfoProviders such as InfoCubes or ODS structures See Figure 6.3 for the typical flow of data in the 3.x release. The data starts at the

PSA, goes through transfer rules to an InfoSource, through update rules to an ODS structure, and then through update rules again into an InfoCube that will be used for query processing.

Suppose, for example, that we wish to load sales data from the R/3 or ECC system into BW. This data would use the standard DataSources in the R/3 or ECC system. These extractors allow the data to be extracted out of the source system. When this data is loaded into BW, one option is to have it first loaded into the Persistent Staging Area (PSA) of BW.

In release 3.x, the PSA is an optional part of the data loading process, but does allow a place for the data to be loaded into BW without any possibility of transformation. Simply put, the PSA is BW's *loading dock*. The data in the PSA represents exactly how the data came in from the source without any transformation occurring in this data. The system provides no possibility of transforming data when loading into the PSA. Thus, it is a good place to look at the data to determine if it has been loaded into BW properly.

After the PSA is loaded, the sales data is typically loaded into an ODS structure. The ODS structure would store all the sales data at a transactional level and would be mapped and loaded from the source system via an InfoSource. This InfoSource has two main parts. One part is the communication structure that represents all the fields that will be loaded as part of the data. The other is the transfer rule.

Transfer Rules

The transfer rules provide two main functions. The first is to map all the fields coming in to BW InfoObjects. In other words, there are various fields coming in on the sales order feed: customer, material, sales volume, etc. Each of these fields represents data that is to be loaded into BW. Thus, each of the fields needs to be mapped to a field in BW. The fields in BW are represented by InfoObjects.

In the transfer rules, the fields can be mapped to their corresponding InfoObject in BW. Thus, in the sales field, the SAP KUNNR field represents the customer, this field can be mapped to the 0CUSTOMER InfoObject in the InfoSource, representing the customer field in the in the data load. Each of the relevant fields from the feeds would be mapped in this manner.

Transfer rules can also be used to map constant values into fields when loading into BW. For example, suppose all sales data is not mapped with the sales organization, but the sales organization is always 1000. The sales organization could be mapped with a constant of 1000 in the transfer rules to allow that value to always appear as 1000 in BW.

The transfer rules are not only used to map fields directly to InfoObjects or as a constant. It is also possible to provide some transformation of data in the transfer rules. Thus, ABAP routines can be created to provide custom transformation of the data in the transfer rules. This transformation of data can be limited to one field or spread across multiple fields depending on the data that needs to be altered in order to load into BW.

Transformation of data is needed if the source data does not match the reporting requirements or if data needs to be changed or transformed in order to harmonize with other sources.

> **Example**
> Suppose a project has two ECC systems, each with different configuration, and both of these systems need to load data into the same BW system. This will require a great deal of transformation in order to harmonize the data.

In the example I just gave, the materials and customers need to be translated into a common customer number or material number to ensure the data can be aggregated and analyzed together. This transformation of the material or customer number can occur in the transfer rules.

There is a great deal of flexibility provided in the system for transformation because the system allows for custom ABAP routines to be developed. This allows for an almost limitless range of possibilities for transformation and validation of data when loading into BW.

Typical transfer rules have logic to determine the values of data that will be filled or read out to other tables within BW to determine the values that should be filled into a specific field. In the example above, where a common customer number is to be determined, often a cross-reference table would be built in BW between the customer numbers in one system and the customer numbers in another. This table can be read while the data is loaded to determine the customer number that should be loaded into BW.

Thus, the transfer rules might register the customer number that is coming in, compare it to the cross-reference table, and determine a new customer number. It can then replace the old customer number with the new customer number in the transfer rules when the data is loaded.

Not all fields that come in from a DataSource need to be mapped to fields in the InfoSource. For example, there might be 300 fields that come in from the sales DataSource. If there are only 100 that are relevant for BW, we only place InfoObjects for the 100 fields in the communication structure, and only those 100 fields are mapped. The other unmapped field values are lost when the data is loaded. This allows for a larger DataSource to be loaded and a subset of data to be used from this DataSource.

It is quite common that multiple fields from a DataSource are not mapped, especially when loading data from the ECC or R/3 system. This is because the ECC and R/3 systems often have fields that are relevant for modules that might not be implemented. If there are no plans to implement the CRM system, the fields from CRM need not be mapped because many of these would have initial values and would not be valuable for BW query analysis. Thus, only the relevant fields need to be mapped when loading data; the rest of the fields can remain unmapped.

Update Rules

Update rules are very similar to transfer rules. However, update rules allow for data to be transformed later in the data loading process. As seen in Figure 6.4, the update rules happen after the transfer rules have been processed. The update rules are used to map and/or transform data when loading data into the InfoProvider, this is typically an InfoCube or an ODS structure.

Like the transfer rules, the update rules are also mandatory in the data model because the update rules are needed to map the various InfoObjects into the corresponding fields in the ODS or InfoCube.

In many cases, the update rules simply map the data directly into the InfoProvider; however, the update rules also allow for transformation and/or constant selection to transform the data.

As with transfer rules, not all fields coming from the source need to be mapped to the destination. For example, there might be 200-characteristic fields in the ODS and 50-characteristic fields in an InfoCube fed from the ODS. The fields that are not required in the InfoCube are simply not mapped into the InfoCubes update rules from the ODS.

Transformation Library Formulas

SAP has made every effort to try to reduce the amount of ABAP coding required in any BW implementation. Many of the most common update rules and transfer rules can be accomplished via transformation library formulas. Using these makes it possible to configure transformations of data without custom ABAP coding.

A transformation library formula is a group of common transformations that are included as part of the transfer rules and update rules in BW. Because these are already pre-coded, there is no need to write ABAP code in order to use them to transform data.

The transformation library has many functions, including mathematical and character value. There is also the ability for projects to create their own customized functions to be added to the transformation library. In many cases, this is not used by many BW implementations. This is because custom transformations that are to be used multiple times usually are handled via custom routines and SAP custom ABAP function modules that can be called from various routines in the system.

Determining When to Use Update Rules vs. Transfer Rules

When to use transfer rules or update rules depends on what InfoProviders need the transformed data. Because update rules happen further in the process and within individual InfoCubes and/or ODS structures, the rules should be used when there are individual InfoCubes or ODS structures that require the data to be transformed. If all InfoCubes and/or ODS structures need the data to be transformed, data is typically transformed in the transfer rules.

> **Example**
> If one InfoSource is used to load the sales data into BW, the data goes through one InfoSource and thus one set of transfer rules. It then is loaded into several ODS structures and several InfoCubes for sales analysis.

To determine if the data should be transformed using the transfer rules or the update rules, we first must look at the InfoProviders and determine if the data needs to be transformed in all the ODS and all the InfoCubes. If so, the data most likely should be transformed in the transfer rules because this would only require configuration to occur in one place.

If the transformation is only required for a subset of the ODS structure or InfoCubes, the data should be transformed only into those InfoProviders. Thus, the update rules should be used for this transformation. This allows for the InfoProviders that require the transformation to have the update rule transformation and those that do not require the transformation to have update rules without any transformation.

6.4.2 Transformation and Mapping of Data in NW 2004s

The transformation logic in the NW 2004s system, as seen in Figure 6.5, is quite different. Instead of the update rules and transfer rules that were available in the 3.x versions of BW, SAP introduced the concept of the transformation area.

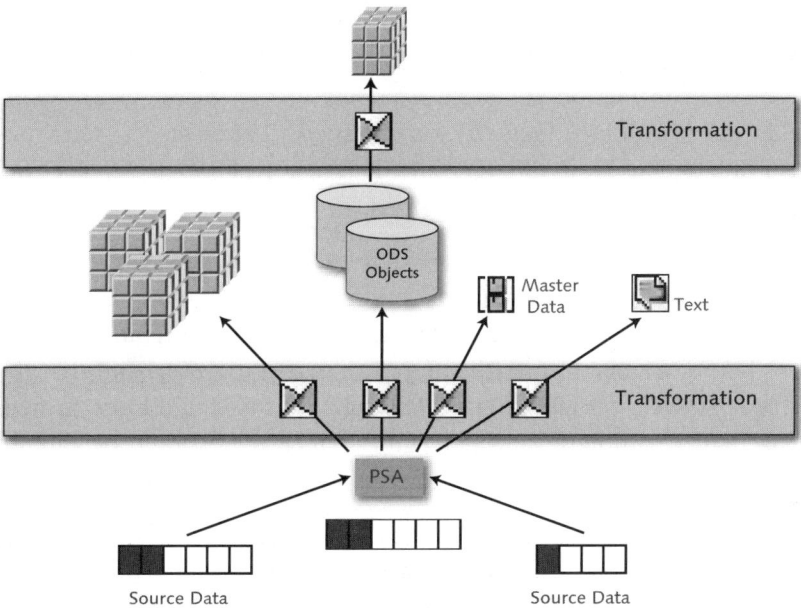

Figure 6.5 NW 2004s Method of Loading and Transforming Data

SAP also makes the Persistent Staging Area (PSA) a mandatory part of the data model. All data that is loaded into the system must first be loaded (untransformed) into the PSA. It can then be loaded into InfoProviders in the BW system.

This transformation area acts very much like the update rules and transfer rules in version 3.x. It allows for direct mapping of fields, constant values, and data transformation of data via ABAP. SAP just simplified the terminology and methods for transforming data into one. Thus, when data needs to be transformed, this can be done only in the transformation area.

6 | Sound BW Development Strategies

Data that comes from the PSA into a Data Store Object (DSO) goes through the transformation area, as does the data from the DSO to the InfoCube. These transformation areas are separate and distinct depending on their source and destination of the data. Thus, there are separate transformation areas that need to be created when loading from one DSO to multiple InfoCubes.

6.4.3 Start Routines

Start routines are places in the transformation that can be used for a mass transformation or filtering of data. The start routine is the first thing that is run during a transformation. This optional area allows you to place complex filtering and transformation for multiple fields in one place, in order for many fields and or complex logic to be performed all at once. The start routines are available in both the NW 2004s transformation areas and the update and transfer rules of the 3.x versions.

Start routines are often used if there are data values that need to be filtered out of data that is loaded, but these filters cannot be easily applied in the InfoPackage load. For example, each record that is loaded into an InfoCube should be checked to make sure it is one of the valid divisions and that the dollar value is above a certain amount. The start routine could loop through all the data that is coming in and determine which data should be filtered and take this data out of the data set. The remainder of the data can then be loaded.

Often the start routines are used when a great deal of custom logic is needed to transform data. For example, sometimes there are many fields that need to be transformed; it can be cumbersome to look at each field to troubleshoot the transformation logic. If all the transformation logic is placed in the start routine, it often is much easier to troubleshoot because all the code for the transformation is in one place.

Thus, as data is loaded, it first completes the start routine, and the code in the start routine loops through the values and transforms those that need to be transformed based on the business rules. Once the data set has been completely transformed, all data is loaded into the destination. The start routine allows for one place for this transformation and filtering logic.

6.4.4 End Routines

End routines were introduced in the NW 2004s version of BW. These end routines run after the start routine and after all fields have been mapped and data is ready for commit to the destination area. These end routines allow for the data to be verified, checked, or transformed one final time.

This is useful if there is complex transformation logic and verification of data is necessary. It is also useful for checking data against a source to make sure all data was properly loaded.

End routines can be quite useful but are not as popular as start routines in most project implementations. In most implementations, the start routines are used to perform most of the complex transformations; the end routines are only used if some verification of data needs to be performed.

6.4.5 Expert Routines

Expert routines were also introduced in the NW 2004s version of BW. These special routines are used to bypass all normal mapping, start routines, and end routines, to allow a complete custom coding of all mapping and transformation of data. These are quite rare and would require very special circumstances to be implemented. Most often, the transformation area of the NW 2004s, in conjunction with the start routines or end routines, provides enough functionality in order to transform data as needed.

In the future these expert routines might be also used by third-party vendors to populate InfoProviders in a specific application running on the BW system.

6.4.6 Implementing Transformations

In most BW projects, it is expected that transformation of data will need to be implemented. This is because transformation data from different sources can be harmonized and joined to allow for homogenized analysis. Typically, these transformations are performed either in the BW system or in the ECC or R/3 source systems. They are most often implemented by the BW team members.

This means that BW a team should have at least one member who is proficient in ABAP. This ABAP is typically rather small, often less than 10 lines of coding. Often it is a simple change of a characteristic value from one to another, or a lookup of a table to determine a new value.

As a general rule, the BW team members who implement the ABAP routines for transformations are not ABAP coders as their primary job. Sometimes, the ABAP code implemented is not as efficient as possible. This can cause issues in large data loads because a small performance issue in a routine is made exponentially worse by multiple iterations reading and running the inefficient code.

A good BW practice is to include an ABAP audit of all custom routines before this code is transported from the development system to the QA system. This allows the code that will be called during higher-volume loads to be checked for efficiency.

6.4.7 Auditing Transformations for Efficiency

There are many ways to check code for efficiency. One of the most popular is to run a trace on the code while a load is running. Typically this is done via Transaction SE30 in the BW, ECC, and/or R/3 systems. This trace is typically performed only on custom-extracted data, not on the standard DataSources or data in BW that is using standard mapping without custom ABAP transformations.

The standard transformations are already tuned by SAP and should be assumed to be efficient. If there are issues with efficiency using standard delivered DataSources, these are typically handled via support messages to SAP via their SAP help desk support.

The Transaction SE30 trace can be run in the ECC or R/3 transactional systems if there are user exits transforming the data on the source system. These transformations are typically implemented in either the user exit RSAP0001 or the BADI RSU5_SAPI_BADI.

It can also be run in the BW system when loading data through custom transformation code. This code is usually implemented in transformations in the NW 2004s release or in transfer and update rules in the BW 3.x release.

6.4.8 Converting from Version 3.x to NW 2004s Transformations

Because the new transformation logic is used only with the NW 2004s release of BW, you may need to migrate the transformations from update rules or transfer rules to NW 2004s transformations after upgrade.

When you create the transformation, the system retains the update rules, Version 3.x InfoSources, and transfer rules. However, it will use the new transformations that are created to map the various sources to their destinations. Instead of the load using the update and transfer rules, the transformation logic are used.

NW 2004s and BW 3.x versions differ substantially on the method to transform data in ABAP code. Thus, in order for any existing 3.x ABAP transformations to work in the NW 2004s system, the coding must be changed to the new type of coding.

NW 2004s uses ABAP OO (ABAP Objects) coding and BW 3.x versions use ABAP coding. There are many similarities in the coding techniques, but there are also some substantial differences. For this reason, SAP has changed the format and variables needed to use 3.x code in NW 2004s; no custom coding that has been developed in version 3.x will work in the NW 2004s version.

When converting from the 3.x update or transfer rules, routines, and custom ABAP code are not automatically transformed. This code must be evaluated and created again manually.

The way routines can be implemented changes when the programming language for routines is converted from ABAP to ABAP OO. Table 1.1 provides an overview of the special features regarding ABAP form routines for the update and transfer rules compared to the routines in the transformation.

Form Routine for Update/Transfer Rule	Routine for Transformation
Parameter COMM_STRUCTURE	SOURCE_FIELDS
Parameter ABORT <> 0	RAISE EXCEPTION TYPE CX_RSROUT_ABORT.
Parameter RETURNCODE <> 0	RAISE EXCEPTION TYPE CX_RSROUT_SKIP_RECORD or RAISE EXCEPTION TYPE CX_RSROUT_SKIP_VALUE
Sub-programs are included in the global part of the routine using an INCLUDE	You cannot use INCLUDES. You can convert these sub-programs in order to: ▶ Convert the subprograms into global, static methods ▶ Create a sub-routine pool in the ABAP editor and execute these sub-programs using PERFORM SUBROUTINE

Table 6.1 Methods for Changing ABAP to ABAP OO

Form Routine for Update/Transfer Rule	Routine for Transformation
	▶ Define a function module that has the logic of the sub-program ▶ Call function modules, methods or external sub-programs in the local part of the routine
STATICS statement	The STATICS statement is not permitted in instance methods. Declared static attributes of the class can be used with CLASS DATA instead.
Addition OCCURS when the internal table is created	▶ The OCCURS addition is not permitted. ▶ You use the DATA statement to declare a standard table instead.
Internal table with header row	▶ You cannot use an internal table with a header row. ▶ You create an explicit work area with the LINE OF addition of statements TYPES, DATA and to replace the header row.
Direct operations such as INSERT itab, APPEND itab on internal tables	You have to use a work area for statements of this type.

Table 6.1 Methods for Changing ABAP to ABAP OO (cont.)

Table 6.1 shows you some of the differences in ABAP OO and 3.x transfer and update-rule coding. You can use this table to help manually change the existing update and transfer rules to the new coding technique.

Auditing a DataSource in R/3 or ECC for Performance

Performance is always a concern whenever custom logic is used for transformation, as one small bottleneck in the transformation can cause a significant performance bottleneck when large volumes of data are being extracted. Thus, it is important to know that SAP has provided several tools to audit the extraction process to determine if there are any performance bottlenecks and eliminate these bottlenecks by adding indices, redefining the ABAP code, etc.

To audit a DataSource for efficiency in the R/3 or ECC system, the first step is to run the Transaction RSA3. This allows for a test extraction of the data from a DataSource. This transaction also runs through any existing user exits in RSAP0001 or the BADI RSU5_SAPI_BADI. Any custom transformations can also be tested using a test extraction in the source ECC or R/3 system.

While the RSA3 test extraction is running, start another session and start the Transaction SE30. This transaction allows tracing of the loads while in progress. Thus, the trace can be run on the RSA3 test load while in progress to determine what part of the extraction process contains the most resource-intensive statements.

The statements that are the most resource intensive will have the highest net percentage in the output of the trace. In order to see the most costly statements, the output should be sorted by the *net percentage* field. The ABAP can then be changed, indices added, etc., to help tune the ABAP to make the process most efficient.

Auditing Custom Transformation Logic in BW for Performance

Transaction SE30 can also be used on BW transformations. To apply the SE30 tool to the transformations in BW, the transformation should be started and while in process, Transaction SE30 should be run in another session of BW. This will allow any transformations that are inefficient to be audited for performance.

Often part of the transformation process will require appending or adding to existing BW objects. Now, I will go on to discuss the method for performing this function.

6.5 Appending or Changing Standard BW Objects

There is a serious misconception about appending objects in BW. Many project managers and developers are first introduced to SAP via the ECC or R/3 transactional systems. In the ECC or R/3 system, whenever you use an SAP delivered object, you do not change the standard objects. If any new configuration changes are needed to a standard object, it is copied and the copied object is changed.

For example, users configuring the sales order area of an ECC system might need their own custom order types. The recommended approach in the ECC system is to take the standard delivered order-type table value and copy it to a new value and configure only this new order type.

This approach differs from the configuration of BW. This is because SAP has designed the standard objects to be used, changed, and appended to if needed. Thus, suppose there is a new custom field that needs to be added to the material master data table for reporting. The recommended approach is simply to append this field to the standard 0MATERIAL InfoObject. Sometimes this is difficult, especially for those that are accustomed to copying objects. The reason it works in BW lies in the design of the standard content itself.

The BW standard content is a series of InfoCubes, InfoObjects, DSO structures, queries, etc. In order to use any of these structures, they must be activated in BW.

In any BW system, there are two types of business content. There is an active version and a delivered version. When business content is activated, the system takes the delivered version of the business content and converts this to the active version.

This provides a distinct advantage. The active version of the ODS and InfoCubes can be used for loading, reporting, etc. in BW. It can also be appended to and modified to meet user needs. Because there is still a delivered version of each object in the BW system, it is always possible to get back to the delivered version of the objects if needed.

When SAP does an upgrade, the only version of the business content objects that are affected are the delivered version. Thus, if several business-content versions of InfoCubes or ODS structures are implemented, these are not affected by the upgrade.

The upgrade only affects the delivered version of the content. You must be careful not to reactivate the business content once an object has already been activated. This is because if an ODS or InfoCube has been modified and content is reactivated, this will write over the existing ODS or InfoCube and the changes will be removed.

The system provides a warning before the content is overwritten, and this warning must be obeyed or existing structures can be destroyed, along with the data that was stored in these tables.

Essentially, the BW content is designed to be activated and modified if needed. There is no need to copy the content to another object in order to perform modifications. The system does not affect any changed content during upgrade because only the delivered version of the objects is changed in the upgrade process.

Once the data has been readied for extraction, the next step is to establish a stable place to house the data in the BW environment. This process is called data modeling. The next section explores strategies for data modeling in BW.

6.6 Data Modeling

The general concept of establishing and maintaining a data model in BW is quite complex, and the rules for determining how the model should function are just as complex. It is not easy to make sweeping generalizations. However, there are many data-modeling tips that can help to make the general reporting more complete.

6.6.1 Loading into an DSO or ODS

The NW 2004s version of BW refers to the ODS as a DSO, and the 3.x version of BW simply refers to them as ODS. In this section, I describe them together because, even though the NW 2004s DSO has additional functionality beyond the 3.x ODS version, the underlying purpose of the structure is the same.

One of the most important rules for working with DSO/ODS structures is to, whenever possible, make sure data that is loaded into BW is loaded into a DSO/ODS first with minimal transformation.

It is a mistake to load data into BW and make sweeping transformations of that data as it is loaded immediately into BW. An example would be extracting and loading data from ECC for sales orders into a sales order DSO/ODS and adding significant transformation to that data into the first DSO/ODS.

If these significant transformations are incorrect, the data must be dumped and reloaded from the source. Because initial loading of data often requires downtime in BW, this can be a difficult task.

To avoid this, I recommend that the first time data is loaded into BW it is loaded into one DSO/ODS and kept as close to the source system as possible. If transformation is needed, this should be done into a second level or secondary DSO/ODS layer. If any transformations are incorrect or inconsistent, they can simply be reloaded in the BW environment without involving any source system resources or downtime. This also ensures that if the transformation requirements change, only BW is affected. The dump and reload only occurs in the secondary DSO/ODS.

In the example above, data could be loaded verbatim (or with minimal transformation) into one DSO, then transformed into a secondary DSO, then loaded onto any InfoCubes for reporting. Although this requires more processing and more batch time, it does allow for a cleaner audit of data and easier dump and reload of data, if needed.

To ensure that data is not lost in the first level DSO/ODS, I recommend that the level of granularity for the first level DSO/ODS match the level of granularity of the DataSource that extracts the data. For instance, if the DataSource is extracting data at a sales-order line item level, the first level DSO should also store this data at a sales-order line item level to ensure that there is a one-for-one match between the data that is being extracted and the data that is being loaded into the first level DSO/ODS in BW.

6.6.2 Create a Consolidation Layer for Data

In general, business-content data is set to load in silos. For this reason, there is a business content DSO for order header and order line, delivery header, and delivery line data. However, reporting is often needed that consolidates data. In this case, often data is needed that would provide an order lifecycle analysis. For example, a user might want to see the order data and its associated deliveries and invoices spanning the lifecycle of the order. This lifecycle analysis is a consolidation of data.

For the most part, the standard business content does not provide a very good consolidation layer of data. This is because it is difficult for SAP to determine what data would need to be consolidated and what data would be measured in consolidated form.

This consolidated layer of the data model can then be used as an information hub to provide data to various InfoCubes or for other analysis needs in the organization.

6.6.3 Extract Once, Use Many Times

As a general rule, it does not make sense to extract the same data multiple times from a source system. This allows for different data marts from within the BW system to develop and consequently can allow reporting of the same data to be reported differently, even though it is coming from the same source.

For example, suppose that sales data was extracted from the ECC system and loaded into two separate DSO structures, then onto two separate InfoCubes. Each InfoCube could have different transformation rules that are being applied to the data as it is loaded into the InfoCube.

The end result would be sales data that is redundant, but also data that is loaded into two different InfoCubes with different transformation logic applied. The reporting off this data might then be inconsistent. Whenever possible all data should be extracted once and used many times.

Sometimes this is not possible, especially if different parts of the organization need the data transformed differently. However, keeping this as a general rule helps make sure that data loaded into BW is as consistent as possible.

6.6.4 Use the Right Object for the Job

There are two main providers and storage facilities for data in BW. These are the DSO/ODS structure and the InfoCube. Understanding the differences in these two main InfoProviders allows the data model to be most efficient and stable. Many times, projects have data-modeling issues because they are using the wrong tool for the job. The following steps through the two InfoProviders and highlights each of their strengths.

DataStore Objects (DSO) and Operational Data Store (ODS)

First let's look at the DSO and ODS, below:

- **Consolidates Data**
  The DSO/ODS is primarily designed as the main storage area for data in BW. This is typically where the largest volume of BW data resides. This is also a very good place to consolidate data from multiple subjects or DataSources into one harmonized data set. Many projects use different layers of ODS/DSO structures to provide this type of consolidation. For example, sales data might be loaded from the ECC system into one first level ODS/DSO structure. This data is typically not transformed in any way. The data is then loaded from the ODS/DSO into a secondary ODS/DSO. The data is transformed and harmonized with other data into the secondary DSO. This consolidation layer of data can then be used to load into one or many InfoCubes for reporting by the end user.

- **Transactional or Document Level Data**
  Typically, the DSO/ODS contains detailed level data, often at the document level. In most cases, the DSO/ODS stores many detailed fields from the transactional data. These transactional data fields are typically stored in the DSO/ODS and later aggregated into one or many associated InfoCubes. For example, a typical sales order DSO would contain almost all fields for the transactional order information. Often, only a subset of these fields may actually be loaded into a related InfoCube. The other fields are there either for more detailed reporting or for any future analysis needs.

6 | Sound BW Development Strategies

▶ **Overwrite or Addition Enabled**
The DSO/ODS can be enabled either to be overwritten or added to. This allows each key figure value to aggregate or overwrite the values that are loaded into the DSO/ODS. For example, if a value for sales is $10,000, and a new value of $100 comes in from the source, should the new number be $100.00 or $10,100? This depends on the source and the data presented from the source. When loading the DSO or ODS, the overwrite or additive option can be chosen individually for each key figure value. It is possible to have one key figure overwrite and another additive in one DSO or ODS. This allows for a great deal of flexibility with the data as it loads.

▶ **Relational Database Structure**
The ODS or DSO is a relational database structure, meaning that the data is stored in various tables and linked by this key structure, much like the ECC or R/3 system. This differs from the InfoCube that uses a star-schema methodology.

▶ **High Level of Granularity**
Typically the ODS or DSO has a high level of granularity because the data is often quite detailed and often is at an individual transactional level. This means that the data in the ODS or DSO is quite detailed and granular.

InfoCubes

Now we can proceed to the InfoCubes:

▶ **Aggregates Data for Multi-dimensional Reporting**
The InfoCube aggregates or gathers up data and adds these values into one central area for reporting. The InfoCube is the most common repository for reporting in the BW data model.

▶ **Used for Analytic and Strategic Reporting**
Most often the InfoCube data is used for strategic reporting because the data is often aggregated and not presented at a transactional level of granularity.

▶ **No Overwrite Allowed—Only Additive**
Contrary to the ODS or DSO, the InfoCube does not allow for individual InfoCubes to be loaded with an overwrite option. This is because the data always aggregates into the InfoCube.

▶ **Extended Star-Schema Design**
The InfoCube has a star-schema database design with one central fact table and multiple dimension tables surrounding this central fact table.

The different attributes of the DSO/ODS and the InfoCube designs allow the two different InfoProviders to be used to exploit their strengths. The InfoCube is primarily designed for providing reporting of many aggregated values. The DSO/ODS is designed to store large amounts of data and pass this data onto existing InfoCubes for analysis.

Strong projects do a good job at tracking and resolving issues. The next section covers some common methods to track and resolve issues that occur in BW.

6.7 Issue Resolution and Issue Tracking

One of the most important processes in any project is the tracking of the issues. Projects often create very elaborate means in order to track and measure the issues on the project. The most important thing is to make sure that each issue is tracked with a priority, date, and the responsible person or owner of the issue.

In many cases, it is best to make sure that the person who is responsible for each issue is an employee, not a consultant. This provides some ownership by the project team of the issue lists and also keeps the issues in the hands of the employees and not the consulting organization.

6.7.1 Reporting Issues via SAP's Service MarketPlace

Service Marketplace formerly called On-line Support System (OSS) is SAP's method for tracking and reporting software issues. Understanding how to report issues properly and — more important — how to search for and use issues that have already been reported and solved help ensure that projects can quickly overcome software issues that are inevitable with any SAP project.

Service Marketplace should be used to report any software issue or anomaly to SAP. A user can search through the existing SAP help desk tickets to see all the reported fixes by SAP. These fixes are called SAP Notes. SAP provides SAP Notes that can be applied to project system to fix various issues. Periodically, SAP batches up a large number of these notes and puts out a support package. The support package contains all the note fixes from one support package to the next.

When a problem arises with the software, an SAP message is created. This is a project trouble ticket that has been reported to SAP. SAP takes the message and may respond by recommending one or many SAP Notes be applied to a customer system in order to fix a software issue.

6.7.2 Response Delays

A number of factors can delay having messages responded to by SAP. Here are some tips to get an SAP message responded to quickly with a quality answer:

- Before any message is answered, spend time researching the existing SAP Notes. More often than not, the same problem you have has already been reported and solved.
- If you cannot find any SAP Notes that reference the software issue you encountered, enter a very detailed SAP message. Many SAP messages fail to give the proper detail and thus produce days of back-and-forth between support personnel and the customer, delaying resolution of issues.
- The SAP message should include a full description of the issue, the steps to reproduce the problem, and any background information needed to understand why and how the problem is occurring.
- Often, SAP help desk representatives will log into a customer system to reproduce the problem. Expect that this will happen with any SAP message that is created. Make sure that all messages have clear login instructions with user ID and password specified.
- Proper care should also be taken to assure that the user ID provided to SAP has security to troubleshoot the issue.
- For SAP to log into a customer system, the SAP connection must be opened. It is typically a Basis task to open the line of communication from SAP to the customer system. Make sure that this connection is open before any SAP message is created. This confirms that if SAP needs to log into the system the connection to log in is open.
- Use the proper priority on SAP messages. I have worked with many projects that enter many, if not all, their SAP messages with a high priority. They are many times quick to complain that SAP takes a long time to respond to their messages. It helps SAP to be able to prioritize messages if the correct priority is assigned.
- Some of the more common issues that occur in BW involve performance. The next section will help you understand some of the tools that can be used to solve performance issues.

6.8 Query Performance Analysis in BW

The most important thing to understand about performance in BW is that the data model needs to be designed from the beginning with performance in mind. Performance, both in query analysis and the load performance, often cannot be retrofitted. Therefore, proper care should always be given to ensure that performance is one of the utmost concerns in any BW implementation.

The following subsections cover some of the most important performance data-modeling tools and issues and some information on how to overcome performance problems in the BW implementation.

6.8.1 Data Model Does Not fit the Data Volume

Often, projects fall into the trap of trying to do too many things or store too much data in one BW object. If one InfoCube contains 100 million rows of data, performance will always be a concern. Thus, understanding and planning for data volume becomes a very important task in any project.

Before any InfoCubes or ODS/DSO structures are built in the system, the data volume that will be loaded should be clearly understood. This means that not only the initial volume of data should be analyzed but each data load that will end up in the model should also be tabulated to make sure that the true data volume is understood.

This data volume helps determine how to create InfoCubes and ODS/DSO structures. SAP provides a very easy method to help performance of high volume data loads. The single best approach to handling high volume is to break up this volume into multiple identical structures. Rather than having one InfoCube or one ODS/DSO structure with 50 million rows, separate this out into four separate but identical ODS/DSO structures or four separate InfoCube structures.

This allows the system to use parallelism for data loads or query access. The end user will never be aware the data that is being queried comes from multiple InfoCubes. He or she will, however, get the benefit of faster performance when the database can use parallelism to read the large volume of data in smaller sets because the data is physically separated. This process is known as logical partitioning of data.

In order to join the various InfoCubes or ODS/DSO structures for reporting, a MultiProvider can be used to provide this join. Any number of InfoCubes and/or ODS/DSO structures can be added to the MultiProvider to provide parallel query processing.

This method should be used any time that volume of data is a concern. It is used to a very large extent with projects that have many terabytes of data in their BW systems. It does add to development time, and any changes have to be repeated to all the destination structures; however, the benefit can be quite pronounced.

6.8.2 Poor Query Definition

Another common concern in BW projects is poor performance with queries. One of the most common reasons for poor query performance lies in the way queries are constructed.

Queries in BW should take advantage of the tools to slice and dice data in BW. This means that, instead of bringing back large quantities of data on the initial view of a query in BW, the project should instead be designed to provide a small amount of data at a much aggregated level. This will allow for a quicker response time for the query.

If a user is looking for a more detailed set of data, he or she can then choose the specific characteristics of the desired data. Users should be trained to filter the data as much as possible in order to limit the data that is shown.

Another way to make sure a query is defined well is to make sure that it has mandatory variables. Variables are the parameter screen that can first appear when any query is run in BW. The variable screen allows the user to first choose the data filters that will be used on the query.

> **Tip**
>
> It is recommended that all queries have at least one mandatory variable.

These mandatory variables serve several purposes. They provide a filter of data and thus make for better performance. However, they often help performance even more in other ways. If there are no mandatory variables on a query, users typically run the query without filter values in the variables. In other words, they run the query on all data in the system.

This can be quite a strain on the system, if all users are constantly running queries in this manner. When a user is presented with a mandatory variable, this causes them to reflect on the data that they actually need in the query.

This forces them to limit the data, thus helping performance for them. This also helps other users who now have freed-up system resources to run their queries.

Often the most effective mandatory variables in queries are the date fields. This is because there are very few queries that are run in the BW system that do not involve date criteria. If these date fields are used as mandatory variables, the filters can help to make queries run much faster for the users.

6.8.3 Lack of Aggregates

Understanding the tools to improve performance helps to make sure that any performance bottlenecks can be mitigated. If most of the performance slowdown involves gathering the data from the InfoCube, the best way to speed this query performance is via aggregates.

> **Note**
>
> Aggregates, as the name implies, aggregate or pre-group the data during the data load process to greatly speed up the data-retrieval process.

In other words, if a user has developed a query to see the sales for the entire country by sales division, there are two ways of gathering this data. It can either be gathered up at the time that the query is run, or pre-summarized into BW aggregates so the data is read off the aggregates rather than the larger InfoCube itself. Typical aggregate sizes are less than 10 percent of the size of associated InfoCube fact tables.

For example, an InfoCube might exist with 50 characteristic values. However, 80 percent of all queries use the same six characteristics. This is very typical in many BW implementations. Thus, an aggregate or series of aggregates can be created to pre-summarize the data for these six oft-used characteristics.

When a query is run, the system automatically checks to see if there is an available aggregate that can be used to report this data. If one exists, the system uses the aggregate rather than the InfoCube fact table. This results in better query performance.

There is, however, a cost for this better performance. The cost lies in the loading process. Whenever aggregates are created, time data for each is loaded into an InfoCube (aggregates are not currently available on ODS or DSO structures), and a step must be performed to *roll up* that data into the associated aggregates. This roll-up step slows the load time, causing the loading to take much longer than it would without the roll-up step.

This allows for the aggregates to be populated with the most current data. This extra step does slow the load process, but the extra time added to the load process can allow for much faster query performance.

Aggregates can also be used on navigational attributes. These are attributes of master data characteristics in the InfoCube. For example, if there is a division on the material master that is needed for many reports, the division on the material navigational attribute can be added to the aggregates.

This allows for a much faster access to navigational attributes, which by nature are slower than the characteristics that exist directly in the InfoCube.

There is one more process that is slowed by navigational attributes in aggregates. The attribute change run job is scheduled after each load to activate the master data object values. It also has another task. If there are aggregates that exist containing navigational attributes, the change run populates these aggregates with any new data values.

This can cause this change run process to run longer during the batch load window. It does, however, typically allow for much better query performance because the queries only need to look to the aggregates, rather than the fact table and the attribute table, to get the data.

Aggregate Maintenance

You should assume that aggregates are not a one-time task. All aggregates should be analyzed to evaluate their usefulness. The best way to see the usefulness of the aggregates is to look at the aggregate maintenance screen. This allows a view of which aggregates are used and which are not. It is very typical that many iterations of aggregates are tried until a good set of aggregates are chosen.

I recommend that aggregates be created in the development system and transported to the production system, and then filled in the production system. Any adjustment of the aggregate would also be done via transport.

Any aggregates that are not being used often should be deleted because of the extra overhead they are costing the system during the data load process.

6.8.4 OLAP Cache

OLAP cache was first introduced in BW Version 20B. Caching is a means of improving query performance. As with most performance-improvement techniques, there are costs as well as benefits to caching.

Caching takes a snapshot of the query results and saves them. When a user has a scenario that requires the same result set, the cache can be read rather than the system re-running the query from the database.

The cost with OLAP cache lies in the organizing and retention of data in the cache. The cache data can be held in the main memory or distributed to an application server or a network. In general, good candidates for caching are complex, popular queries that are run on a data set that is not often refreshed.

The query cache mode determines if and how the system caches the results of the query. It can be set as a default by InfoCube and also individually by query. The cache mode can be set up per query, because it allows the query author to determine if cache would be advantageous for the query.

> **Example**
>
> If a query is created that will be run by a small group of users who never run the same query variables twice, the users would not benefit from cache because there is no repeated query data set to be read from cache. Thus, it would make more sense to turn off cache via the cache-mode setting for this query. Otherwise, the system would incur the overhead of filling cache that would be rarely, if ever used. Thus, it is up to the query author to evaluate each query to determine if there are multiple users who would run the same query for the same results. If this is the case, the query should be set to cache.

The cache setting by query is in the Query Monitor (via Transaction RSRT). The cache mode determines if cache is used at all. If the cache mode is 0, no cache is used and the query will not benefit from cache. The other options for setting up cache are explained below. There are five different modes of query cache in BW.

- **0: Cache is Inactive**
  Queries are not set up for cache at all.
- **1: Main Memory Cache without Swapping**
  Queries save cache entries into shared memory, but does not permit swapping. Swapping is the act of moving the cache from main memory to a file or cluster table when the memory cache is full. Therefore, if the memory cache is full, no cache is saved.

6 | Sound BW Development Strategies

> ▶ **2: Main Memory Cache with Swapping**
> Queries cache entries into shared memory, but allow 'swapping' or saving overflow values to disk.
>
> ▶ **3: Persistent Cluster/Flat File Cache For Each Application Server**
> Queries save cache entries into a cluster or flat file on each application server. In a multi-server environment, the cache is saved on each application server.
>
> ▶ **4: Persistent Cluster/Flat File Cache Across Each Application Server**
> Queries save cache entries into a cluster or flat file to be shared by all application servers. This setting is preferred when multiple application servers are used in a BW landscape.

The cache settings specify how cache is to be saved. It can be in memory cache or persistent cache. Main memory cache saves query results in shared memory. Memory cache uses main memory to store result sets, thereby taking this memory from other BW processes. In an active BW environment, typically persistent cache is used. This allows the cache to be saved either to a flat file, cluster table, or binary large object (BLOB) table. As a general rule it is most advantageous to use a persistent cache using cluster table or BLOB table across applications server. This allows main memory to be avoided while also enabling users who access queries via different application servers to take advantage of OLAP cache.

The query results can even read subsets of the OLAP cache. If one query was run early in the day for all divisions of the company, each division is shown in the result set. If the identical query is run later in the day for one division, the system can read the division subset of the cache to get results for only one division. This can be a significant feature of OLAP cache.

Some projects use their reporting agent and/or the information-broadcasting feature of BW to schedule high-volume queries to be run in batch. When these queries are run, the data is saved to cache. This allows many users who run the report throughout the workday to take advantage of the cache, and thus provide better query performance on this query.

It should be noted that because cache is set and stored per query, it works well in environments where very few queries are run by multiple groups of users. In organizations where many queries are run by few people, the cache is less effective because there is little redundancy to help the performance.

To recap, the OLAP cache allows for saving of query result sets so future queries can take advantage of queries run previously. The data in the cache is automatically made invalid after a query is regenerated or a data load takes place. The cache is therefore typically good for only one day in an environment where data is refreshed daily. However, it is very easy to implement and can provide significant performance benefits.

Compression Not Run

One frequent reason for poor query performance is the fact that the compression jobs have not been run on high volume data sets in BW. This compression job is important for reducing the data volume, thus providing better loading and query performance. It is important to understand compression and the consequences of compressing data in BW.

The goal of compression is, as the name implies, to compress or reduce the amount of data that is stored in an InfoCube. Compression is only possible on an InfoCube, not with ODS or DSO structures. Every InfoCube has two fact tables for storing data. These are the **F** fact table and the **E** fact table.

Initial data loaded into an InfoCube is first loaded into the F fact table. The system assigns a unique request identifier to each data package that has been loaded into the InfoProvider. This is set as part of the key of the data load package. The reason for the request identifier is to designate and separate the different data requests that have been loaded into the InfoCube.

Once a request has been compressed, the system flags the request as compressed in the Manage screen of the InfoPackage. Thus, there can be multiple requests in an InfoCube, some compressed and some not compressed. Those that are compressed are stored in the **E** fact table; those that are not are stored in the **F** fact table.

If an InfoProvider has not been compressed, the system keeps the request identifier as part of the key structure of data. This causes tremendous inefficiencies when reporting, because the same data can appear multiple times in the uncompressed InfoProvider.

For example, an order InfoCube is created with the characteristics customer, material, calendar month and year, and order quantity. If data is loaded daily into the InfoProvider and one transaction record's order quantity has been changed in the source system five times on five different days, the corresponding data that is loaded into the InfoCube will appear five separate times in the **F** fact table of an uncompressed InfoCube.

The system keeps the key of the request identifier in the data each time the data is loaded. Because there were five different loads of that same order, there are five different request identifiers and thus five different records in the **F** fact table. A query that is created on this order data would be forced to aggregate the five requests at query runtime. This adds significant performance overhead to the query processing.

If this order InfoCube is compressed, the system physically moves the data from the F fact table that is keyed by the request identifier to the **E** fact table that is not keyed by the request identifier. This compresses the data because the request identifier is eliminated, and the five records noted above exist as one record in the compressed E fact table of the InfoCube.

The system combines and aggregates all records with the same master data keys. Typically, this results in a 20–30 percent reduction in the amount of data. The percentage varies based on data, but query performance on compressed data is usually much faster than performance on the uncompressed data because of the reduced data volume.

It should be noted that compression runs sequentially on each data package. Thus, if many data packages need to be compressed, this could take a long time because each request is compressed in order and no compression parallelization is possible.

InfoCube compression is completely transparent to the end user. There is no evidence that compression has been performed other than improved query performance due to the reduction of data. Data is automatically kept consistent after compression.

Disadvantages of Compression

There is a very distinct disadvantage to compression, one that stops many people from compressing data. Once data packages have been compressed, there is no way to back out, or remove individual compressed packages from the InfoProvider. For example, data that has been loaded into an uncompressed InfoCube can simply be deleted by package.

Once an InfoCube has been compressed, it is impossible to remove one individual request. The system has eliminated the request identifier from the key once the compression job has been run. Since the request identifier is gone, you cannot delete one request. Thus, the only way to remove the data from InfoCube is to selectively delete InfoCube data based on other keys. This can be very difficult in some circumstances.

It is possible to have some compressed and some uncompressed data in an InfoCube. The system will aggregate the compressed data in the **E** fact table with the uncompressed data in the **F** fact table automatically. To compensate for this disadvantage, many projects keep a few data loads uncompressed. This allows them to have the flexibility to back out recent loads if needed while keeping most of the data in the InfoProvider compressed.

Compression with Zero Elimination

Zero elimination is another performance-enhancing function that can be performed by the system during compression. Depending on the data model and source system data, records can be loaded into an InfoCube with characteristics populated but zero values in all key figures. This is inefficient because these records provide no reporting value and slow the overall reporting performance.

To eliminate these records, the option for zero elimination during compression can be chosen. If this option is checked, the system will remove any records with all key figure values equal to zero during compression. This reduces the data volume and thus provides better query performance. I recommend that the zero elimination flag is set whenever compression is run to ensure the zero records are eliminated from the InfoCube. The only exception is if zero values are valuable for reporting. This is common in planning functions, where a zero plan is used for reporting.

To achieve the optimal query performance, it is recommended that InfoProviders be compressed as quickly and as often as possible. Compression can greatly improve query performance by reducing the amount of data that is accessed at query runtime. However, this benefit needs to be weighed against the inability of backing out data from the InfoCube.

6.8.5 Partitioning Not Set

Partitioning is a performance-enhancing technique that separates the InfoCube into multiple transparent database tables to enable parallelization and provide better query performance. This occurs because the partitions each contain a series of the data and queries across these partitions can gather data in parallel, thus improving performance. Partitioning can be set in the InfoCube on the InfoObjects calendar month or the fiscal period.

It should be noted that only the InfoCube **E** fact table is partitioned when the partitioning option is set. Thus, if data has not been compressed and moved from the **F** fact table into the **E** fact table, the data is not partitioned. Simply put, if compression is not run there is no partitioning of data in the InfoCube, even if the partitioning option is set.

To achieve optimal reporting performance and enable parallel processing of queries across partitions, InfoCubes should be compressed. This will ensure that the system is partitioning the data in the InfoCube.

6.8.6 Database Statistics Not Up-to-Date

Database statistics are used by the underlying database platform in order to optimize query results. The more up-to-date the statistics, the better view the database has on the size of the tables and the better the database optimizer can suggest a join or a path to gather the data.

Every effort should be made to keep these database statistics up-to-date. The best way of doing this is by running the statistics job after the batch loads have been complete. Sometimes, in a system where the batch window for loading data is not long, these statistics are run weekly rather than daily.

The database statistics should not be confused with the BW statistics. The BW statistics are tables and InfoCubes in BW meant to report the speed of processing in the BW system. The database statistics are used to report the table sizes and lengths of the data to the database optimizer.

6.8.7 Virtual Characteristics and Key Figures

Virtual characteristics and virtual key figures are used to determine values at run-time by reading out to other values in BW or even outside systems to show values in a report. These use a virtual key figure or virtual characteristic because they are created during the building of the InfoCube and/or ODS or DSO structure but not actually filled using transformations. They are filled using ABAP code in SAP enhancement RSR00002 or BAdI RSR_OLAP_BADI.

There are several reasons for using a virtual characteristic or virtual key figure. For instance, a sales organization may determine the salesperson's assignment based on the volume of sales to a series of customers. If the sales go over a certain dollar amount, a different salesperson is determined.

Typically, the salesperson is assigned during the time of loading. For example, a sales organization may wish to assign the responsible salesperson who gets commission for sales based on the volume of sales made to a series of customers. In the example above, the salesperson cannot easily be determined at the time of data load because the salesperson is determined based on volumes of sales for groups of products. Only after the entire InfoCube has been loaded can we determine which salesperson should be determined.

In this case it is not very easy to load the salesperson data on each record in the InfoCube. The other way of determining the salesperson is during the time the query is run. When the data is shown, based upon the specific values of the data, the salesperson data is displayed on the report and not stored in the InfoCube data at all.

The virtual characteristic makes the most sense in this example because the only time the salesperson can be determined is after the volume of sales has been aggregated. Unless the InfoCube or ODS/DSO is loaded completely each day, the salesperson cannot be determined on each load but rather by using the query.

Thus, the virtual characteristic is added for the salesperson. If the volume is over a threshold, stored in a custom table in BW, the salesperson is determined from the volume of the sale and the custom table gives the salesperson value. The code determines the salesperson's value.

This approach works well to determine this value, but because of the value being determined at run time, there is often no way to use aggregates or OLAP cache on the report. This can slow the reporting dramatically. Thus, in order to stay away from slower reporting, virtual characteristics, and virtual key figures should be avoided if possible or limited to very few queries to help query performance.

6.8.8 Time-Dependent Master Data

Time-dependent master data allows for the display of master data snapshots for a specific time or in its present state. This can be a very useful feature if multiple views of master data are part of the reporting requirements. However there is a cost for storing these snapshots of master data. This cost should be weighed against the reporting benefits.

The need for time-dependent master data arises because of the nature of master data itself. Each loaded record either creates a new record or replaces the attributes of the old master data record. After loading, the former master data view is lost. Any reporting analysis of past data—i. e., sales—reflects the sales using the current view of the attributes and hierarchies of master data, not the view of these at the time of the transaction.

For example, you might need to see sales reports showing the material division of the past month before reorganization was done. The master data will not allow this to occur because it only shows the data as it currently is stored. Master data is replaced each time the master data is loaded.

This can be frustrating if reporting analysis is desired showing the master data as it existed in the past. This is especially frustrating if there are frequent realignments of master data. If we analyze prior sales using current master data, we could come to incorrect assumptions on this data. To be able to see the master data as it was in the past or when the transaction occurred makes for a more complete view of the data.

Time dependency can be set on InfoObject attributes, hierarchies, and texts. The time dependency is established on the configuration screen for the InfoObject.

Performance is an important factor in determining when and how to add time dependency to the data model. The addition of the new key to the master data increases volume, and often adversely affects query performance.

> **Tip**
>
> All efforts should be made to avoid time dependency in any BW data model.

Once time dependency has been introduced into a data model, it is often very difficult to remove it. Once implemented, the increased data volume that is generated often adversely affects query performance. Time-dependent master data does provide a useful process that allows for queries from snapshots of master data. On the other hand, the performance concerns should be weighed against the potential benefit of this BW feature.

There are some ways to speed up the reporting of time-dependent data. One is to add time-dependent aggregates. This allows data to be aggregated using a certain key date. This data is set in the aggregate and all data is summarized by this date. As long as the queries are processing based on that date, the aggregate is available for use. This often helps to speed up the time-dependent query performance.

One other way to speed up the query performance is to limit the time dependency to only those attributes that require it. For example, if there are only two fields that are needed for time dependency, only these two attributes should be turned on for time dependency. Many developers make the mistake of turning on all or most attributes for time dependency when only a few are needed.

One other way of preventing the time dependency from adversely affecting reporting is to have a shadow attribute that is non-time-dependent for each time-dependent attribute. For example, we can require the division on the material master data to be time-dependent. We can set the division field to time-dependent, but also have another division attribute that is non-time dependent.

Typically, most queries do not require the time dependency, so those queries should use the non-time dependent attribute to show the division. Only the queries that need the time dependency should use the time-dependent attribute of division. This limits the impact of the time dependency to those queries that require it, thus limiting the impact of the time dependency in the data model.

6.8.9 Complex Authorizations

Adding complex security authorization checks to a data model can often slow the query processing. This occurs because the system must check the authorization objects in the 3.x version and/or authorization analysis in the NW 2004s version of BW. The more complex the authorization strategy, the more this has a potential to slow the query results.

To avoid authorizations slowing the query processing, a clear strategy for security with an eye toward performance should be considered. Often the security requirements are non-negotiable. For example, if one division of a company cannot see another division's budget numbers, this should be considered as a requirement in BW. The strategy needs to include these requirements.

If the data model involves lower volumes of data, this is not a concern. But, as the system is required to access many millions of rows of data and check security on each one, this can cause query processing to slow. Authorizations can be implemented and secured on the following:

- Query level
- InfoProvider level (ODS/DSO InfoCube)
- Characteristic level
- Characteristic value level

6 | Sound BW Development Strategies

- Key figure level
- Hierarchy node level

The list above is sorted by the least resource intensive to the most resource intensive security strategy. If the security requirements can be fulfilled using a security strategy that is broad rather than more detailed and system intensive, performance can be better.

In this example, security requirements are established to allow for one division not to see the other division's budget information. This can be handled by setting security at a characteristic value level, in this case at the division level. In a high-volume data environment, this can slow the query processing as the system checks each division and compares that with the role of the user running the query.

With some data modeling, this can be handled at a higher level. For example, the division can be secured at an InfoProvider level if the data is segregated into like InfoCubes by InfoProvider. This would allow for a parallel processing of the data and provide only one check at the InfoCube level rather than at the characteristic value level.

The system keeps statistics on the time used for authorization checks. So, to pilot several methods of security, each can be evaluated to determine its load on the overall query performance. Often, this is difficult to judge in the development system, but at least we can estimate the cost of authorizations.

There are many different circumstances for security implementations, and thus each needs to be evaluated individually. Performance should be one consideration when developing a security strategy.

6.8.10 NW 2004s BI Accelerator

There has been a lot of discussion and excitement over the BI Accelerator appliance that has been announced and rolled out by SAP. This allows for Google-type indexing of data in the data model. Running in place of aggregates, this accelerator can index data and provide quite startling query performance.

The basic issue with the BI Accelerator is the cost. There are limited lists of hardware vendors that build this appliance. They have created a custom chip in order to run the appliance. To make implementation profitable, the price is steep for many projects.

At the current time, this does appear to be a very exciting performance enhancing tool. However, it may be outside the budget of many projects. Even with the appliance in place, it is still recommended that sound data-modeling practices be followed to ensure that, even in the absence of this hardware, the model will perform well.

6.9 Conclusion

Although the actual building and configuring of the BW system can become complex, it is important to understand the way that data flows through the system and the methods that are typically used in order to transform data. By understanding these tools, it is easier to anticipate the various issues that might occur with these tools. This will help the project manager be more proactive in problem solving.

Because the BW product itself is quite robust, a project manager would have a very difficult time managing the project while also providing substantial configuration. This reduces some of the effectiveness of the project-management staff because they find themselves limited in their configuration experience of the product. This is typical in any BW project.

The most experienced project managers rely on an experienced data architects and BW developers to keep the solution and design intact but also to keep a close eye on the requirements. If the project management understands the requirements fully, it can keep the team focused on what the solution should deliver.

This allows the project managers to assert themselves during the design phase and then again even more strongly on early unit tests. If the unit tests do not appear to match the known requirements, the project management can step and redirect the design to better match those requirements. This does not require significant configuration strength, but rather requires one eye on the business and the other eye on development.

In Chapter 7, I will discuss some of the challenges associated with a project after the configuration is complete. Planning for the rollout of BW during the build phase helps to allow for a smooth transition to go-live.

"The victory of success is half won when one gains the habit of setting goals and achieving them. Even the most tedious chore will become endurable as you parade through each day convinced that every task, no matter how menial or boring, brings you closer to fulfilling your dreams."
– Og Mandino

7   Preparing for Go-Live and the Go-Live Process

After the configuration of BW is complete, the BW team is not finished work. Typically, the next logical step in the process is to do a review of the entire model to ensure that it follows the naming standards, design standards, etc. Once this is complete, the BW configuration can be transported to the QA environment for testing.

After this testing is complete and all issues resolved, the BW configuration can be then transported to the production system. In this chapter, we will explore the various challenges presented during the process of actuating the data model in the production system. This involves setting a clear strategy for publishing queries to the portal for end user processing.

7.1   Data Model and System Review

As mentioned in Chapter 5, the data model and system review is vital for consistency and should be performed after the BW development configuration is complete. The BW data model design review walks through an existing data model in BW prior to transport to QA, or other systems, in order to make sure that the design is sound. As project teams grow, it is often hard to make sure that each design being populated into a BW system is stable and conforms to standards.

This is because new team members are not always aware of the design and naming standards of the project. I recommend that as new team members join, part of their orientation includes a walk though a design-standards document. It should also be clear to all team members that design reviews will be conducted to keep the designs consistent.

The data model design review process includes formal evaluation to determine if standards have been followed and if the model seems sound from both a business and technical standpoint. This is designed as a two-part working session. One of the reviews occurs in the analysis phase but before the build; the other occurs after the build but before any transports are released. This allows all data models in BW to be formally checked to make sure that they follow development standards.

This design review should be a formality in most projects, because the data architect or design lead should be reviewing the design throughout the project. However the review allows for a more formal check covering several aspects. A full formal checklist of each is found in Appendix B. The following team members need to be present during the design review:

- Business team representative or SME
- Data architect or design lead
- BW project manager
- BW developers for the model

It is very important that this session not be seen as a group evaluation of the design work and should not be performed in a confrontational environment. It should be seen as a collaboration to confirm and verify the design. The design review team works together to make sure the data model conforms to the following:

- Naming standards followed
- Security requirements understood
- BW design standards followed
- Business expectations and requirements understood
- Documentation complete

The overall goal is to make sure that there are no design issues with the model. Making sure the model adheres to BW best practices helps to avoid restatements and dumps and reloads of data later.

Making sure that all documentation is complete is a vital part of any review process. Understanding and enforcing adequate documentation can make the transition of any BW project from the BW development team to a SAP Center of Excellence (COE) or production support organization much easier.

Let's explore some of the most common configuration documentation and its main sections and goals.

7.2 Documenting BW Configuration

Documenting of the BW data model should occur throughout the BW data-modeling and development process. However, the data model review is a good time to make sure that this documentation is up-to-date and matches the system configuration.

There are four main documents that I recommend to describe the configuration design in BW. Each project typically has its own documentation standards and templates; some have more documents, and some have fewer documents. These are as follows:

- Functional Model Document
- DSO/ODS Technical Design Document
- InfoCube Technical Design Document
- ETL Technical Design Document

Samples of these documents can be found in Appendix C.

These documents are usually used to bring new developers on board in such a way that they understand the current development environment. It can also be used to transition the development to the COE or production support organization. In some cases, these documents are also used to show the project management organization the data models at a high level.

Let's now explore the most common ways of documenting BW configuration.

7.2.1 BW Functional Model Document

This document, described in Chapter 5, gives an overall understanding of the business and organizational needs for the BW model. This serves as the functional design document for an entire subject area. This document should answer the following questions: Why did we do this? What needs were we trying to fill? What was the goal of this model?

7.2.2 DataStore Object/Operational Data Store (DSO/ODS) Technical Design Document

This document is designed to provide the business use for a DSO or ODS. NW 2004s uses the term DSO, while the BW 3.x release uses the term ODS, but the purpose of both structures are very similar. The same document can be used for both. This document should clearly define and document the type of data in the DSO/ODS and the overall part that the DSO or ODS plays in loading the data model. For example, when loading purchasing data, the data might first load into one DSO, then to another DSO, where it is transformed to meet specific reporting requirements. In this case there would be two DSO documents, each explaining the role of its DSO, its use, transformation logic, and how the data flows between each object.

This document is also designed to provide a profile of the data that is loaded. The overall goal of this document is to answer the following questions: Why did we create this DSO/ODS? What is its purpose in the data model? What kind of data is stored in this DSO/ODS? What data flows in and out of this DSO/ODS? How is data transformed before or after this DSO/ODS, and why?

7.2.3 InfoCube Technical Design Document

The InfoCube technical design document is designed to document the InfoCube, its contents, and its use. This document contains information on how data is being fed into the InfoCube. It also details the type of data, its volume, and whether there are any historical data that has been loaded into the InfoCube at the time of go-live.

This document also has information on the partitioning settings of the InfoCube and any aggregate designs associated with the InfoCube to provide faster reporting to the end user. If InfoSets are used, these are also documented using this template. InfoSets are another kind of InfoProvider used to present data to the end user.

7.2.4 Extraction, Transformation, and Loading (ETL) Technical Design Document

The ETL technical design document is helpful in a complex BW environment. There often are many different InfoCubes and DSO/ODS structures in a BW model that are used for many different purposes. The data flows through the various structures for use in analysis reporting, and one DSO/ODS may be used for many different tasks. Therefore, when looking at the overall flow of data in the organization, it is often difficult to understand which DSO/ODS structures feed which InfoCubes, etc.

Transformation introduces further complexities. Sometimes because transformation occurs between a DSO/ODS and an InfoCube, it becomes difficult to fully describe the transformation. This is because you do not know where the transformation should be documented, or whether it should be documented with the source or the destination structure.

The ETL document prevents any debate over where the documentation should reside for the complete flow and transformation of data in the data model. By creating one ETL document for each subject area, the ETL documents can be used to follow the data through the BW system from DataSource all the way to query analysis.

By using these four main documents, the data model in BW can be fully documented. In many cases a signoff is added to each document to formally finalize it.

Figure 7.1 BW Timeline for Documentation

As shown in Figure 7.1, a document needs to be completed at a particular phase in the project. That is, there are specific times that each document needs to be created and delivered. Samples of each document can be found in Appendix C.

One of the other documentation features of BW is in the Metadata Repository. This is a function that can be run either from within BW or as a web front end that shows the different structures in a data model. Let's see how this can be useful in a BW project.

7.2.5 The MetaData Repository

One of the more useful features of BW is in its ability to self-document. The MetaData Repository can be used to show all the different structures that have been activated and loaded in the BW environment. The MetaData Repository also shows those structures that have not been activated. These represent the business content that is available for activation in the BW system. See Figure 7.2 for a screenshot of the **Metadata Repository**.

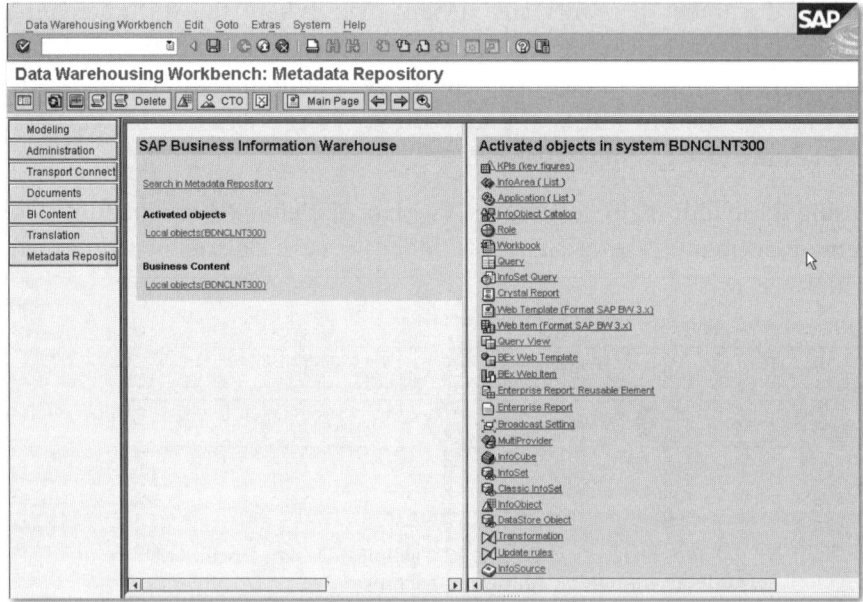

Figure 7.2 The MetaData Repository

The **Metadata Repository** also shows the full flow of data through the data model. This will allow the viewer to see the different DSO/ODS structures that are being loaded as part of a data model. If multiple structures are being loaded from one source, the MetaData Repository has this information.

One of the mistakes that some project organizations make is not taking advantage of the Metadata Repository to help document the BW solution. They create their own design documents that painstakingly map out each InfoObject for each structure in the design documents. This not only is a very tedious process, but really is unnecessary because of the MetaData Repository.

Rather than spending a lot of time cutting and pasting the various InfoObjects that make up the InfoCubes and DSO/ODS structures in BW, it makes much more sense to leverage the MetaData Repository for this type of documentation. The focus of the InfoCube, ODS/DSO, and ETL documents is not to show every InfoObject and field associated with each structure in BW. The goal is to understand the flow, transformation, and purpose of data to provide the analysis for the end users.

The documentation should not be used to track and document each and every InfoObject that makes up a BW structure. This not only requires a major effort in creating the initial document, it also makes it more difficult to keep the documentation up-to-date as new fields get added to the structures.

The MetaData Repository allows a user to look at the configuration and fields for each InfoCube, DSO/ODS, and query in the system and enables a greater understanding of each structure as data flows through the organization.

The MetaData Repository is designed to provide the fields and flow of data through BW. This tool does not show the business questions that the model represents and the various reasons for transformation, field supplementation, etc. Thus, the documentation should reflect this information.

The MetaData Repository can also be exported to the web to be used as a portal link so the entire organization can see the existing data model. This makes the MetaData Repository more useful because it opens it up to more users.

Another popular tool for documenting configuration is SAP Solution Manager. This allows documents to be posted to one central documentation area that is open to all users. In the next section, we will explore what works well in BW for Solution Manager and what areas need some improvement.

7.2.6 SAP Solution Manager

Solution Manager is a stand-alone SAP product designed to serve as a document repository and also provide documentation of configuration steps used in an SAP system. The product is designed mainly to centralize the place that the process teams go to complete their configuration. Instead of performing the configuration steps in the actual system itself, the developer would log onto Solution Manager to enter the configuration and record documentation with each step.

Many projects use Solution Manager in order to keep the process teams organized around the use of one tool in order to document and perform all configuration tasks. For this reason, Solution Manager is a very useful product when used by the ECC and R/3 environments because much if not all the configuration is done in the Implementation Guide (IMG) section of the product.

The IMG is a series of tables and settings that are used to tune, add features, and set up the ECC and R/3 systems. In the R/3 and ECC systems, the users would log on to Solution Manager and perform their configuration steps in the Solution Manager environment and this would set the configuration in the associated ECC or R/3 systems.

Because the BW system also has an IMG that is used for some central settings, some projects believe that they can use the features of Solution Manager to provide in the BW environment the same kind of central configuration and documentation available ECC and R/3.

Unfortunately, this is not currently advisable. Although the BW system does have an IMG, it is used quite rarely. Of all the configurations done on the BW system, fewer than 5 percent are actually done in the IMG. Because Solution Manager currently only documents the configuration in the IMG, it is not very useful to use for configuration centralization and documentation in BW.

Therefore, for those project teams that plan to use Solution Manager, I do not recommend using Solution Manager to provide centralized configuration documentation. There is, however, a common use for Solution Manager in conjunction with BW. It is as a BW document repository. Solution Manager does a good job at centralizing document management, help desk tracking, and document version control.

Solution Manager can provide a place for all in-process and completed BW configuration documentation. Solution Manager typically keeps documents better organized and with better version control than we could achieve by keeping the equivalent data in a shared drive. It allows documents to be locked while editing, thus providing a convenient way to publish documentation that can be reviewed by the project team.

Some projects also use some of the features of Solution Manager for issues tracking in BW. The Solution Manager is evolving as a product and does allow for some very useful features for document management, but in its current form is not useful for centralizing the configuration management in BW.

Another challenging area in BW is transport management. Transport management is used to move configuration from one BW system to another. Let's explore some of the challenges this presents.

7.3 Transport Management in BW

The BW Transport Management System (TMS) allows you to transport or move your work from one system to another. For example, an InfoCube that was created in the development environment can be moved to the QA environment via the TMS. Configuration, objects, roles, and Business Exchange (BEx) objects (queries) can and should be transported from the development system to the QA system, and then onto the production system.

Figure 7.3 Typical Transport Path in BW

As shown in Figure 7.3, the transport path in BW—as with any SAP system—originates in the development system. All transports move from the development system to their intended destination system. In order to move configuration, a transport is created.

A transport in BW can contain one or many configurable items that need to be moved from one system to another. Each transport is automatically numbered by the system in a sequential manner with a prefix of the source system. Let's take the example of BDN900010. This transport number will be used to track the status of the transport as it moves from one system to another. If there are issues with the transport, the transport number serves as a tracking tool to find the issue and view the failure log for the transport.

Typically the BW transport is first moved to the QA environment, tested fully, and then the same transport is moved to the production environment. If the tests fail, another transport is usually created to fix any issue; this transport is sent to the QA environment again and re-tested. If it passes, both transports are usually sent to the production environment. The first transport establishes the configuration and the second transport fixes the issue,

7 | Preparing for Go-Live and the Go-Live Process

keeping the configuration in the QA environment in sync with the production environment.

The most popular way to create transports in the BW system is to go into the Transport Connection screen in BW; this is found as a menu item from Transaction RSA1. Figure 7.4 shows a detailed screen shot of the **Transport Connection** in BW. This transaction is found as a menu option on the bottom of the Transaction RSA1 screen.

Figure 7.4 Transport Management in BW

The Transport Connection also does a very good job pointing out any prerequisite objects that need to be activated before other objects. This allows the user to avoid some of the common errors that are associated with the BW transport process. There are several tips to remember when using the BW transport system. These are noted in the subsections that follow.

7.3.1 BW Transport Management System Tips

BW is known for transport issues. The typical issues involve transport failures when transports are being sent into a destination system. This is the nature of the BW system itself, because much of what is done in BW is leveraged from previous work. For example, when creating an InfoCube, various InfoObjects need to be either activated or created.

If the InfoCube is transported before the related InfoObjects, the transport will fail. The only way to fix the transport is to create another transport with the missing InfoObject and send the original transport again. There is no way to append the missing InfoObject onto the original transport because the original transport has already been released. SAP does not allow appending to transports that have been released.

Many project teams make the mistake of allowing little time for the BW transport process. Often it takes several days to get the entire BW configuration from one environment to another. Because BW transports are quite challenging, the expectation should be set immediately that BW transports can and will fail. I have worked on projects with people who are accustomed to working with ECC and/or R/3 transports, and they are amazed at the difficulty of BW transports and the expertise and effort needed for troubleshooting.

If possible, it helps to have a developer or data architect who is very familiar with the BW transport process to help guide the transports and troubleshoot their failures.

7.3.2   General BW Transport Tips

The following are some general tips for BW transports:

- To avoid multiple transports, do not begin transporting until development is complete and stable.
- Wait until as long as possible to transport.
- Do prototyping and playing in the sandbox and try to keep the *junk* out of development. Delete any unneeded objects to prevent them from being included in a transport accidentally.
- Be very mindful of the transport order. The sequence in which transports are sent to the QA system is the same in which they should be sent to the PRD (production) system.
- Do not try to create one large BW transport. Instead, separate the BW transports into smaller transports grouped by object type

7.3.3   Separate BW Transports into Logical Groups

Errors and transport failures can be reduced if, instead of trying to group all BW objects into one transport, you add the BW objects to transports based on their object types.

Although there is no functional reason that transports cannot be grouped together with unlike objects in one transport, it is not a best BW practice. For example, the system would allow an InfoObject and InfoCube to be placed together in one transport and sent to the QA system. The issue that can sometimes be encountered is that an InfoObject is needed for another InfoCube that is in a different transport; these transports are dependent and must be sent in the proper order.

If unlike objects are stored together in different transports it is very difficult or impossible to determine what transport order should be used. Thus, if all InfoObjects are kept in one transport, they can be sent first, allowing all InfoObjects to be generated in the QA system first before any InfoCubes are sent. The following is a list of the object types and the order in which the transports should be sent to the destination system:

1. ECC and/or R/3 DataSources and structures (replicate after transporting)
2. Application components/InfoAreas
3. InfoObjects
4. DSO or ODS structures
5. InfoCubes/InfoSets
6. Security authorization objects (if applicable)
7. Stand alone Ztables and ABAP (if applicable)
8. Transfer rules (3.x logic)
9. Update Rules (3.x logic)
10. Transformations (NW 2004s)
11. MultiProviders
12. Aggregates
13. Web templates
14. Variables from BEx
15. BEx web queries
16. Portal objects

The transports can be released in any order; however, the transports should only be imported and executed in the order above. Thus, if there is one subject area with multiple DSO/ODS, InfoCubes, and queries, the objects should be split up into transports based on their type. All DataSources are sent first, followed by all InfoObjects, etc.

After any ECC or R/3 DataSource activation or DataSource transports, a manual step of replication should be included to make sure that the new DataSources are available in the destination system.

7.3.4 Keep Careful Watch of Transports—Take Good Notes

Because of the tendency of BW transports to fail, it is necessary to keep a careful log of each transport and its status and order. The order of the transports in the QA system should be exactly the same order as the transports into the production system.

Some projects opt to keep this order intact for each system. If transport into the QA system fails, they track and document the failure. During cutover, they send the same transports in the same order and allow those that fail in the QA environment to fail again on the way to the production system.

> **Example**
>
> Suppose the order is Transport A fails, transport B succeeds, and transport A is sent again. This should be exactly the same order in which the transports are sent to the production system, to ensure that the system stays in sync.

Some project organizations opt to reorder the transports slightly between the systems. For example, when building the QA environment, the transport A is sent first and fails because it is missing a dependent InfoObject 0PLANT. Transport B is created to transport 0PLANT. Transport B is sent to the QA environment, and then transport A is re-sent. Transport A succeeds the second time because 0PLANT now exists in the system from the transport B.

Some project organizations opt to reorder these transports when sending them to the production environment. Rather than letting transport A fail, they reorder the transports: sending transport B first, then sending transport A, and allowing them both to move successfully into production.

Both processes work. The decision which to use depends on how strict the project team wants to be in sending the transports to production in the exact order in which they were sent to the QA environment.

7.3.5 Never Leave a Transport Behind

It is a best practice to make sure that all transports that are released and imported are tried again and again until they are transported successfully. It is not recommended that a new transport be created each time a transport fails.

For example, transport A is created with two InfoCubes inside it. The transport has been released, and the Basis team has attempted to import and execute it into the destination system. The transport fails because of a missing InfoObject. This missing InfoObject can be included on a new transport, released, imported, and executed in the destination system. Now the original transport should be executed again. This ensures that everything in the transport exists in the new system.

If a new transport is created each time a transport fails, it is very difficult to troubleshoot and track the transports to make sure that all objects are transported. If anything is missed on subsequent transports, the systems can become out of sync. It is recommended that, each time a transport is released, every effort be made to make sure the transport is imported and executed successfully in the destination system.

7.3.6 Final Cutover Recapture of Transports

Typically transports are sent into subsequent systems in exactly the same order. Sometimes there are issues with this process. In the case of BW transports sometimes it is not advisable to follow this procedure. This happens when the same objects have been sent from development to QA many times. For example, one InfoCube, if changed many times, might have been captured in a transport several times. If all these transports are sent, the InfoCube will be created over and over. This increases the time that it takes for the transports to be sent to production.

This can mean that when it is time for cutover to production prior to go-live there are many hundreds, if not thousands, of BW transports for each iteration of the design. Sending each transport into production in the exact order that it went to QA can take a great deal of time and effort.

Some projects decide to re-gather these transports into a brand new grouping and resend them rather than use the existing transports to send to the production system. For example, in the process of developing an InfoCube, this InfoCube could be sent to the QA system 10 times, 15 times, or even more, depending on how many changes happen to the InfoCube in the lifecycle of the development.

If the transports are sent in the same order from QA to production, this InfoCube is regenerated 10 or 15 times. Often the cutover to production occurs on a weekend shutdown, and time is of the essence. If the same InfoCube is created and recreated, this can take up a great deal of time.

It may be advisable to recapture the transports for cutover. This process involves gathering up all the objects from the development environment into new transports. These transports will be sent in place of the large volume of cutover transports noted above.

This allows the transport process to complete more quickly and smoothly. Every effort needs to be made to make sure that no objects are missed. After going live, the production system can then be copied to QA to keep these two systems in sync.

7.3.7 The Mock Cutover

Some customers opt to have a mock cutover. This involves creating a new server that would mimic production. Sending all transports over to the new mock cutover system ensures that the actual cutover will go smoothly. This mock cutover is often the best way to ensure that the actual cutover goes smoothly and without issue.

Typically, the mock cutover is performed after all transports are sent to QA. The list of transports is now intact, and the mock cutover can be performed to send all transports from the development environment to another non-production box as a dress rehearsal for sending the transports to the production system.

This allows the project to estimate the timeline of the transports and make sure that any issues during the actual cutover are minimized. This is often performed in projects where there is limited time for cutover to production. Most often, the cutover to production takes place when the production system is down.

If the downtime has a very short window, there is very little allowance for errors and issues with the transports. The mock cutover allows these issues to be understood and fixed without the time constraints of the typical production transport downtime. After the cutover has occurred, the data must then be loaded into the BW environment.

After the data is loaded, it can then be verified and reconciled against its associated source system data. In the next section, I will walk through a common testing scenario for BW.

7.4 Testing in BW

After the transports have been loaded into BW, the next step is to populate the data in the various systems and measure this data against the desired data model. There are several different processes that can be established to reconcile and test the data in BW to ensure accuracy.

7.4.1 Develop at BW Test Plan

The first step in testing BW is to create a test plan based on the scope of the project and the functional requirements of the system. This should include the testing resources, testing goals, and timeline.

Several different types of tests are required in a BW system. Each test is designed to test that the system is ready for production and that it meets the defined business, technical, and validation requirements. The following paragraphs describe different types of BW testing:

- **Unit Test**
  Ensures that development activities work in line with the functional and technical design documents.

- **Integration Test**
  Ensures that development objects hand off data in a manner that is consistent and correct. It will also ensure that the BW application design works end-to-end, including all applications with input to BW and all applications receiving output from BW.

- **Stress Test**
  Ensures that the system and application components meet performance requirements. This is designed to make sure that the system can handle the intended volume.

- **Operational Readiness Test**
  Ensures readiness of the organization to support the system in production. Test issues include error management, disaster recovery, and system availability.

7.4.2 Developing Test Scripts for BW

The following guidelines should be followed while writing BW test scripts and executing the test process. A sample integration test script is found in Appendix F. Every test script should have the following:

- Testing cycle
- Source system
- Created by
- Creation date
- Tested by
- Tested date
- Verified by (business person)
- Primary developer

The test purpose should be clearly defined to explain the reason for the test and the expected outcomes. This should include the inputs and outputs to the process. Any setup requirements should be clearly spelled out in the test script. These setup requirements include all of the following:

- Business Information Warehouse setup
- Other source system setup (if applicable)
- Transactional data requirements
- Master data requirements
- All BW test scenarios should be developed to ensure that all mandatory and important requirements identified in the functional specification are tested thoroughly. The test scenarios should walk through all the steps of the process in detail. Assume that the executer of the test script is familiar with BW and the processes of BW.

All custom-developed objects should be tested in detail for all fields. Standard InfoObjects need not be tested in detail. Test script should list all the transformation routines that are used in the respective objects. The script should clearly list the expected results and the actual results. All test results should be saved together for future reference.

It is advisable that someone other than the primary developer or test-script author should execute the test scripts. Thus, the test script should be detailed enough for others to run the test. In most cases, the test script will involve both BW and legacy roles.

For example, a test script might be used to prove the sales order data is loading properly into BW. A new sales order should be created and this followed into the BW system and verified against that ECC or R/3 transactional data to make sure that it matches. All order values should then be loaded to test that all orders are coming in properly. List functionality can be used on the ECC system and compared with BW queries to make sure that the total order quantity and order values match.

In all cases where delta loads are used, the full load of data should be tested along with the delta loads of data to make sure that the delta loads are working properly.

Query testing should include validating all relevant data values. Fields that are transformed may be validated before and after each transformation. Every effort should be made to get a sample of production data. For example, a process that works fine with a standard purchase orders may fail when drop-shipments are used. Every effort should be made to include as many data scenarios as possible. Screen captures of all steps should be included as documentation of the testing. These can be attached to the test script.

All issues that are encountered during the test script execution should be recorded on the test script and also using the project issue-tracking process. The scripts should be clearly denoted as PASS/FAIL, and those that fail should be designated for re-test.

Because query performance is a very big consideration in BW, the test scripts should also focus on performance. When possible the performance should be documented in the script. These can be used for benchmarking against what could be expected in the production landscape. It is not always possible to benchmark against the production environment, but every step possible to validate performance should be performed.

7.4.3 Automated Testing Tools

There are many automated testing tools on the market that can aid in the testing of transactional systems. These systems work well to simulate users entering values into the system. Typically, automated testing tools do not work well for BW testing.

The problem with attempting to use an automated testing tool in BW lies in the nature of BW reporting itself. Unlike iterative processes like entering in sales orders or making journal entries, BW is a more interactive process.

Once live, users have many different ways of drilling into and filtering reports based on need.

Thus, because the uses of BW vary so greatly, it often does not make sense to use an automated test tool to test BW. An automated testing tool cannot reflect and show a series of users with many differing analysis patterns. BW also needs to be checked against the source during the testing process. The automated testing tools often cannot perform these types of tests.

Thus, the most popular way of using automated testing tools in the BW environment is to run a stress test on the system. The automated testing tools can often give an idea how many users are capable of running analysis queries in the BW system, thus gauging the potential workload.

Typically most testing in BW is done manually. The BW testers often work closely with an R/3 or ECC counterpart to provide transactional data additions, changes, and deletions in order to test and reconcile the loaded data into BW.

In some projects, the transactional processing teams teach the BW team to enter, change, and delete transactions, and the BW team performs the transactions and reconciles the data into BW.

Now, let us proceed with understanding organizational change management in a BW implementation.

7.5 Organizational Change Management

Many projects see training as a necessary evil of BW implementation, and for this reason they do not spend much time or energy on the training process development and execution. In reality, a sound training strategy can reduce both costs and user frustration by ensuring that work can be done right the first time.

7.5.1 Training

One of the biggest challenges in delivering BW training is the timing. Typically many end users need to be trained on the BW system in a short time. This can make it very difficult to find enough trainers to handle the regular workload. To compensate for that, many project organizations opt to perform the training well in advance of go-live to ensure that all users can be trained. This presents challenges because it means that all configuration must be fairly complete to create the training material. Also, many users who are trained early need refresher training because so much time has passed since their training.

Another challenge to the training of BW is the lack of good data to use for training. Many times the training group is forced to create data in order to show some valid data in the system. The configuration is often changing during the training process, as issues are being uncovered and solved.

I recommend that project managers opt for a *train the trainer* approach. This involves picking a group of qualified people at each of the sites and training them on the system, then having them train the end users. This serves two purposes: it gets more people training the system, and it develops super users who can be used to help support the system during the production support phase. These super users become the first level support for any issues that occur after go-live.

7.5.2 A Separate Training System

Many project organizations opt for a separate training system. In most large organizations this is vital because trying to train users using either the QA or development systems invite so many issues. The development system is changing frequently and often is much too unstable to bring in end users for testing.

Furthermore, development systems often are unsecured, so that a user could inadvertently change configuration, causing issues for the development team. The QA system is often too volatile for training. The testing of BW often requires a lot of dumping of data and reloading. This cannot occur during the training process, so if training is going on, testing typically must stop.

To counteract these issues many customers opt for a separate BW training system. This guarantees a steady environment that can be locked down and used for training exercises. The biggest difficulty typically encountered with a training system is getting staff from the BW development team to build this system and populate it with data.

Many projects opt to fill the QA system with data and then copy this QA system to another system and use that for the training system. This lessens the burden on the BW team to populate the training system.

7.5.3 Do I Really Need Hands-On Training?

The value of a *hands-on* vs. a *hands-off* training is simple. Hands-on training provides a much more complete understanding by the end users but requires a much more patient training team and a much more complete training environment.

However, it is very difficult for users to really understand the functionality of the BW system and the query-processing tools without hands-on time on the system. They can use this time to run queries, perform drill downs, etc.

The general rule with BW end user training is to try to get some real or close to real transactional and master data loaded into a BW system. Users typically respond better to data that approximates what they will be seeing after the go-live.

The training should be structured to first include an overview of the data that has been loaded into BW, along with a multi-generational plan on the data that will later be in scope. Often, training focuses exclusively on the BW tool set and ignores the more important questions related to data strategy.

7.5.4 Training Budget

Lack of funding is one of the biggest reasons that SAP BW customers' training initiatives fall short of their goals. Most BW projects begin with a plan and rather significant budget for training the end users. But as contingency needs arise, the training budget can often be raided to supplement shortfalls elsewhere.

It is the nature and timing of training that causes this to occur. At the end of the project, there is no other place to find contingency money, so training gets the deepest cuts.

It is important to make sure that the BW training budget is set from the beginning of the project and holds steady throughout so the training needs are not compromised by a lack of budget.

Let's continue proceeding in our path towards a go-live by discussing cutover planning.

7.6 Cutover Planning

The next step in preparing for go-live is to create a cutover plan. This document is designed as a project plan for the go-live. A sample cutover plan and associated checklist is found in Appendix B. The document in this appendix serves as a list of all tasks the typically need to be performed.

The main purpose of the cutover plan is to make sure each task is fully documented so that when the go-live cutover occurs there are no tasks that are missed.

In many cases the cutover team is under a great deal of pressure to complete the tasks correctly and quickly to ensure the least downtime of the BW and associated transactional systems. The more organized the team can become at communicating the various tasks and their responsibilities, the more smoothly the cutover will progress. Some of the most important tasks in the cutover plan are as follows:

- Activities and tasks that need to be performed in both the BW and any source systems to prepare the systems and data for the go-live should be clearly listed. For example, if there are several flat files that need to be generated from a source system, this task should be scheduled and planned to make sure the file is available when needed.

- All data loading requirements should be documented in detail with the approximate duration of each load process. Many projects have a dress rehearsal for the initial data loading procedure in either the production system or a copy of the production system to ensure that the initial data load procedure is sound.

- All data load jobs should be listed with a clear task list in the order that they should be performed. This is especially important because many BW jobs have predecessor jobs. For example, in order to load the initial delivery data from the ECC system, the delivery-creation job should be run to make sure that all deliveries in the system are being prepared for loading into BW.

- Outages for any systems need to be clearly stated. In many initial loads from the ECC or R/3 transactional systems, it is required that no transactions occur while the initial loading programs are running. Ensuring that there is some quiet time planned for the transactional source systems is vital to cutover planning.

- Batch windows of loading time should be clearly stated. If the users are promised the system on Monday morning at 7am EST, this should be clearly understood by the cutover team in order to make sure data is loaded and verified before the users log on to the system.
- A reconciliation plan should be established to document how the initial loads into BW are going to be matched with the equivalent data on the source system. This allows for the data to be verified and *blessed* by the business SMEs associated with the process.
- Assignment of a responsible person for each data load process is vital. This allows a clear understanding of who is responsible for the tasks and how escalation can occur if critical tasks are not complete in time.
- A communication plan of all tasks and their current status should be created. This allows the project management to clearly see each cutover step, its status, and state of the process.
- A security plan should be developed and included in the cutover plan. Often when the cutover occurs, several jobs need to be run on the ECC or R/3 system to start data initialization. Team members performing these jobs need to have proper access to complete the jobs. The security plan should also cover any external systems needed for extraction or reconciliation along with the BW system. Planning for these authorization issues can help to prevent issues and delays during the cutover.
- An escalation plan needs to be established to understand clearly how issues are to be documented and resolved. This plan should include escalation for application, Basis, database, and business-process issues.
- SAP should be informed of the go-live plans and timing. SAP keeps a list of those customers that are going live. This helps their support organization prepare and prioritize those issues that are reported to SAP.
- A data purging, cleansing, and cleanup procedure should be documented, if applicable. In some cases during the cutover, some setup tables or data load tables need to be purged during or after the cutover. These tasks should be clearly listed in the cutover plan.
- Contact numbers and cutover schedules should be clearly documented and posted.

Once the cutover plan is established, the next step is to make sure that the system is prepared for this go-live. This involves making sure all system settings are correct and the overall health of the system would support go-live.

The best way of making sure the system is ready for the go-live is via a go-live checklist.

7.7 Go-Live Checklist

Several things need to be checked in any system prior to getting it ready for a cutover. This checklist is typically called the go-live checklist. It differs from the cutover plan because it provides a list of all the things that are needed in order to begin transporting. This list can and should be used for any new system that has been created or copied.

Here are some of the important activities that need to be performed or checked when a new BW system is built:

- **SAP Notes Checked for High Priority Fixes**
  When a new system is built, this is a good time to look at the SAP Notes for the current support package in the Service MarketPlace to ensure that SAP has not released any high-priority fixes. These can be found by searching on the support package number in the Service MarketPlace.

- **Database/Kernel/Operating System Patches Applied**
  Many times the focus of BW projects is simply on the application, but there are several underlying patches that should be checked to make sure they are consistent with the QA environment. This is typically performed by the Basis or technical staff. It is a good idea to have these tasks on a new system checklist to make sure that these checks are performed whenever a new system is built.

- **Technical Infrastructure Checked**
  All users systems should include whatever they need to access BW including the proper GUI, portal links, etc. This involves checking the user setups and ensuring that their desktop and network access is optimal to access the system. One of the more common issues are obsolete or outdated releases of MS Excel or MS Internet Explorer. These can sometimes cause issues with running BEx Analyzer or some of the Java tools.

- **Connections to Source Systems Established**
  Check that the connections to all source systems are sound and functioning properly. This involves setting the connections to any external system including the SAP and non-SAP systems. If flatfile data is to be loaded, a source system connection should be established to allow this data to be loaded into BW.

- **Transfer of Global Settings Performed**
  Each R/3 or ECC source systems should have their global setting transferred so the UOM, currency, and calendars are populated in the BW system.

- **Permitted Characters Checked**
  Check the permitted characters setting in Transaction SPRO to make sure that the permitted characters match in QA and Production

- **Default Packet Size Checked**
  Check the settings in the BW IMG to make sure the default packet size is identical to the QA system. This is needed for loading data from ECC or R/3 into the BW system.

- **Flat File Parameters Verified**
  Check the flatfile loading parameters to make sure the QA system matches with the production system. This setting is needed to load the flat file data into the BW system.

- **All System Traces Switched Off**
  If there are any system traces in Transaction ST01, these should be turned off. These traces can slow performance.

- **All User Logging Switched Off**
  If user logging has been turned of in Transaction RSRTRACE, this should be turned off. These traces slow performance if not needed.

- **Security Checked**
  One of the most popular help desk issues post go-live is security. Checking and rechecking of the roles can make the security issues less painful.

- **Transports Completed**
  All transports complete and system setup matches the QA environment

- **Process Chains Checked**
  Check to ensure that the process chains have been migrated properly and run properly on the BW system. Issues often occur because there are no valid connections or not enough processes or database log size to complete the process chain.

- **OLAP Cache Turned On**
  Most OLAP cache settings are performed in each system. Check the cache settings on all queries to make sure they are correct and functioning properly.

- **Statistics Turned On**
  The BW statistics Cubes can be used to track the performance of the BW

system. The statistics need to be checked and turned on in each system. Verify the settings and ensure there is a process chain to load the statistics cubes.

- **Aggregates Filled**
  Any aggregates that are part of the data model need to be filled. Aggregates are used to speed up the query performance.
- **DB Statistics Run**
  Database statistics should be run on all InfoCubes and ODS tables to ensure that they are up-to-date. This allows the database to know the size of tables and makeup of their data to allow for faster query processing.
- **RSRV Checks Performed**
  Transaction RSRV has many tools with which to check the system prior to go-live. Run the various checks to ensure that indexes are built and the table structures are sound.
- **Portal Content Checked**
  Check to see that all portal links are working properly and that BW queries exist properly and function properly on the portal.
- **SAP Go-live Check Performed**
  SAP provides a service to check a system to determine if it is ready for go-live. These technical checks can give a sanity check to determine if the system is ready.

Once the testing has been completed, the data is ready to be loaded into the production environment.

In the next section, I will explain the loading process in BW and some of the common issues with loading data.

7.8 Run Initial Loads in BW

When the production transports are complete, the system is ready for loading. In most projects, the initial loads of data are performed manually in the production system. In the case of a delta load, the BW system is loaded and delta queues are generated on the ECC or R/3 system. Once the delta queue is established, any new delta records will be added to the delta queue.

In the event of data where a delta is not possible, a full load is kicked off. These loads typically are performed manually as well. The BW team should take proper care to monitor the data loads and reconcile the data back to the ECC, R/3, or legacy source system.

In some cases, setup programs must be run in order to initially fill the data queues in the ECC or R/3 system. These are common with those DataSources that involve the logistics extractors; i.e., those extractors that are configured in ECC in the Transaction LBWE. Look at the documentation or configuration guide to determine the appropriate initial loading program needed for the specific DataSource used.

Most customers opt to have BW live for a few weeks prior to inviting the users onto the system. This allows for BW to be loaded and tested and the batch loads to run for a few weeks to work out any issues that might occur.

The initial loading of data is performed manually because the steps that are performed for the initial loading of data in BW are usually only performed once. Once the initial load of data is complete there is no reason to run it again unless there are major issues or a realignment of data for a reload of data. Thus, once the data is loaded for the first time manually, the next step is to establish process chains for the periodic loading process in BW.

7.8.1 Create and Schedule Process Chains in BW

The process chains are used to schedule the data loads in BW. In order to automate these loads the various process chains to load both master data and transactional data must be configured and scheduled. These process chains allow the many different jobs to be scheduled, either in parallel or serially as part of the nightly batch window.

In a typical BW implementation, there are hundreds of jobs that need to be run nightly. These jobs may include loading master data or transactional data, or running database statistics. The role of the process chain is to organize and kick off all these loads in a consistent manner.

It also allows for one place to monitor and watch the jobs for failures. The process chains have functionality to notify the administrator of any failures. This notification allows administrators to fix any job failures quickly before the end users get on the system.

When loading data in BW, it is necessary that all master data be loaded first and then the transactional data. This allows the master data to be established so that when the related transactional data is loaded it can leverage these entries.

In most projects, the process chains are administered and created by one individual or a small subset of the BW team. This is because the complex web of jobs that need to be run nightly can become difficult for all the members of the team to understand.

In most projects, I have recommended that one steward be in charge of all the process chains. This steward is responsible for gathering all the loading requirements from the process team members and assembling that into the process chains. This allows for a consistent organization of all new jobs and one person to contact when new jobs are needed.

The task of monitoring the nightly batch jobs for failures and acting on those failures is typically the responsibility of the production support team. However, until the production support team starts to support an environment, the BW development team often monitors the data loads for a stabilization period. This role is usually shared by several members of the BW team.

Because monitoring the batch loads takes place in the evening, and often this requires the team to work late into the night, the project manager should be very careful about who monitors the data loads. For example, in one project, the team had some of their most qualified people monitoring the data loads at night, and these team members thus were not available to tackle other issues that occurred during the day.

All ECC and/or R/3 transactional loads should also be considered before scheduling the BW process chains. For example, if a process chain is created to load invoice data, the process chain should only be scheduled to run after the invoices have been created in the R/3 or ECC systems. In many cases, the process chains are not scheduled until after midnight to make sure all entries for the previous day have been processed and can be loaded into BW.

Many times, dependent jobs need to run on the ECC or R/3 transactional system. These dependent jobs are needed before any BW jobs can run. Let's explore some of the most popular ECC jobs that are related to the BW batch.

7.8.2 Schedule ECC Jobs

In most BW implementations there are several ECC or R/3 jobs that must run on the transactional system. Some of these jobs are part of the normal transactional workday in the ECC or R/3 system. For example, in order for the system to be able to load the invoices into BW, the billing generation program must be run in the ECC or R/3 transactional system. Only after this job has been run can the BW system pull these billing documents.

There are several other transactional jobs that must be run on the ECC system before the BW system can load data. Many times these are the responsibility of the ECC or R/3 process team to schedule. The BW team simply needs to know when these jobs will run in order to ensure that BW does not try to load its data before these other jobs are complete. If the BW system pulls data too early, it will not be available for the end users for that day.

For example, the billing documents are typically run at 11pm each evening. If the BW system pulls the billing documents at 10pm, they would only get the documents that have been run throughout the day since the last invoice run. However, the billing documents that are generated on the 11pm run would only be available for the next day's load. BW batch loads frequently do not even start until midnight to ensure that all the processing in the transactional systems is complete for the day. This gives the end user a complete picture of the day's transactions.

Another popular kind of job that is scheduled in most BW implementation is known as the V3 job. These jobs are used to gather up the recent changed logistics data and move this data into the logistic delta queues. For many of the common logistics transactional data loads, this process must be scheduled on the ECC or R/3 system each evening before the BW system loads the data. In some cases, project teams opt to run the V3 job multiple times in the work day, depending on the volume, however, it must be run before the BW system can pull that day's delta records.

The V3 jobs are only necessary if the logistics extractors are being used in BW. The logistics extractors are setup and V3 jobs scheduled using Transaction LBWE on the ECC system. Figure 7.5 provides a view of the V3 process in the transactional system.

The V3 job moves the data from the updated records file to the delta queue. This delta queue is then used to load the data to the BW system. If the V3 job has not been run for the day, there are no delta records in the delta queue; thus, the data load in the BW system would load zero records.

The BW team needs to coordinate with the ECC or R/3 teams to make sure that this job runs consistently during the evening before BW loads data. This allows all the logistic delta records to be loaded into BW.

Once the process chains have been created and scheduled, the data is now ready for reporting. The next step is to make sure that the queries are ready to provide this data to the end user. These queries are typically launched via the portal. The next section discusses the various strategies for the portal and publication of queries into the portal.

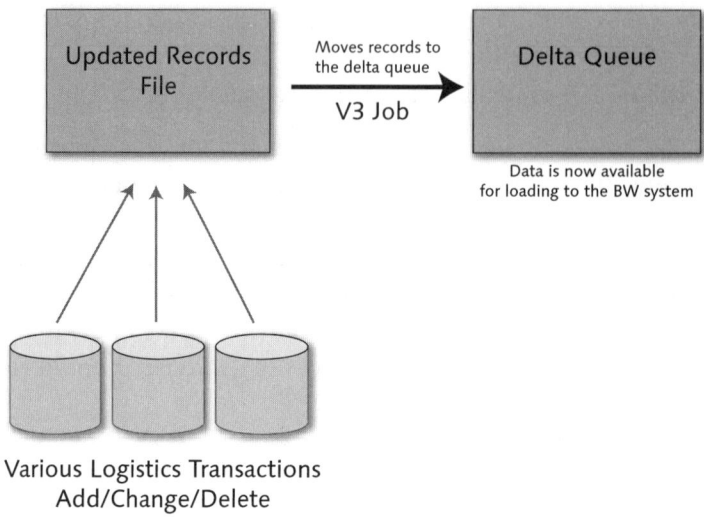

Figure 7.5 Description of the Logistics V3 Process in ECC or R/3

7.8.3 Portals and BW

In general, a portal is the transactional launch pad for the user in order to run transactions and analysis, or to view data from multiple sources in one place. The need for a portal came about because as SAP and other vendors introduced more and more products, the users became increasingly frustrated with the need to log on to multiple systems to do their work.

To add to this frustration, the user also needed to go to several places to perform analysis in these systems. The need quickly arose to have one place that users could log on that would provide them access to multiple systems, links, documents, and transactions across the enterprise. Basically, the user wanted one place to go to do their job. Thus, the portal was born.

There are many different portal software solutions to choose from in the marketplace. The most common choice among SAP customers is the SAP Portal. This makes sense because the SAP Portal comes with the SAP NetWeaver products along with the BW system. In fact, as part of all NW 2004s systems, an enterprise portal is loaded as part of the installation.

The SAP Portal, although designed to work and integrate with all SAP products, is not limited to only SAP products. This can be used to launch documents, reports, and analysis from virtually any web-based solution. This provides users with a wide range of content that can be used for their portal.

The portal is a very important part of the BW environment because it is needed in order to present the analysis to the end user. Only after queries are complete can they be published to the portal, so this is typically the last step in the query-development process in a BW implementation.

In the 3.x releases of BW, the portal team and BW team had very limited interaction. In the cases where customers were using a portal, the BW team typically developed their queries on their own and then passed these queries to the portal team via a uniform resource locator (URL) link or as an iView. The portal team placed this link on the portal, and the user could access the query.

In the NW 2004s environment, the BW team and portal team are much more integrated. This is because all BW reports are now published to the portal via a standard publishing process in the BW report designer. When publishing queries, the BW team needs to work with the portal team to develop a clear publishing strategy that allows the BW content to be developed and presented to the end user in accordance with the portal strategy.

For example, suppose the BW team develops several unrelated queries, one for sales, one for finance, and one for purchasing. The publishing strategy needs to ensure that the queries show up properly on each of the various portal views and that the queries have a consistent look and feel. They also need to be published in accordance with any security and authorization strategy developed by the portal team.

This requires clear communication between the BW team and the portal team and a clear portal strategy.

7.8.4 Developing a Portal Strategy

To ensure that the various users have a consistent tool in order to perform their jobs, a portal strategy needs to be developed. This strategy mainly looks at the different audience of the portal and determines what is needed by each group and how this should be presented to the end user. This strategy also ensures that the users can access the various transactions and analysis in accordance with the security model.

It is recommended that any portal strategy be developed and owned by a portal resource, in conjunction with the business representatives and the change management team. Portal strategy decisions are not primarily performed by the BW team. However, because the BW queries are often launched via the portal, and the portal is the end user's first view of the BW solution, it is vital that the BW team be very involved in the portal strategy.

Portal strategy should take into account any other systems that will be accessed by the end user and act as a launch pad for these applications as well. BW can then leverage these roles and this strategy to make sure that the users not only have one common place for all transactions, but that their reporting needs are also met in the same area. In general, a portal strategy has several goals:

- Provide one central point of entry to view, analyze, and transact data across multiple systems
- Expedite user log-on and entry into systems
- Reduce the number of log-ons by using a single sign-on (SSO) process
- Centralize important documents and links and make these available to the user
- Provide one place to run all analysis regardless of the source system

Another very important aspect of the portal strategy is governance. This helps to determine and maintain the content that will be shown on the portal. Since the portal is a very public place and gives the users their first and most common view of the organization, these portal governance decisions are quite important in preserving user confidence in the organization. This confidence often comes from a well-designed and useful-looking portal. These decisions come from portal governance. There are several goals for portal governance:

- Defining and understanding the portal users and key stakeholders
- Determining the content administrators
- Creating a governance model to develop portal content and provide this to the end user
- Integrating with any authorization or security strategy
- Communicating with the various systems owners about how to connect and where possible providing single sign-on (SSO) for the users
- Prioritizing and completing portal work

A common place to start developing the analysis portion of the portal strategy is in the BW landscape. If BW reports are to be presented to the end user via the portal, there are two main approaches for providing these portal links. These two strategies are as seen here:

- **BW Portal Display Strategy**
  Because the SAP Enterprise Portal (EP) comes as part of the NW 2004s installation, this portal can be used as the BW analysis launch pad. In this strategy, only the BW portal as part of the NW 2004s system is used as a portal. No other portal systems are installed. This provides the user one basic method of providing a fully functional portal to the end user.

- **Federated Portal Strategy**
  In a federated portal strategy, a completely separate portal environment is established that is separate but mirrors the BW system with an EP development, EP QA, and production stand-alone systems. This stand-alone system is called the Federated Portal, and resembles the illustration seen in Figure 7.6.

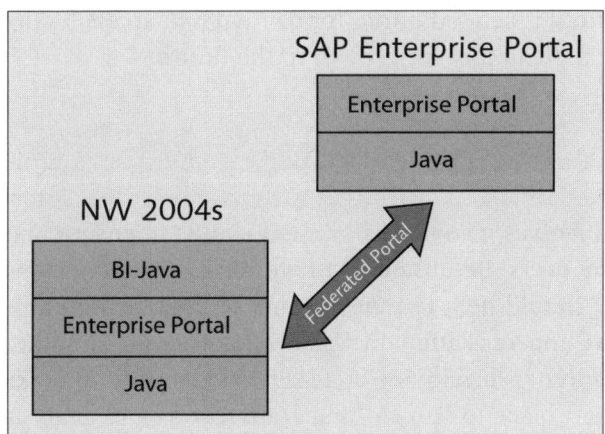

Figure 7.6 Portal Design in NW 2004s and SAP Enterprise Portal

In most cases, the federated portal strategy is preferred to using the BW portal display strategy. In most cases, it is recommended that a stand-alone EP system be used as the portal for the organization rather than relying on the BW portal.

There are several reasons that the federated portal strategy makes sense. A project team may start to build its content into the BW portal rather than a standalone EP implementation. If a project team opts to use the BW portal and develops a great deal of content in that portal and then decides to use another SAP software product like CRM or APO, it may find that these products have limitations regarding the version of the portal that can be used. In some cases there are severe limits on how these systems can be linked.

However, if the federated portal approach is used, the systems can be linked in the federated portal by each of their underlying EP products. For example, the BW system can link to the federated portal via its EP; CRM can link via its EP, etc. This provides much more flexibility for linking systems.

So why not begin using the BW Portal for end user access, develop content and configuration on this system, and then convert to a federated portal later? The answer is that it takes a lot of effort to migrate to a federated portal from a BW portal. Often, this means that once a federated portal is needed, the organization has to redevelop all the portal content on the federated portal.

Therefore, it is not advisable to begin using the BW portal as the main portal for the end users. Instead it makes sense to opt for the stand-alone EP implementation and use the central federated portal for content and access by the end users. This provides the flexibility for growth in the future.

7.9 Conclusion

Preparing for the go-live involves many decisions and checks to ensure that the system is ready for the users. Because the cutover tasks are often quite stressful, proper planning should help to relieve some of the stress by providing the right resources and escalation in the event of issues. Another important aspect of going live is developing a clear portal strategy to make sure users have a consistent place to launch their transactions and analysis needs.

In Chapter 8, I will discuss what is needed after the project goes live to ensure that any future BW rollouts will be successful.

"Nice guys finish last, but we get to sleep in."
– Evan Davis

8 After BW Go-Live

BW projects like R/3 or ECC projects are not complete once they go live. There are many jobs that need to be done after the users start using the system. These include establishing periodic tasks to reconcile the data and keep the system healthy, and transitioning the solution to the production support organization for ongoing maintenance.

This can be a challenge in many organizations because budget resources have not been adequately allocated to post go-live activities. Often, the budget that is allocated is used as a contingency for other activities that are over-budget. This makes post go-live tasks even harder.

To add to the frustration, many of the project team members either leave to work on other projects or go back to their former jobs. Others may be burned out from the long hours spent during the implementation process and go-live. Keeping a core team motivated to help on the post go-live activities requires planning prior to the go-live and coordination after the go-live.

In order to plan for these activities, we first need to understand the typical project responsibilities after go-live and the challenges faced in this phase of the project lifecycle.

When a project goes live, the BW development team is often the first level of support for issues that occur. After the stabilization period is complete, the next step is to transition the solution to the production support group or Center of Excellence (COE).

8.1 Building a Production Support Center of Excellence (COE)

A production support Center of Excellence (COE) is a central organization used for ongoing production support after go-live is complete. It is important that the COE be seen as a long-term organization and reinforced with staffing and budget. All the ongoing support for the product should be coordinated and organized through the COE organization.

Figure 8.1 Lifecycle and Responsibilities of the COE

The COE has many different responsibilities, and once established it should be considered a vital part of the organization. Figure 8.1 illustrates the lifecycle and the responsibilities of the COE. The typical COE has a core staff but relies on many extended team members to provide the support needed to keep the BW system functioning properly. Some of the primary goals of the COE are to:

- Understand the existing BW environment, the sources of data, transformation, and presentation of this information to the end user
- Optimize the existing system and processes to make sure that the business goals continue to be met
- Staff and maintain a help desk to gather incident reports and provide support to assign, track, and resolve incidents
- Escalate issues to the various organizations including the Basis, database, development, business, and to SAP
- Track, troubleshoot, and implement fixes for issues and deviations from the business goals
- Manage, optimize and stabilize the existing BW environment

- Monitor the loads to the BW system
- Coordinate maintenance of the system
- Provide a proactive approach to system issues to help find problems before the users do
- Provide ongoing user-support and training for new users
- Act as a conduit for user feedback on desired features and functionality

The challenges in setting up a COE are to find the right resources and to transition the knowledge from the BW development team that built the solution to the COE that will be maintaining the system.

In order to build a successful COE, there must be a very organized and planned transition from the development team to the COE.

8.2 Transitioning from BW Development to Production-Support COE

Transitioning from the development role to a production-support COE can be difficult. In most projects, the development team provides the production support on all new objects for several weeks until the new development is stabilized. After the stabilization period, the newly developed objects are transitioned to a production support team that handles the ongoing monitoring and maintenance of the solution.

Several tasks must be performed in order to have a successful handoff from the BW development group to the production-support COE.

8.2.1 Transition the Knowledge

A clear communication plan and plan for transition to production support can allow for a clean transfer of knowledge and a handoff of the responsibilities of the design. However, the transition of the BW design often does not go smoothly. New development frequently suffers because the BW development team spends a great deal of its time working with and supplementing the production support team on issues.

Thus, once the development build is completed, it is vital to start the knowledge transfer of the solution to the production support team, keeping it engaged in the solution. The BW development team members need to make themselves available to the production support team, but not to the extent that they are unable to perform the new development required by the project.

It is also necessary to make sure that the COE staff is able to understand not only the technical configuration of the system but, more importantly, the business needs and goals of the organization. In many organizations this means that the COE works very closely with the business subject matter experts (SMEs) and business stakeholders to ensure ongoing communication.

The best way to ensure a smooth transition of the business and development knowledge is to plan this well in advance of go-live. Many projects wait until late in the process to begin the transition to the production-support COE. This also occurs when the COE is not staffed until well after go-live. By then, many of the developers have either left or are busy working on other enhancements and it is difficult to get their time to aid in the support of the system.

8.2.2 Determine Measurement Criteria

Once the knowledge has been adequately transitioned to the production support team and they are comfortable about beginning to support the solution, a process must be developed to measure and track the success of the COE and its processes.

In order to provide adequate BW support, some measurement criteria for the production-support COE are needed. This enables us to understand how well the COE is meeting the needs of the organization. Some of the measurements and processes that should be established and agreed upon are as follows.

- **Service Level Agreement (SLA)**
  This is for query-processing performance, and is typically set as an average query response time across the organization. This can be tracked and measured in BW via the statistics InfoCubes.

- **Issue Tracking Agreement**
  This helps in understanding how issues will be logged, prioritized, tracked, and resolved in a timely manner. This strategy will also include a strategy on how the COE will communicate the resolution of issues.

- **Roles and Responsibilities Agreement**
  These help the COE to draw a clear line between the support organization and the new-development organization. This allows each group to concentrate on its assigned tasks. In many organizations, the new-development team is called in often by the COE to work on production support

issues. This takes time away from the development lifecycle. A clear procedure and plan should be established to make sure the development team can provide some background and expertise to issues while also concentrating on their main role of new development.

- **Total Cost of Ownership (TCO) Agreement**
  This calculation allows the organization to understand and track the ongoing cost for maintenance of the system. It is useful for the ongoing project budget and to benchmark the project against other projects.

Establish a Help Desk

Most often, issues are reported to the COE via the help desk. Help desks establish a phone line, email address, and/or website to track incidents reported by the end users. These incidents are tracked, assigned, and prioritized by the BW help desk.

Typically this requires software to track incidents, status, and resolution. Some companies use a basic MS Access database; some opt for an off-the-shelf package for a more sophisticated tracking of incidents and help-desk calls. Here are the most important things to understand about the BW help desk:

- Understanding the source systems is vital to troubleshooting a BW issue. This is often where we encounter the gap of knowledge in a help desk. Many times we find someone who is very knowledgeable about the BW environment but who is not as proficient in the ECC or R/3 system.

- Many of the issues will be the result of master data or transactional data in the source system. Many of the help-desk tickets simply show that the data in the BW system matches the data in the source system. Although this does not always solve the user's issue, it does provide the proof that BW matches the source.
  This is then passed on to the COE for the associated ECC or R/3 system for repair. Suppose, for example, that a user runs a report and wonders why the sales for his or her division seem low. The BW team matches the sales figures by division to the ECC system, but some of the sales are from the wrong division. Although this appears to the user to be a BW issue, the issue can only be resolved on the ECC system by adjusting the sales divisions in the transactional data.

- Understanding the latency of the data in BW is also vital. Because BW data is typically loaded once a day, the data is not current with the source system. Often, users expect that the data in BW is more current than it is. Many issues are resolved by making sure that users understand this latency.

- Knowing the flow of data through the BW system will help in troubleshooting the issues quickly. Many help desk incidents are resolved by working backwards through the data loads. For example, a user sees values that appear to be incorrect in the *Net Sales* key figure. In order to resolve this incident, the query is run to verify the data.
  The Multi-Provider is then examined to determine if the issue is in the joining of the data. Next, the InfoCube is studied, then the DSO/ODS structure, and then the PSA. Finally comes the comparison to source data. This requires an understanding of the data and the flow of the data through the BW system. It also requires a clear vision on how the data is transformed at each step in the process.

- Sometimes the data in BW will be mapped incorrectly. This may require a dump and reload of the BW data. This occurs when transactional data has been loaded into a BW InfoProvider incorrectly. These activities are a normal part of the production-support COE, but obviously need to be avoided, if possible.

- Leveraging the organization's development resources from time to time is an effective say to resolve the more difficult issues. Although it is important not to go to the development team for most issues, it can be helpful to enlist the people who built the solution to help on some of the more difficult issues. Many projects schedule sessions with the development team weekly to deal with open issues. There should also be an escalation process for timely involvement of the development team in critical production issues.

- Turnover in the COE can be very frustrating. Keeping a good COE staffer for a long time can be difficult, as many of these people move to other areas of the organization or into the development team. Keeping the team motivated is important.

One of the ways a strong COE organization becomes more proactive to the end user needs is to spot issues and fix them before the end user is even aware the issue exists.

This requires a process of reconciliation and validation. This process compares the data in the various systems to see if the data differs between systems of if other issues exist.

8.3 Ongoing BW Reconciliation and Validation

In order to keep the COE working toward a proactive role in understanding and preventing issues, a process needs to be established to periodically reconcile the data in the BW system with the ECC or R/3 system.

This process can be used to validate accuracy and ensure that all related data is being loaded into BW. This process should be considered an ongoing and vital part of the BW post-production tasks. Thus, it should occur on a scheduled periodic basis.

The mistake many BW project organizations make is to consider BW reconciliation to be a one-time pre- and post go-live activity. They verify that the initial loads of data correctly match the R/3 or ECC source, and then they assume that all future loads will follow suit. Because BW is typically the reporting system for management decisions, it needs to be periodically reconciled.

The reconciliation allows the BW team to proactively manage the BW system to make sure that the data does indeed match with the ECC or R/3 system. This is not always an easy task. Often, the R/3 or ECC source data is not found in one table or one report. Thus, in order to match the data from the BW or ECC system, multiple sources of data may have to be read in the ECC system and matched against the equivalent data in the BW system.

Rarely is the process of reconciling data between BW and the transactional source systems automated. Thus, most methods of reconciling data in the ECC or R/3 system to the BW systems involve a manual process of running reports periodically in the BW system and comparing the reports to equivalent data in the source system.

8.3.1 Develop a Reconciliation Strategy

There are several elements that go into the ongoing reconciliation strategy. These are discussed below:

- **Sources**
  All important and vital sources of data should be checked against the equivalent BW data. Typically this involves not only transactional data but also master data.

- **Granularity**
  Transactional can exist at many levels of granularity. Typically the strategy is to check the data at a more detailed level and to spot check the transac-

tional data. This is because it is not reasonable to assume that each transactional record can be verified with the source.

- **Scope**
  In a BW data model, there are many characteristics and key figure values that make up a BW InfoProvider. Again, it is not usually practical to verify all data fields; the data fields should be prioritized to make sure the reconciliation efforts are expended wisely.

- **Frequency**
  The frequency of reconciliation depends on the granularity of the data and the frequency of the loads. For example, an InfoCube that is kept at a monthly level in an InfoCube is typically not reconciled more frequently than once a month.

- **Time**
  The reconciliation needs to occur at an inactive or low-activity period to ensure that the systems are synchronized. This may not be easy in a very dynamic environment. In some cases, it involves using data from the past and ignoring the recently changed data.

- **Testers**
  Many environments use the BW team to provide the testing of BW. This process should be owned and executed by the business-process teams. This fosters ownership of the BW reconciliation and data and ensures that those who use the data most and understand the information being presented best are checking that information for validity.

- **Steps**
  The reconciliation steps need to be developed and documented. These steps depend on the data that is in BW and also the availability of the data in the related source system. These steps cover the detailed procedure to reconcile the data in BW with the data in the source system.

- **Prerequisites**
  Often, reconciliation can only occur after specific jobs or tasks are complete on the BW and/or source systems. These should be clearly understood.

- **Documentation/signoff**
  The reconciliation should have a clear documentation procedure and a signoff process to make sure that all parties agree on the reconciliation.

8.3.2 Reconciling the Data to ECC or R/3

It is recommended that a periodic and systematic verification of the data in the BW system and its source data be checked in either the ECC or R/3 system. This is to make sure that the data in BW is valid and reflects the equivalent data in the ECC or R/3 transactional systems.

This effort should be proactive. Rather than waiting for users to report any issues with missing data, the team can run periodic checks to make sure that the characteristics and key figures match between the systems. The most frequently used methods of gathering data from the ECC or R/3 source systems include the following tools:

- SAP Standard reports
- Report-painter/report-writer tools
- Virtual InfoProviders (remote InfoCubes)
- Transaction SE16 and/or manually inspecting SAP source tables
- Logistics Information System (LIS) reconciliation
- SAP Queries, which are queries run on the SAP system using the SAP Query functionality (this is not the BW query functionality)
- Custom ABAP reports

Although there are multiple ways of reconciling data from SAP systems to the BW system, many COE organizations rely on only few of the tools mentioned. The first place to check for a source of reconciliation is in the SAP standard reports. There are many list-functionality reports that allow for totaling and comparison with BW data. The report-writer and report-painter reports can also be used for this reconciliation. Typically these reports are run and compared to specific BW queries.

This is the most common way of reconciling and is the easiest because no development needs to take place in order to begin the reconciliation process. The issue that often occurs is that there are no SAP reports that match the data in BW. This happens because the BW data is often transformed or harmonized with other data in the BW system. This makes reconciling the data from standard reporting difficult.

Another common way to reconcile data is to use Transaction SE16. This allows a user to inspect table contents in the SAP source system to look at various table contents. This output can sometimes be compared to the BW transactional data to ensure that the data matches. This allows the totaling up of transactions for some key figure values, and these can be compared to the

BW system to see if the totals match. Although this is not a perfect method of reconciliation, it does provide a way of checking against the data.

Providing reconciliation via a remote or virtual InfoProvider is another common method. This process involves creating a virtual view of source data on the ECC or R/3 system. This view can be used as a DataSource to look into the ECC or R/3 system. For example, the sales data can be sourced as a DataSource and this DataSource queried in BW as a virtual InfoCube. Comparison queries can then be created to verify this data and compare it with its source data.

This method does involve some development on the source system to create the view needed to look at the data. However, once this view is established, this method does provide a very user-friendly reconciliation of data because BW queries can be run by the COE to compare the data in the various systems to ensure they match.

The biggest issue that occurs with most reconciliation is that BW is a batch system. It gets its loads periodically, typically nightly. When reconciling, however, it is looking at live data. In order to properly reconcile, the latency of the BW solution must be considered in the reconciliation process. Most of the time, this means that data from the current day is excluded from the reconciliation process. This is typically done because that data has not been loaded to BW.

This subsection summarizes some of the typical issues with reconciling data to SAP systems. In most projects, there are also non-SAP systems that need to be checked. There are other methods that are used to reconcile these systems.

8.3.3 Reconciling Data to External Systems

Reconciling BW data to external systems is much more difficult. Most projects opt to run either standard or custom reporting programs on the external source system and compare that to the data in the Persistent Staging Area (PSA) or via queries on the BW system.

However, this process is completely reliant on the toolset provided in the external system in order to create a reconciliation process. Because many external systems use flat files to load data into BW, this provides a place to do some reconciliation. Periodic checking of the flat files against the BW data helps to ensure a level of accuracy.

External systems should have some process to reconcile their data against the BW system and a periodic audit of the data to ensure the users are seeing the data properly.

Along with data reconciliation, there are other ongoing tasks that the COE needs to either perform or oversee other groups' performance in order to support the system. In the next section, I highlight some of the most popular periodic processes that need to be performed.

8.4 Periodic Jobs to Run in a BW Environment

In order to keep a BW system running properly, there are several ongoing and periodic jobs that need to be planned and scheduled. Here are the most important periodic jobs:

- **System Backup (Daily)**
  All BW environments need to be backed up and a backup-and-recovery strategy should be implemented and tested periodically.
- **Basis Monitoring (Daily)**
  All system logs (Transaction SM21), ABAP runtime short dumps (Transaction ST22), operation monitor (Transaction ST06), and database monitor (Transaction DB02) should be checked daily to assess the overall health of the BW system.
- **Application Load Monitoring (Daily)**
  All process chains used for the loading of BW data should be monitored for errors. Any errors in data loads should be logged and fixed. This often means reloading or re-running a delta load process again to fix an error.
- **Run Database Statistics (Daily)**
  The database statistics are vital to ensuring that the underlying database optimizer can determine the proper run path for queries. This should be run on all InfoCubes, DSO/ODS tables, and any other large or dynamic tables in the BW system. In some cases this is run from the BW application itself; in others it is run from the database system.
- **Load-Performance Statistics InfoCubes (Daily)**
  The performance statistics InfoCubes are used to report and measure performance. All InfoCubes and ODS structures should be turned on for reporting and all performance InfoCubes should be loaded in batch nightly. In order to use these statistics InfoCubes, they need to be activated from the business content.

- **Compression**
  This is done periodically, typically daily. Compression should be performed on the data packages in BW to speed the query performance and reduce the data volume in the InfoCubes.

- **Aggregate Rollup (Daily)**
  When data is loaded into an InfoCube that contains aggregates, the data must be rolled up into the aggregates before the new data is available to be reported. This rolling up of the data must occur after each data load.

- **Query-Performance Monitoring (Periodically)**
  The statistics InfoCubes should be monitored to determine the level of query performance. Those queries that are performing poorly should be tuned.

- **View SAP EarlyWatch Alerts (Weekly)**
  SAP provides a service called EarlyWatch that can provide some system monitoring and warnings. The report should be checked and any recommended actions be performed. This is typically run and monitored by the technical Basis team and not by the applications team, as most of the recommendations are more technical in nature.

- **RSRV Checks (Periodically)**
  There are many checks in the Transaction RSRV. This transaction can be used to check the overall health of the BW system. In many cases, the system has a function to fix any issues that are shown during the checks. These processes can either be run manually or scheduled periodically.

- **Check InfoCube Fact-to-Dimension Ratio (Periodically)**
  The optimal fact-to-dimension table ratio in any InfoCube is 10 percent. If a dimension table goes beyond this limit, query and load performance can suffer. In order to monitor the fact to dimension table ratio, the program SAP_INFOCUBE_DESIGNS can be run. This is run using Transaction SE38. For this program to work, all database statistics must be run first. This program gives the current ratio of all BW InfoCubes. In order to fix any skewed dimension, the InfoCube can be dumped and characteristics can be shuffled. In the NW 2004s release, the remodeling workbench can be used to shift the dimensions without dumping and reloading data.

- **Purge the Persistent Staging Area (Periodically)**
  The PSA tables can become quite large. After data loads have been verified, the persistent staging area is typically not necessary. This frees up some disk space in the system, and keeps the file system from filling up.

- **Check and Verify Aggregates (Periodically)**
  Aggregates can help query performance; however, any aggregate that is being used infrequently or not at all causes unneeded overhead in the system. Thus, all aggregates should be checked periodically to determine their usefulness. The aggregates can either be checked via the statistic queries or via the aggregate-maintenance screen.

- **Delete DTP Temporary Storage (Periodically)**
  In the NW 2004s version, the Data Transfer Process (DTP) has temporary storage tables that can be used for troubleshooting. The deletion of temporary storage can be set from DTP maintenance by following this menu path: **Settings for DTP Temporary Storage • Delete Temporary Storage**.

- **Delete Unused Queries and Workbooks (Periodically)**
  Transaction RSZDELETE allows unused queries to be removed periodically.

- **Near-line Storage (Periodically)**
  BW allows for near-line storage of data. This means that a subset of some little-used data is offloaded to another storage device. This allows this data to be available for reporting; however, using an alternate storage device, the data is taken off the primary database server. Typically queries of this near-line data are slower than the data in the primary database server, but offloading that data does allow for the primary database server to perform faster.

- **Archive Data (Periodically)**
  Archiving of data reduces the data volume and thus allows for better performing system. An overall archive strategy should be developed and implemented.

Another responsibility and ongoing task is to apply the various support packages when they become available. Determining when to apply and how to perform the needed regression testing on the solution often involves the development, Basis, and COE teams. Developing a sound strategy in order to continually keep up-to-date with support packages is crucial.

8.5 Develop an Ongoing BW Support Package Strategy

Developing an ongoing support-package strategy is important to the overall health of the BW system. There are several components of a typical BW system, and each requires support packages for the following:

- Java support packages (NW 2004s and above)
- ABAP support packages
- Basis support packages
- BI content support packages
- BI front-end support packages

> **Tip**
> In order to find out the timing of and get information about each SAP support package, visit SAP's Service Marketplace website at. *www.service.sap.com/bi*. This site gives information in detail on all support packages.

SAP delivers fixes to the software via individual SAP Notes. Periodically, SAP gathers up all relevant SAP Notes and provides an ABAP support package as one large grouping of many fixes to the software. The ABAP support packages are designed to fix or enhance the software application and have the biggest direct impact on the support team of all the support packages.

The frequency of the ABAP support packages depends on the stability of the software and the complexity of the related area. This support package schedule is quite arbitrary and is set based on SAP's support timetable.

Often there are quite a few prerequisites and dependencies in the BW support packages. Proper care should be taken to assure that all the dependencies are satisfied prior to installing a support package. SAP has developed a support-stack strategy for recommending the various Basis, ABAP, and Java support packages that are needed and should be upgraded together. This takes some of the guesswork out of determining which components should be upgraded together.

Each support stack is tested manually and via automated tools by BW support. Because of the complexity of the product and the many different ways that customers use and configure the BW product, however, there are often new issues that occur with each new support stack.

For this reason, each new support stack requires regression testing prior to implementation in the production environment. Because this effort can be so time consuming, customers often find themselves many support stacks behind, despite SAP's recommendation that they stay no more than two support stacks behind. Regression testing of BW is split into two specific types, as seen here:

- **Data Loading**

  Typically, the data loading testing is done using process chains. Most customers simply run their normal batch processes in the development and/or QA testing environment for several weeks under the new support stack to ensure that it does not adversely affect the batch loading.

- **Query Processing**

  Query processing testing is much more difficult and time consuming. Most automated testing tools do not work well for regression testing. This is because BW query regression testing requires a lot of user interaction regarding different queries and comparison of these results with other queries and with the source system itself. Automated testing tools typically do not allow for a great deal of user interaction, so most BW query testing is done manually.

To test the query results, the query statistics can be used to determine the most-used reports and the focus of the testing can be on the most mission critical and most-used queries. These queries should be run with a series of different users with different authorizations. This will allow the security authorizations to be checked along with the query data.

Typically, support stacks are added first to the development system and tested in some detail. After a few weeks of stabilization, the support stack is applied to the QA system. The testing occurs again with QA data. This support stack is then stabilized until it can later be added to production.

The latency of the support stack allows for a challenging production support environment. If the development, production, and QA systems are not using the same support stack, testing issues can be hard to resolve because the systems often do not act the same way under different support stacks.

For this reason, many customers opt to wait until any new major functionality is being developed for BW prior to upgrading the support stack. This allows them to create a new completely separate BW development environment. This new environment can be upgraded to the newest support stack while leaving the production support development, QA, and production at the old support stack.

When the new development is ready for cutover, the production environment is then upgraded to the newest support stack. This strategy has several advantages. It allows the support stack to be implemented in an environment outside of the production support environment, ensuring the integrity of that system. It also allows for new development to occur on the newest support stack. If issues occur, SAP Notes can be applied to the new development landscape independently of the production support systems.

Since all new development needs to be regression tested prior to bringing the functionality to the production system, this regression testing serves two purposes. It tests the new functionality that is being delivered and also tests the new support stack to determine it stability and validity.

This strategy only works for those environments that perform new development in a new separate BW environment. If this is not feasible, the only other strategy is to stagger the support stacks as stated above and regression test in each environment. This also assumes that any risk of the development, QA, and productive systems being at a different support stack is understood.

There are also other non-SAP patches needed in any implementation. These include kernel patches, operating system patches, database patches, etc. These should not be overlooked when developing a support-stack strategy.

8.5.1 Front-End Support Packages

Front-end support packages are challenging in a BW environment. This is because these front-end packages are required to be loaded on the various desktops that are using and accessing BW. Although the BW front-end support packages are typically very small, the process of pushing out the support packages to a large audience can be quite challenging.

The front-end support packages are only needed if users are developing or accessing BW reports via the BEx Analyzer. If the users are not developing queries and all queries are accessed via the Java or ABAP web interface, the front-end patches are not needed for these users.

The front-end patch is only used during query development and running using the BEx Analyzer. Because the web queries are being processed in the web browser and nothing else is running on the desktop, the front-end patch is not needed for these users.

To support those users who need the front-end patches, most BW customers use a push technology to send these patches to the various desktops in their organization. There are several software packages that allow the pushing out of these patches to the end user. This allows the packages to be organized, scheduled, and queued for periodic rollout out to the end users.

For those project organizations that do not want to deal with the overhead of the front-end patches for all users often use a Citrix or other shared environment. This environment allows multiple users to run the same front-end patches to keep some consistency for these users. If there is an upgrade necessary, only one instance needs to be upgraded. This reduces the overhead of rolling out multiple front-end patches to users.

No matter which access method is used, a clear front-end strategy should be decided upon and planned as part of the BW implementation to ensure that new front-end patches can be pushed out to the end users.

One of the other tasks that should be performed after go-live is a lessons-learned session. The goal of this session is to go over the implementation and determine where the process could have been more efficient and highlight some of the things that were done well. This helps to make sure the team can build on some of the lessons of the past.

8.5.2 Conduct a Lessons-Learned Session

A lessons-learned session is important to gather, analyze, and document feedback on events that happened during the BW project so they may be beneficial to others in the future. During these sessions it is important not only to speak about some of the things that the project could have done better, but also to focus on the things that went well.

Conduct this session as soon as possible after go-live to get the clearest and most pertinent feedback. Include the project management and the stakeholders in the discussion. If possible, it helps to have a facilitator who has not been directly involved in the project.

It is also important to set some guidelines and rules for the lessons-learned session to ensure that the discussion stays focused. Keep the focus on the process not on the people involved in the process. Where possible, in addition to the discussion with the group, allow people an opportunity to provide anonymous feedback

These sessions can either be run with the entire project team or with each process group. I have worked in projects where these sessions are used to find issues with the entire project as one group. I have also worked in teams where we as the BW team held these sessions to look at only the BW implementation issues. The lessons-learned discussion should include the following:

- What went well, and what steps should continue in future implementations?
- Are we doing things the right way?
- What recommendations would you have for others that would do a like project?
- Are we focusing on the right things?
- What did not go well? How would you have changed it?
- Are we getting the benefits that we expected?

After the lessons-learned session, document the feedback and provide a clear action plan on how the lessons will be included in future implementations. Communicate this to the project team.

This is often where the lessons-learned process breaks down. In order to have a clear and effective strategy for learning from past implementations, a formal plan and communication medium need to be developed. This shows the team members that any feedback that is given is used constructively to build a stronger team.

I worked on a long-term implementation that continually scheduled these sessions after large go-lives. The change-management group met with many of the key project members to get their input in several group settings. These were then assimilated into one large document of all the feedback from all the groups.

The problem was that this feedback was then never acted upon by the project-management organization. This was extremely frustrating because many of the issues and problems were then repeated in the next implementation. For example, one of the big issues we presented was a lack of a consolidated project plan and many issues with lack of business involvement in decision-making. After the session, the next phase of the implementation started. It started without a consolidated project plan and with little business involvement. This was extremely frustrating for the team because these challenges had been addressed clearly in the lessons-learned sessions.

However, the change-management team was not able to convince the project- management organization to find a systematic way of implementing the suggestions. I think the team would have been less frustrated had the project-management organization explained why suggestions were not being implemented. Simply ignoring the lessons-learned sessions caused a lot of frustration within the team.

The most important step in the lessons-learned process is to clearly spell out all the things that were mentioned and give clear steps on how these will be implemented or what steps are being taken in the future to make the process more efficient.

This helps to keep the staff motivated and helps retain good team members. There are other things that can be done to retain good team members. Let's explore some in the next section.

8.6 Retaining and Motivating Staff for Future Rollouts

After the go-live has occurred and the initial software issues have been addressed, the pressure starts to mount again. Often there is functionality that was not addressed in the first go-live and that has been delayed for a subsequent release. Typically, there are also some elements that require a redesign or change based on user feedback.

In order to provide these changes and also roll out future functionality, a new project-scoping exercise and new staffing plan are needed. Often the people that worked on the first project may be slated to return back to their original jobs, or they may be burned-out from the hours spent getting to the latest go-live.

In order to retain the staff, it is imperative that the people that made the go-live successful are rewarded for their work. I have seen several actions that help to motivate and recognize those that were vital to the project. Here are some of these:

- Provide some money in the form of travel vouchers to use on vacation travel. This helps to recognize the employees and their families' sacrifice for the project.
- Create a *wall of fame* for outstanding project team members.
- Have various members of the team present some lessons learned to upper management. This gives some credibility and recognition to the team in front of their top managers.
- Provide project related items such as shirts, mugs, etc. Although this seems like a small gesture, an unexpected gift like this can sometimes go a long way.
- Set a meeting time and use this time to thank individuals for their contributions. Do not discuss any other issue at this meeting.

The main thing to understand is that often those employees who were the most productive now have very valuable skill sets. The management team needs to recognize and understand that keeping these people motivated and challenged will go a long way toward retaining them.

Once the staff has been chosen, the next step is to prepare for rolling out new functionality. There are several things to keep in mind about rolling out new functionality. Let's discuss this process next.

8.7 Prepare for Future Rollouts

BW projects are seldom considered completely finished. Often after a go-live there is a hand-off process to production support and then an evaluation of the existing environment and a prioritization of the unfilled analysis needs. In many cases, the existing reporting environment may need to either be enhanced or redesigned.

Although frustrating, this is quite typical. Once the business users begin to see the information provided by BW and start to use this to aid in business decision-making, the emphasis and focus often shifts to other areas of improvement in the same functional area. Depending on the scope of the initial implementation, this may require redesigning the existing environment in order to provide this analysis need. This should be considered normal and should be expected.

Of course, the more the BW team is able to foresee any new analysis needs, and incorporate this into the existing design, the better the team will be able to meet new demands.

8.8 Conclusion

Understanding and providing a clear go-live strategy requires careful planning before the go-live to make sure that the COE can provide definite value to the end user. This is often the only view the user gets of the implementation team. It is important that, through the proactive steps mentioned, the COE provides value to the organization and helps to keep the users focused on their responsibilities and not on issues with the software.

Now, let's proceed to the final chapter of this book, Chapter 9, and bring our exploration of BW projects to an end.

9 Epilogue

BW implementations are often complex and can easily become quite political because of the analytical needs that are involved. Understanding these needs and planning to meet the challenges help to make sure that the project manager handles them gracefully.

This involves understanding the typical issues and mistakes that are commonly made as well as the most common systems issues that are encountered. Familiarity with these allows the project manager to make good decisions and steer the team quickly toward resolution.

This book walked through many of the challenges that are typically faced in the implementation process. Of course, every project has its own particular challenges and unforeseen issues. However, a clear methodology, as spelled out in the preceding chapters allow the project to clearly assess the scope, deal with new scoping questions, prioritize, and implement a solution. It also aids with the transition from development to production support.

9.1 Using this Book

The various methods outlined in this book to help with requirements gathering, transport management, cutover, etc., should be used to develop the end-to-end project management strategy. This book can help you to highlight the most important challenges and recommendations, this information can be used along with knowledge of the various project requirements to create and evolve a clear implementation methodology. A large part of this methodology involves gaining understanding of the typical challenges and planning properly how to respond when faced with these issues.

Another important goal is to make sure that the requirements-gathering process is clearly understood and well planned. There are several documentation templates in the appendices of this book that will also help with building and defining this strategy. You can return to this book at any time, using it as a reference guide.

9 | Epilogue

I would now like to give you some additional insight into the common issues and challenges you are likely to face in your BW project.

9.2 Common Issues and Challenges

In general the most common issues that BW projects face is typically not in the actual configuration tasks of the BW system. Many of the biggest challenges are typically project management, scope, and requirements-gathering issues. That is the main reason this book focused more on project management and not as much on the functionality and system configuration features.

SAP provides many classes and documentation on the features of the software; however, there is very little emphasis on the tools and methods needed to successfully implement the product. Ironically, these are the most common reasons that projects fail. They rarely fail because the system cannot satisfy clearly understood requirements. They fail because these requirements are either not understood or there is not a clear direction to scope, prioritize, staff, and implement these requirements.

These tasks are where a project defines its success. This means providing sound tools in order to capture the current requirements in detail and modeling the solution so as to meet not only these needs but also the unnamed needs that will emerge in the future.

The best way to understand these needs is to clearly understand today's needs and work with the business users to help predict the future requirements. I hope this book provided some guidance on typical issues encountered and methods for requirements-gathering and scope management. These should give your project a head start on their methodology decisions.

Let's now recap the important things to remember for your BW project.

9.3 Important Things to Remember

There are several important things to understand and remember during any BW project. I have covered these in the subsections that follow.

9.3.1 More Challenging than an ECC or R/3 Project

The reasons for these challenges lie in the extreme flexibility of the BW product and many different systems involved. Most ECC or R/3 projects do one conversion of data from external systems during the go-live phase. In a BW project, these conversions happen nightly. Added to this is the political nature of BW projects and the diverse audience that it addresses, which can make project management difficult. The most important thing to remember is to have a clear communication with the business partners to ensure you have their full understanding and guidance.

9.3.2 Management Commitment Needed from the Beginning

Projects need the right sponsorship to get over the inevitable issues that will occur. Management needs to be updated frequently. This commitment is built through establishing clear missions and strategies for data acquisition and data delivery and also through a thoughtful prioritization of scope. This prioritization should take place under the guidance of management to ensure its buy-in and also to ensure that the steering committee understands how BW would address some of the business pain of the organization.

9.3.3 Project Management: User-Focused, Not Technology Focused

Sometimes teams focus too much on the system issues and the technology and not enough on the business drivers behind the solution. This can cause the team to deliver a product that does not match the end user requirements. Understanding and keeping the team focused on the end solution can keep the team working toward this solution. In many ways, the technology issues are more micro in nature compared with the macro issues of meeting the end user needs. Project management needs this macro-focused approach.

9.3.4 Clear Methodology Needed to Determine Requirements

Many projects attempt to begin configuration too early. This forces them to make decisions on the user requirements before they understand them. Having a clear methodology with clear ways to document and agree on scope can help this process. Often, the more time spent up front developing these methodology documents, the better the end result.

9.3.5 Understanding Data Load Volume and Granularity

Once the data volume is known, it is much easier to develop a sound data model. One factor that directly impacts the volume is the granularity of the data. This is important because it impacts the overall loading time and query performance. It also sets the scope for user reporting in the future. This is because the decisions made early in a project regarding the level of granularity affect the availability of data in the entire solution. Knowing as much as possible about the volume and granularity requirements help to ensure that data is loaded and analyzed properly.

9.3.6 Manage Expectations for BW

BW should not be considered the only reporting solution. Proper management of expectations can make sure that the transactional data process teams do not assume that BW will provide their end users with all the reporting they need. Although BW does excel at many analysis tasks, there is some reporting that is better left on the transactional system. Recognizing this early in the project will help to keep the scope of BW better matched to its strengths.

9.3.7 Fix Bad Data at Its Source

From the beginning of a BW project, there is pressure to fix data that is incorrect on the source systems. Mainly, this pressure comes from the source system teams because they do not want to spend the effort fixing data that is already complete. Instead they look for the BW solution to fix this data. What starts as a few lines of code to make a few fields consistent often turns into complex logic and custom coding. Setting the precedent early that data should be fixed at its source helps to reduce or even eliminate the data-fixing process.

9.3.8 Build a BW System, Not a Series Of Data Marts

There is a temptation to maintain the BW system as silos of data in the same way as do the transactional systems from which BW sources. This is a mistake. The more the BW solution works to consolidate data from multiple sources and report this data together, the better the solution will be at providing a clear picture of the business as a whole.

9.3.9 When the BW System Is Live, the Solution Isn't Finished

The work is not done after go-live. A sound BW system is constantly evolving with enhancements to the existing solution and new scope added. This should be expected and embraced.

9.4 Conclusion

I hope this book fulfilled your BW project-management needs. Remember that your work is not complete, even after go-live. It is now time to work with your BW system and to help it achieve your business goals.

I welcome any feedback or questions you have on the book and hope that you gained valuable insight that can be applied to your project.

Appendix

A	Sample Project Plan	335
B	Important Checklists	351
C	Document Templates	367
D	Common Issues When Upgrading from BW Version 3.x to NW 2004s	383
E	Sample BW Naming Standards Document	389
F	BW Integration Test Script	393
G	Bibliography	397

A Sample Project Plan

This is a sample project plan that can be used as a base for developing your project plan or for understanding the typical tasks involved in project planning. The core of this project plan came from an initial project plan developed by SAP. I have changed several tasks, reordered others, and added typical tasks needed in a BW project. This can be used to help in planning or for reconciling with your project plan.

Phase 1: Project Preparation and Planning

Create and Issue Project Charter

- Define Project Mission Statement
- Define Business Warehouse Project Objectives
- Define Business Drivers
- Identify Business Measurements (Key Figure Matrix)
- Identify Project Measurements (Define Success Criteria)
- Create Project Charter Document
- Approve Project Charter Document

Define and Review Implementation Strategy

- Define Basic Requirements
- Define End User Requirements
- Define Data Requirements
- Define Technical Landscape
- Define Implementation Approaches and Alternatives
- Define Project Scope
- Create Implementation Strategy Document
- Review Implementation Strategy

- Confirm Implementation Methodology
- Check Strategy for Corporate Rollout

Establish Project Team Working Environment
- Plan Environment
- Set Up Environment

Determine Project Organization
- Define Organization and Roles
- Assign People to Roles
- Create Project Team Organization Document

Prepare Project Plan
- Create Project Work Plan
- Create Project Budget Plan
- Create Project Resource Plan

Create Project Team Training Plan
- Identify Business Warehouse Training Requirements
- Evaluate Need for Business Warehouse Workshop
- Register/Schedule Team Training
- Create Training Plan Document

Approve Project Planning Documents and Project Procedures
Define Project Management Standards and Procedures
- Identify Project Communication Plan
- Define Project Documentation
- Create Issue Management Plan
- Create Scope Management Plan
- Create Team Building Plan
- Define Project Planning and Monitoring Standards

- Define Strategy for Using SAP Services
- Determine Quality Assurance Standards
- Define Project Management Standards and Procedures Document

Define Implementation Standards and Procedures
- Develop Business Warehouse System Configuration Standards
- Define Functional Model Document
- Define End User Training and Documentation Strategy
- Define Testing Strategies
- Define Post Implementation Service and Support Strategy
- Define System Authorization Standards for Project Team
- Determine System Problems and Errors Handling Process
- Define System Enhancement and Modification Approval Process
- Define Naming Standards Document
- Define Data Administration Standards
- Create BW Implementation Standards and Procedures Document

Approve Project Procedures Documents
Project Kickoff
- Kickoff Meeting
  - Prepare for Kickoff Meeting
  - Conduct Kickoff Meeting
  - Conduct Companywide Project Introduction

Technical Requirements Planning
Identify Technical Requirements
- Complete Technical Questionnaires
- Define Technical Infrastructure Needs

Procure Hardware
- Develop High Level, Preliminary Sizing Estimates
- Review System Sizing Results

- Approve Sizing Results
- Order Initial Hardware
- Order BI Accelerator

Project Preparation Phase Quality Assessment

- Define Quality Assessment Process and Parameters
- Conduct Quality Assessment
- Create Project Preparation Quality Assessment Document
- Sign Off Project Preparation Phase

Phase 2: Business Blueprint and Analysis

Project Management Business Blueprint Phase
Conduct Project Team Status Meetings

- Prepare for Status Meetings
- Attend Status Meetings
- Follow Up on Action Items
- Correct Project Variances
- Refine Project Plan

Conduct Steering Committee Meetings

- Prepare for Steering Committee Meetings
- Attend Steering Committee Meetings
- Follow Up on Action Items

General Project Management

- Change Management
- Conduct Team Building Activities
- Define End User Roles and Responsibilities

Project Team Training Business Blueprint Phase

- Conduct Project Team Training

Phase 2: Business Blueprint and Analysis | **A**

- Refine Training Schedule
- Prepare for Training
- Attend Project Team Training
- Review and Assess Post-Training Skills

Business Process Analysis Phase

- Prepare for End User Requirements Workshops
  - Schedule Requirements Workshops Based on Categorization of Key End Users
  - Develop Agenda and Approach for Each Workshop
- Conduct Key End User Requirements Workshops
  - Review/Refine Business Drivers and Critical Success Factors
  - Determine Executive Information Needs and Key Measurements
  - Determine and Document Decision Support and OLAP Requirements
  - Determine and Document Operational Reporting Requirements
  - Determine and Document Application Functional Areas Involved
  - Determine Cross Application Functional Areas Involved
  - Determine and Document Global Decision Support Requirements
  - Complete Functional Model Document

Assess Current Data Warehouse and Information Access Environment

Identify and Assess Current SAP and Non-SAP Reporting Environment

- Identify SAP Sources
  - Identify Information in R/3 or ECC Sources Necessary to Satisfy Requirements
  - Complete R/3/ECC DataSource Section in Functional Model Document
- Identify Non-SAP Sources
  - Identify Data from Non-SAP Sources Necessary to Satisfy Requirements
  - Develop Plan for Capturing Non-SAP Source Data into Flat Files
  - Assign Resources to Obtain the Data
  - Complete external DataSource Section in Functional Model Document

- Identify Master Data Requirements: Create Master Data Requirements Document
- Define Data Conversion Rules
  - Define Transformation Rules
  - Define Aggregation Rules
  - Define Staging Requirements
  - Define Granularity Rules
  - Estimate Volume
  - Define Filtering Rules
  - Complete Data Section of Functional Model Document

Business Process Analysis Documents and Business Warehouse Design
Data Design for Each Functional Area

- Identify Key Figures Required for Each Functional Area
- Identify Characteristics Required for Each Functional Area
- Identify Dimensions Required for Each Functional Area
- Identify Compound Characteristics Required for Each Functional Area
- Identify Calculated Key Figures Required for Each Functional Area
- Identify Hierarchies Required for Each Functional Area
- Identify Business Rules by Field for Each Functional Area
- Create Data Design Document
- Data Access Design
  - Identify Presentation/Layout Preferences
  - Identify Summarization Level Requirements
  - Identify Data and Retention Requirements
  - Complete Analysis Section of Functional Model Document
- Model Business Warehouse Environment
  - Determine Uses of Business Content DSO, InfoCubes, and Reports
  - Identify New InfoProviders to be Created
  - Define and Document Business Warehouse Data Model
  - Identify Data Integration Requirements
  - Create Business Warehouse Environment Document

- Create Technical Design
  - Identify Major Technical Components Required (Hardware/Software/Network)
  - Identify Technical Components Not Required in SAP-Only Solution
  - Develop Plan for Assessment of Non-SAP Technical Components
  - Assess and Select Non-SAP Technical Components
  - Define Printing Infrastructure
  - Define Network Topology
  - Define Business Warehouse Interfaces
  - Define Change Request Management
  - Define Release Management Strategy
  - Determine Desktop Deployment Strategy
  - Define Desktop Management Strategy
  - Design Archiving Management Strategy
  - Define Business Warehouse Detailed Physical Technical Design
  - Create Technical Design Document

Procure Technical Components
- Develop Sizing Estimates
- Approve Sizing Results
- Configure Hardware Environment
- Define Software Environment
- Configure Network Environment
- Order Hardware
- Order Software
- Order Network Facilities

Establish Business Warehouse Development Environment
- Install Initial Hardware
- Install Operating System on Business Warehouse Server
- Install Business Warehouse Software
- Install Business Information Warehouse Plug-in on ECC or R/3 System

- Establish ALE System Connectivity
- Install Desktop Components for Project Team
- Install Additional Components for Project Team

System Administration
- Define System Administration for Business Warehouse
- Define Business Warehouse System Monitoring Strategy
- Define Backup Strategy
- Define Table Space and Reorganization Strategy
- Verify System Administration Functions
- Define Periodic System Maintenance Procedures

Approve Business Warehouse Documents
- Business Blueprint Phase Quality Assessment
- Define Quality Assessment Process and Parameters
- Conduct Quality Assessment
- Create Business Blueprint Quality Assessment Document
- Sign Off Business Blueprint Phase

Phase 3: Realization/Build
Project Management Realization Phase
Conduct Project Team Status Meetings
- Prepare for Status Meetings
- Attend Status Meetings
- Follow Up on Action Items
- Correct Project Variances
- Refine Project Plan

Conduct Steering Committee Meetings
- Prepare for Steering Committee Meetings

- Attend Steering Meetings
- Follow Up on Action Items

Initial Planning for Production Support and Cutover
- Determine Production Support Plan
- Determine Cutover Plan

Conduct Project Team Training
- Refine Training Schedule
- Prepare for Training
- Attend Project Team Training
- Review and Assess Post-Training Skills

System Management
Develop System Test Plans
- Develop Unit Test Plan
- Develop Volume Test Plan
- Develop Integration Test Plan
- Develop Stress Test Plan

Define Service-Level Commitment
- Determine Possible Failure Scenarios
- Define Disaster Recovery Procedures
- Establish Service Level Commitment
- Create Service Level Commitment Document

Establish Business Warehouse Administration Functions
- Develop Testing Procedures for Business Warehouse Objects
- Develop System Monitoring Procedures
- Develop Database Reorganization Procedures
- Verify Transport Procedures

- Verify Backup and Recovery Procedures
- Create Business Warehouse Administration Functions Document

Create Functional Model
- Develop ETL (Extraction/Transformation/Loading) Document
- Develop DSO Functional Model Document
- Develop InfoCube Functional Model Document
- Develop InfoSet Functional Model Document
- Develop Master Data Spreadsheet
- Build Development Environment
  - Activate DataSources in the ECC/R/3 System
  - Replicate DataSources
  - Activate Business Content
  - Create InfoObjects
  - Configure DSO Objects
  - Configure DSO Transformation
  - Configure InfoCube Objects
  - Configure InfoCube Transformation
  - Configure InfoSet Objects
  - Configure Analysis Query Objects
  - Configure Master Data Loads
  - Configure Process Chains
  - Load Development System

Set Up Quality Assurance Environment
- Verify Business Warehouse Systems Technical Environment
- Install Quality Assurance System
- Set Up User Master Records
- Secure Quality Assurance System
- Set Up Client Management and Transport System

Define Productive System Management

- Define Productive System Security
- Define Productive Operating Procedures
- Define Productive System Administration
- Define Productive System Printing Environment
- Define Productive Database Administration Procedures
- Create Business Warehouse Systems Operations Manual
- Create Productive System Management Document

Set Up Production Environment

- Install Production Hardware
- Verify Production Systems Technical Environment
- Install Production System
- Install and Configure Network Environment
- Install Desktop Hardware and Components
- Secure Operating System and Database
- Install Printers and Configure Printing Services

Approve System Management Documents

- Conduct Business Warehouse Unit Testing in Development
  - Resolve Discrepancies from Unit Testing
  - Prepare Transport List and Reconcile with Basis Group
- Migrate Objects to QA Environment:Troubleshoot Transports
- Build and Load the QA Environment
- Conduct Integration Testing
  - Resolve Discrepancies from Unit Testing
  - Sign off on Integration Testing
- Migrate Objects to Production Environment:Troubleshoot Transports

Prepare Final Confirmation

- Prepare Final Confirmation Scenarios
- Develop Final Confirmation Agenda

- Prepare for Final Confirmation Session
- Perform Final Confirmation
  - Perform Final Confirmation Scenarios
  - Review and Sign Off Final Confirmation

Develop Production System Environment
- Schedule Process Chains
- Test Data Extraction
- Establish Authorization Concept
- Create Authorization Detailed Design
  - Review Company Security Philosophy
  - Define Access Required by Job Functions
  - Conduct Authorization Interview with Data Owners
  - Identify General Information Access and Service Usage
  - Create Authorization Management Procedures
  - Create Authorization Detailed Design Document
- Implement Authorization Concept
  - Create Activity Groups
  - Generate Authorization Profiles
  - Create User Master Models for Job Roles
  - Test User Masters
  - Create Authorization Profiles and Job Roles Document
- Validate Authorization Concept
  - Identify Activity Groups for Individual Users
  - Create All User Masters
  - Validate User Masters for Job Functions
  - Refine Authorization Design
- Approve Authorization Design Documents
- Assign Authorizations

End User Documentation and Training Material
- Prepare End User Documentation Development Plan
  - Define End User Documentation Requirements
  - Create End User Documentation Development Plan
  - Approve End User Documentation Development Plan
- Create End User Documentation
  - Conduct End User Documentation and Training Workshop
  - Create End User Documentation
- Develop End User Training Materials
  - Create End User Training Materials
  - Create End User Training Instructors Guide
- Prepare for End User Training
  - Organize Training Facility, Equipment, and Logistics
  - Confirm End User Enrollment

Realization Phase Quality Assessment
- Define Quality Assessment Processes and Parameters
- Conduct Quality Assessment
- Create Realization Phase Quality Assessment Document
- Sign Off Realization Phase

Phase 4: Final Preparation

Project Management Final Preparation Phase
Conduct Project Team Status Meetings
- Prepare for Status Meetings
- Attend Status Meetings
- Follow Up on Action Items
- Correct Project Variances
- Refine Project Plan

Conduct Steering Committee Meetings

- Prepare for Steering Committee Meetings
- Attend Steering Committee Meetings
- Follow Up on Action Items

End User Training

- Prepare for End User Training
  - Finalize Logistics for Training
  - Initialize End User Training Environment
  - Load Training Data into End User Training Environment
- Conduct End User Training
  - Review End User Training

System Management

- Establish Productive System Administration
  - Configure Business Warehouse System Monitoring for Production Environment
  - Configure Productive System Printing and Spool Administration
  - Train System Administration Staff
- Conduct System Tests
  - Conduct Volume/Stress Test
  - Conduct System Performance Tuning (if needed)
  - Implement BI Accelerator
  - Conduct System Administration Tests
  - Conduct Disaster Recovery Test
  - Conduct Going Live Check

Detailed Project Planning

- Create/Refine Cutover Plan
  - Create Conversion Checklist
  - Determine Production Readiness
  - Approval for Cutover

Create/Refine Production Support
- Define Help Desk Procedures
- Create Help Desk Facility
- Reorganize Team for Post Live
- Staff Help Desk
- Define Long-term Production Support Strategy
- Create Production Support Plan Document

Cutover
- Perform Cutover to Production System
  - Transport to Production Environment
  - Perform Load Conversions
  - Perform Manual Entries
- Final Approval for Going Live
  - Approve the Production System
  - Secure Productive Environment
  - Verify Users are Ready
- Final Preparation Phase Quality Assessment
  - Define Quality Assessment Process and Parameters
  - Conduct Quality Assessment
  - Create Final Preparation Phase Quality Assessment Document
  - Sign Off Final Preparation Phase

Phase 5: Go-Live and Support

Production Support

Provide Production Support
- Direct Problem and Issues
- Manage and Resolve Problems

Validate Live Business Process Results
- Monitor Daily and Weekly Transactions

- Resolve Issues
- Confirm Live Environment

Optimize System Use
- Conduct Early Watch Sessions
- Optimize Technical Environment
- Optimize Business Warehouse Data Model Star Schema

Post Go-Live Activities
- Follow Up Training
    - Attend Advanced Training
    - Train New Employees
- Define Long-Term Plans
    - Refine Technical Upgrade Plan
    - Create Enhancements or Additional Implementations Document
    - Execute Long-Term Service and Support Strategy
- Upgrade Live System Landscape
    - Conduct System Upgrade
    - Conduct Database Upgrade
    - Execute New Release Migration Plan
    - Perform User Acceptance Testing
- Perform On-Going System Operations
    - Perform Computer Center Daily Operations
    - Perform Database Administration Daily Operations
    - Refine System Administration Procedures
- Project Review
    - Review and Close Open Issues
    - Review Business Benefits
    - Sign Off and Close Issue List
    - Conduct Lessons-Learned Session

B   Important Checklists

This appendix contains important checklists that you can use during the course of your BW project implementation.

B.1   New BW System Validation Checklist

This is a preliminary checklist that can be used to make sure the initial system settings are enabled and correct before the system is used. This assumes that the system has been installed properly and should not be considered an exclusive list.

B.2   Preliminary Checks (Prior to Any Transports)

- [ ] All users created in system with proper security
- [ ] Connections to each source system established
- [ ] SAP notes that have been applied in development and QA systems applied to production
- [ ] All kernel/DB patches applied in development and QA systems applied to production
- [ ] Check of each source system performed as green (**RSA1 • Tools • Manage Source Systems**)
- [ ] Replication green for relevant source systems (**RSA1 • Tools • Manage Source Systems**)
- [ ] Source system name assignment (**RSA1 • Tools • Source System Assignment**)
- [ ] Transfer global settings complete on each system (**Source System**)
- [ ] Number of parallel processes limit checked (coordinate with Basis for this)
- [ ] Conversion of local systems names set, only on a development system (**RSA1 • Tools • Conversion of Local System Names**)

- ☐ Printers are set up (Transaction SPAD)
- ☐ Permitted character settings (Transaction SPRO)
- ☐ Default packet size checked (Transaction SPRO—Links to Other Systems -Maintain control parameters)
- ☐ Flat file parameters checked (Transaction SPRO)
- ☐ Switch off all system traces. Trace status should be set to **Trace switched off** (Transaction ST01)
- ☐ Check trace tool—Verify there are no users activated for logging (Transaction RSRTRACE)
- ☐ ECC or R/3 Source System load parameters (Transaction SBIW in ECC or R/3)

B.3 Query/Portal Checks

- ☐ Check mail server to see if active (Transaction SPRO)
- ☐ Check Internet Graphics Server (IGS) to see if active (Transaction SPRO)
- ☐ Check web template to see if active (program SE38 RS_TEMPLATE_MAINTAIN_70)
- ☐ Activate personalization in BEx (Transaction SPRO)
- ☐ Check OLAP Cache global settings (Transaction RSRT)

B.4 Loading Checks

- ☐ Check traffic light color settings (Transaction SPRO)
- ☐ Set traffic light waiting time (Transaction SPRO)
- ☐ Check permitted character settings (Transaction SPRO)
- ☐ AL11 flat file locations setup
- ☐ ALEREMOTE and connection user IDs set-up with proper security

B.5 Transport Settings

- ☐ Development Package Established
- ☐ Function Groups Created

B.6 BW Query Development Checklist

This checklist serves as a design standard and validation procedure for good query development standards. It helps to make sure that queries are following good BW query standards.

- [ ] Query design should be consistent with the requirements document and the functional model document and should be reviewed often with the business SME(s). This allows the query development to stay in sync with the business requirements.
- [ ] Naming standards of the query matches naming standards document for all key figures, characteristics, query technical name, and description.
- [ ] Abbreviations of key figures and characteristics are consistent within the same queries and existing queries and follow standard project abbreviations. For example, amount = Amt, Count = Ct, etc.
- [ ] Capitalization of key figures and characteristics are consistent in order to give the user the same look and feel for each queries.
- [ ] Queries should utilize variables. This ensures that all queries include a variable screen. This encourages filtering of the data for performance purposes.
- [ ] Mandatory variables exist to limit the first view of data for performance, if applicable. This is typical for higher-volume MultiProviders.
- [ ] Mandatory variables should appear at the beginning of the variable list that is presented to the end user. This prevents the mandatory variables from being found in the middle or at the bottom of the variable screen.
- [ ] Variables are in order of most commonly used and should appear at the top of the variable screen. Because almost all queries are filtered by date, this typically means that the date variables appear first in all query variable screens.
- [ ] InfoObjects related to the variables should be checked to ensure that their F4 settings are consistent with the user values. If there is no preference, the setting to *show only values in the InfoProvider* should be used. This setting is found in the InfoObject screen (Transaction RSD1). This option tells the system if all master data values or just the InfoProvider relevant values should be shown when the user hits the F4 button in the variables.
- [ ] The initial view of data should be limited; the user should be encouraged to filter and/or drill the report by the free characteristics for better per-

formance. Typically, this means that the fewer data values that are pre-drilled down in the rows, the better the performance of the query.

☐ The developer should be mindful of the totals shown and verify that the user needs to see result totals. Result subtotals at a detailed level can be very distracting

☐ UOM and Currency queries should present the data in a consistent UOM or currency value, if possible. This ensures the consistency of the data in the report.

☐ Initial sorting of the query should be logical based on business needs.

☐ OLAP cache should be turned on for the query in Transaction RSRT.

B.7 BW Data Model Conceptual Review Checklist

This checklist includes all tasks that need to be completed for the BW Data Model conceptual review.

B.7.1 Items Needed Prior to Conceptual Data Model Review

- [ ] Completed Key Figure Matrix: Detailed documentation of the key figures that will be used and their calculations
- [ ] Completed BW Functional Model Document
- [ ] Understanding of current reporting requirements
- [ ] Understanding of the DataSources
- [ ] Mockups of the reporting requirements (either physical or conceptual)
- [ ] Preliminary data model diagram complete (this will be the foundation for the review)

B.7.2 Conceptual Data Model Review

- [ ] Analyze preliminary data model diagram and discuss touchpoints with other functional models.
- [ ] Ensure that the overall model is reviewed for any possible reuse of existing data. This can be reconciled against the global data model data diagram.
- [ ] View all DataSources to determine which sources are new and which are leveraged from existing feeds or from other models.
- [ ] Analyze the data model diagram to determine if data is integrated or siloed. Where should the various information from differing sources be joined and how?
- [ ] Discuss how the levels of granularity differ in the sources and how this can present a challenge in the consolidation of the data.
- [ ] Discuss need for a conceptual DSO layer and where this might aid the future requirements. This is a layer of the DSO that consolidates data from multiple areas for a more holistic view of data. There are multiple ways of doing this, but each requires some thought on the consolidation of that data. The integration of this data should be understood, and the linking of the data should be verified.

- [ ] Ensure that the cross-model requirements provide an end-to-end view of the data (if applicable) and establish the owner of the end-to-end view of data.
- [ ] Ensure that every key figure in the key figure matrix has a clear owner.
- [ ] Ensure that the data model goals are clearly understood by developing a mission statement for the data model review. What questions is the model supposed to be answering? How will this provide business value now and in the future?
- [ ] Discuss the possible future requirements? What are the reports that will likely be required or needed for future analysis?

B.8 BW Data Model Review Checklist

The BW Data Model Review is designed to check the planned data model after the configuration build is complete and before any transports are sent. This allows the data model to be verified against typical best practices to ensure that the model is sound and sustainable.

B.8.1 Items Needed Prior to BW Data Model Review

☐ Completed documentation, including functional model document and any other related functional specifications

☐ Detailed knowledge of the source data volumes

☐ Knowledge of the source data relationships including data dependencies, compounding characteristics, parent-child relationship, and hierarchies

☐ Diagram of InfoCubes and DSO that are being planned (MS Visio diagram)

☐ Knowledge of the business requirements and DataSources for the purpose of answering questions about how the information will be used and the data will flow.

B.8.2 Items Checked During BW Data Model Review: Overall

☐ All required documents are completed.

☐ Master data feeds are documented on the master data lists for use creating process chains, all master data fields configured and tested.

☐ All data is loaded to first level DSO without transformation (or extremely minimal transformation) on first pass of data into BW.

☐ All objects follow BW naming standards per the naming standards document.

☐ Security strategy is clearly understood and included in the design.

☐ Reflexive or recursive loads on transactional data avoided for performance reasons

☐ Data volume of rows coming into BW for transactional and master data is understood. This is used to ensure that the performance of the model will be sound.

☐ Model is checked for possible dump and reloads later via restatement. This requires the developer to understand the possibility for restatement.

- [ ] Navigational attributes are included when necessary and/or required.
- [ ] BW database storage parameters are updated on all objects.
- [ ] Logical partitioning is used, if necessary, to allow for parallelization of queries across multiple InfoProviders
- [ ] Loading requirements documented and implemented into process chains.
- [ ] ECC job requirements are captured and implemented into ECC loading schedules.
- [ ] ABAP Code review is complete; all ABO follows good ABAP standards for performance, syntax, and documentation.

B.8.3 DataSources/Feeds
- [ ] Generic DataSources delta-enabled, where applicable
- [ ] Flat Files using ASCII (text) files, NOT CSV (if possible, for performance)
- [ ] FTP procedure determined and planned for flat files; if archiving is needed, this is planned and implemented

B.8.4 DSO
- [ ] DSO settings are checked for reporting, data quality flag, etc. to see if these settings are correct.
- [ ] DSO key is verified to ensure no entries are lost.
- [ ] DSO key figures are checked to determine overwrite vs. addition.
- [ ] DSO delta capabilities are properly designed.

B.8.5 InfoCube/InfoSets/MultiProviders
- [ ] InfoCube dimensions were reviewed for multiplying effect between characteristic values, this includes checking for the 10% rule on dimensions.
- [ ] InfoCubes designed for multiple use; i.e., not one InfoCube for one query, etc.
- [ ] InfoCube key figures were reviewed to verify /understand the needs (summarization versus non-cumulative).
- [ ] Check that MultiProviders meet the requirements.
- [ ] Physical partitioning is implemented on each InfoCube (if applicable)

☐ InfoCube compression is planned.
☐ Aggregates are implemented (if applicable, data volume).

B.8.6 Query Processing Checklist

☐ Check for NOT clause in filters; remove if possible.
☐ Initial query result should be limited in number of rows.
☐ Summation should be suppressed if not needed.
☐ Read mode should be set to H (Transaction RSRT).
☐ Cache mode should be set to cache the query, if query is reusable and large results are expected.
☐ No virtual key figures or virtual characteristics should be used, if possible.
☐ Initial view of query should hit aggregate, if applicable. (Transaction RSRT).

B.9 Cutover Plan Checklist

This checklist highlights the most common tasks needed in a BW project before cutover. Often projects have other specific tasks that are unique to their implementations, so this list should not be considered complete for all projects. However, it can serve as a template for a project cutover plan.

B.9.1 Administrative Tasks

☐ Schedule Downtime of ECC or R/3 systems for initial loads
☐ Determine test queries to be used for data validation
☐ Schedule application resources for cutover
☐ Schedule Basis resources for cutover

B.9.2 Security Requirements

☐ Set up cutover role for BW
☐ Set up cutover role for source systems
☐ Assign user authorizations for portal (if applicable)
☐ Set up ALEREMOTE and connection user Ids with proper security
☐ Test cutover roles

B.9.3 System Requirements

☐ Verify technical steps for connections to source systems have been completed
☐ Set up BW systems and make all connections to source systems
☐ Validate source system connections
☐ Check FTP directory for flat files (Transaction AL11)
☐ Manually configure in BW via Transaction RS_PERS_ACTIVATE per SAP Note 754206
☐ Apply all SAP Notes to production that have been applied to test and development systems
☐ Apply all database/kernel patches to production that have been applied to test and development systems
☐ Check the number of parallel processes limit
☐ Set up printers (Transaction SPAD).
☐ Permitted character settings (Transaction SPRO).

- ☐ Check default packet size (Transaction SPRO—Links to Other Systems—Maintain control parameters)
- ☐ Check flatfile parameters (Transaction SPRO)
- ☐ Switch off all system traces. Trace status should be set to **Trace switched off** (Transaction ST01)
- ☐ Check trace tool
  Verify there are no users activated for logging (Transaction RSRTRACE)

B.9.4 Transport Requirements

- ☐ Change source system name after transport (Transaction RSA1)
- ☐ Maintain source system IDs (Transaction RSA1)
- ☐ Transport R/3 or ECC DataSources
- ☐ Transport DataSources in ECC
- ☐ Replicate DataSources in BW to keep systems consistent
- ☐ Transport InfoObjects
- ☐ Validate InfoObjects
- ☐ Transport InfoProviders
- ☐ Validate InfoProviders
- ☐ Transport transformations
- ☐ Validate transformations
- ☐ Transport data transfer processes (DTP)
- ☐ Validate data transfer processes (DTP)
- ☐ Transport or manually create InfoPackages
- ☐ Validate InfoPackages
- ☐ Transport process chains
- ☐ Validate process chains
- ☐ Transport queries and query elements
- ☐ Transport reporting roles
- ☐ Transport web templates
- ☐ Validate reporting

B.9.5 Portal Requirements

- ☐ Set up portal system
- ☐ Technical set-up of portal

☐ Save Iviews to portal
☐ Set up personalization and history

B.9.6 Prior to Load Checks
☐ Check traffic light settings (Transaction SPRO)
☐ Set traffic light waiting time (SPRO)
☐ Check permitted character settings (Transaction SPRO)
☐ Lock users out of ECC system (except ALEREMOTE and Admin users) for initial loads
☐ Transfer global settings complete on each system (**Source System** tab)

B.9.7 Prior to Query Testing
☐ Check OLAP cache settings for each query (Transaction RSRT)

B.9.8 Validation
☐ Validate reporting roles
☐ Validate web template (if applicable)
☐ Validate process chains
☐ Validate data loads
☐ Validate queries and analysis

B.9.9 Data Loads
☐ Run setup programs in ECC for initial loads (if applicable)
☐ Schedule jobs for V3 updates on ECC system (if applicable)
☐ Run delta initializations for master-data deltas
☐ Run delta initializations for transactional data
☐ Schedule periodic loads
☐ Schedule process chains
☐ Monitor loads
☐ All queries should come from a multi-provider, even if only reporting from one underlying InfoCube

B.10 BW Performance Checklist

This checklist can be used to check the various performance settings in BW. It is broken down into loading and query performance. Often there are several reasons for performance issues, so all should be checked. The most common cause of poor performance is the data model itself. In general, it is better to have many smaller objects than a few larger objects. This checklist gives the most common things to check when experiencing slow or substandard performance in BW.

B.10.1 Overall Tasks

☐ Turn on statistics for all queries (**RSA1 • Tools • Settings for BI Statistics**)

☐ Install all performance InfoCubes and DSO structures (NW 2004s statistics found in the **Business Information Warehouse • BI Statistics InfoArea**)

☐ All ABAP coding should be tuned per ABAP best practices and standards

B.10.2 Query Performance

☐ Check data model to ensure that volume is not too great. When in doubt, use logical partitioning to separate data into multiple InfoProviders.

☐ Check the InfoProvider, and if running from an ODS/DSO make sure indexes are added to query access fields. If possible, build queries from InfoCubes and not DSO/ODS objects. The star schema model is typically faster for performance than the relational model. Thus, InfoCubes are typically faster than DSO/ODS structures.

☐ Eliminate the volume in the query by reducing the data in the rows and columns. Make the query less granular for the initial view, and add fields as free characteristics. This forces the user to choose the characteristics they want. This typically reduces the volume.

☐ Check the query read mode (Transaction RSRT -> Properties).

☐ Reduce the number of navigational attributes that are used in the query.

☐ Suppress totals lines, if not needed.

☐ Check database statistics; make sure they are up-to-date for the query InfoProvider.

☐ Check support package, and get to newest support package. There are many performance enhancements with each support package.

- [ ] Check database settings to ensure tuning is optimal for star joins, etc.
- [ ] If running a query from an InfoCube, implement compression to reduce the data volume and utilize partitioning.
- [ ] Eliminate *Not Equal To* logic in queries. This can increase performance degradation substantially.
- [ ] Eliminate virtual characteristics and virtual key figures.
- [ ] Eliminate before aggregation key figures.
- [ ] Turn on OLAP cache for each query (Transaction RSRT -> Properties).
- [ ] Check the partitioning setting of the InfoCube; if data query performance is substandard, this can be activated via a transport for most databases.
- [ ] Implement aggregates to reduce the volume of data being accessed. To determine if aggregates are needed, use Transaction RSRT: **Execute and Debug • Display aggregate found**.
- [ ] Check the authorizations. A very complex authorization strategy can cause query performance degradation.
- [ ] Implement line-item dimensions in the InfoCube or shuffle the InfoObjects in the dimensions, if dimension to fact table ratio exceeds 10 %.
- [ ] Keep non-cumulative data in InfoCubes to a lower level of granularity.
- [ ] Implement pre-cache of query, to prime the OLAP cache.
- [ ] Implement pre-calculated web templates.
- [ ] Reduce the number of cell calculations in the query.
- [ ] Examine hardware and memory.
- [ ] Examine network latency.

B.10.3 Load Performance

- [ ] Check the data model to make sure data is segregated so that more parallel loading is possible.
- [ ] Use delta loading whenever possible.
- [ ] Drop indexes before high volume loads.
- [ ] Check process chains to ensure parallel processing.
- [ ] Reduce granularity in the data model.
- [ ] Implement load balancing.

B.10 | BW Performance Checklist

- [ ] Check customer enhancements and custom code to determine where bottlenecks exist.
- [ ] Eliminate LIS as a source for data, wherever possible.
- [ ] Load master data before transactional data.
- [ ] If loading high-volume master data, buffer the number range table.
- [ ] If loading very high-volume transactional data, buffer the number ranges for the dimension tables.
- [ ] If load is slow on the change run (apply job) implement parallel activation.
- [ ] If load is slow on the change run, reduce the number of navigational attributes in the aggregates.
- [ ] If load is slow on the DSO/ODS, turn off reporting flag in the DSO/ODS if possible.
- [ ] Reduce the time-dependent fields in the data model, if possible.
- [ ] Implement line-item dimensions.
- [ ] Implement PSA partitioning.

C   Document Templates

This appendix gives you information about the various documents that you will need to create for your BW project. You can use the information contained in each section in this appendix as a template for these documents. There are four types of documents needed, which are:

- Functional Model Template
- Data Store Object (DSO) Template
- InfoCube Template
- Extraction, Transformation, and Loading (ETL)

Each of these are discussed in this appendix.

C.1   Functional Model Template

The goal of this document is to allow the functional business process teams to communicate their needs. Basically, this functions as a requirements document. Once complete it serves as a functional specification for BW. Once BW is determined to be in scope for a process, this should be the first document completed.

This document allows the BW team to clearly understand the requirements of the process teams. The most difficult part is to make sure that all sections are filled out with the proper level of detail so that you can later model the solution in BW.

There should be one Functional Model Document for each subject area used for analysis in BW. This subject area is not always easy to define. The goal is that the functional model document gives the requirements for one logical grouping of functionality. Examples include: *Sales Analysis Reporting Functional Model* or the *Demand Planning Functional Model*.

The Functional Model Document is not designed to provide information about InfoCubes or DSOs, etc. The goal, instead, is to get agreement on the scope for the subject area. It can then be used as the main input to determine the physical model structures that need to be created in the BW system.

This document should be listed and tracked as a process team deliverable. The reason this is considered a process team deliverable and not a BW team deliverable is to shift the analysis gathering and ownership to the process teams. This gives these teams the incentive to gather and own the functional model document, because without a completed functional model document, no development can take place in the BW system.

Refer to Chapter 5 for some details about this document such as its timing, and some information about major sections of this document. Now, let's examine some of the important sections of this document.

Document Information

Each Functional Model Document should cover one subject area. This section should detail the BW and the business owner of the model. It should also give a name and brief description of the model and its complexity. It is also helpful if this section has some information on the process team that owns it, such as *finance* or *sales*. This helps to group the Functional Model Documents.

Functional Model Description and Audience

In this section a few paragraphs should be written that clearly state the overall goal of the Functional Model and why it is being implemented. This helps to gain some understanding of why the Functional Model is needed, who is the intended audience, and the roles of the analysis users.

Related Documents

This section can be used to list and attach any preliminary requirement documents and/or other supporting documents that help to explain the scope and needs of this subject area. In some cases these are samples of legacy reports and other similar information to help the BW team understand the analysis needs.

Document History and Signoff

This section is used to track any versions of the document. Each edit document should be assigned versions so that changes can be tracked. This is designed to determine who made edits to the document at any stage. This section is also reserved for the signoff. Projects differ on who signs off on this document. However, at the very least, the signoff should be the BW data architect, the process team representative, the process team manager, and the BW project manager. The signoff conveys that these team members have read and understand the structure and data contained in this structure.

Business Functionality Description: Business Questions Asked and Answered

This section is designed to give an overall understanding of the business and the questions that this functional model should answer once implemented. Although this appears to be a very easy section to complete it is often the one process teams have trouble completing fully.

These business questions will also be used as a foundation for the test cases in the future. This ensures that the physical model, once implemented, does answer the questions posed in this section.

Transformations

Often there is some type of transformation of data that is required to meet a business need. This transformation often requires significant time from the BW development team. It is difficult to determine all transformations of data until the data is loaded. However, the transformation that is known early should be clearly spelled out in this section. Some common transformations include unit of measure (UOM) conversion and currency conversion. There is typically more significant transformation with legacy data than with SAP data because it typically requires harmonization with the SAP data.

Filters

If data is to be filtered from the source, this should be documented in this section. This helps to determine if the full or a subset of the source data is needed.

Reconciliation, Validation Needs, and Error Handling

This section should include any potential errors or validation issues. If the data needs to be validated or checked against existing data this should be clearly stated.

Test Criteria

Any special test criteria can be listed here. The test criteria will also be developed based on the business questions mentioned in the Functional Model Document.

Dependencies and Constraints

Typically in any model there are some dependencies. The more important dependencies include external jobs that need to run before the data can be loaded. For example, an external invoice creation program needs to run before the legacy invoice data is loaded. There will be similar constraints on the ECC or R/3 transactional systems to complete certain jobs before BW loads the data. This ensures that BW is getting the most current data. This helps to determine when the data loads should be scheduled and also points out potential issues that can occur if these dependencies do not run or fail.

Compliance Requirements

Apart from other compliance requirements, this section is also where any Sarbanes-Oxley (SOX) or validation requirements should be documented.

Assumptions

Any assumptions about the data model, data validity, or any processes outside of the team's control that need to be assumed should be mentioned here. This helps to show any outside risk.

DataSource Profiles

This is the most important section of the document because the DataSources make up one of the biggest inputs into scope and timeline. It is very important, therefore, that all DataSources used to load this data are clearly recognized and documented. There are several things that should be documented about each source, which are:

- DataSource Name
- Source System (ECC or Flat File, etc.)
- DataSource Description
- Data anomalies or specific information about DataSource that should be known

- Dependencies for this DataSource
- Frequency of loading
- Key Contact for access
- Update Type (Delta/Full Load)
- Data Granularity
- Volume Expected
- History Needed
- Notes about this DataSource

Since this section is so vital, all these subsections should be clearly filled out for each DataSource. This information is only required for each transactional DataSource, not for each maser data source. If the data is being loaded from the ECC or R/3 system and if there are similar DataSources these can be combined into one list. The goal is to understand the main DataSources that will be used as an input to the flow.

Data Flow Diagram

A data flow diagram is helpful to see the flow of data and sources feeding this data. This helps to understand that the feed of the data might come from SAP. However, the data may have originated in a legacy system first, then fed to SAP ECC and then onto BW. Understanding the flow of the data through the organization allows for a clearer understanding of the dependencies involved.

Frequency and Timing

Understanding the frequency and timing of the data loading process and the query analysis timing helps to plan how the model will be loaded. For example, BW is typically loaded once per day, nightly. If the data needs to be loaded multiple times per day, or real-time data is needed for the model, this section can help the BW team understand the requirement. It also helps to determine how the users will use the queries. Do they use them only at month-end or daily? It also helps determine how often they are used.

History Requirements

The history requirements help to define the information and source of data for the solution. If history is required, it is important to understand what history and how much history is required to complete the model. This is most important when there are legacy systems involved.

Security

Since BW security should be considered early in the data modeling process, this section is very important to understand any security requirements. These might be role, by query, or by individual characteristics or key figure values. For example, if users should only be able to see selected company codes, this security requirement should be listed. It is understood that security could differ by report. However, this section gives an overall view of the security for the Functional Model so it can be included in the BW data model.

Sample Reports and Output

This section is used to show some of the sample analysis reports required in this subject area. Although there can be many queries associated with the model, this section is designed to list a few of the most important analysis queries. In many cases these sample reports are created with the use of Excel to show the BW team what to expect.

Issues

Any open issues should be documented here. Any issues should also be entered into the central issues database maintained by the project.

Appendix

Any attachments or other design documents can be linked. Any supporting documents can also be linked or attached here.

C.2 DSO Document Template

The purpose of the DataStore Object(DSO) Document Template is to provide some guidelines for documentation of the DSO or Operational Data Store (ODS) structures used in a data model. It helps to record the business purpose of the structure, its design, and use. It should be completed and signed off prior to any configuration in the BW system.

One document should be completed for each DSO used in the data model. This is an ideal document for transitioning a data model from the development team to the production support team.

Document Information

This section should list the name of the DSO—both technical and functional—and describe the BW team owner and the business SME owner. It should also describe at a high level the subject matter and intent of the DSO

Related Documents

All related documents should be listed in this section. These include documentation on any other InfoProvider(s) (InfoCube, DSO) that is fed or feeds this DSO. This would also include the ETL document(s) that show this DSO as part of its flow. This section is useful to determine where this DSO fits in the entire data model.

Document History and Signoff

This section is used to track any versions of the document. Each edit to the document should be assigned versions so that changes can be tracked using these versions. This will show who made edits to the document. This section is also reserved for the signoff. Projects differ on who signs off on this document. However, the signoff should at least include the BW data architect and the BW project manager. I recommend that a representative from the business also signoff. The signoff communicates that these people have read and understand the structure and the data contained in this structure.

Business Functionality Description

This section shows the business reason for the DSO in paragraph format. It describes why the DSO was created and gives some details about the data being stored in the structure.

Diagram and Data Flow

This diagram shows the flow of data in graphical format from the DataSource through this DSO as well as any other structures that are fed from this DSO. This section helps to illustrate where the DSO falls into the data model and what downstream and upstream objects in the data flow are affected by its use.

Business Content

If the DSO is activated or copied from business content, this section can show that original business content object. This helps you to understand the origin of the structure. If the DSO is completely custom-created, this should be noted here.

Sources of Data

Understanding the sources of data used to fill the DSO is very important to understanding the purpose and use of the DSO. This section describes the DataSources used to fill the DSO. If the data is being filled by an ECC or R/3 DataSource, the DataSource name, description, and a brief summary of the extracted data should be documented. If the DataSource is related to an external source, this section should also describe the external source system and the data being fed from this system.

DataSource Profile

This is the most important section of the document. It describes each DataSource that feeds this DSO, in detail. It shows each source, the type of data, frequency, and method of loading (flat file, DBConnect, SAP API, etc.). The goal is to know the type(s) of data being loaded into the DSO.

Historical Data Profile

If historical data is being loaded into this DSO, this should be noted here. This section is useful if a new DSO is being created and legacy data needs to fill the DSO. For example, a new sales order DSO is created, once ECC is live. It will be filled with ECC orders. Before the ECC system is live, the historical order data needs to be loaded from the legacy system.

This historical data should be documented in detail. Some of the more common issues involving DSOs are with the harmonization of data with other sources and with the ECC system data. This section helps to document historical data challenges and its content.

DSO Data Profile

This section describes the data that will be loaded into the DSO. It should be used to describe the key fields of the DSO and its overall data design.

Reporting

Most DSO structures are not used for reporting. Although the DSO is not intended to be the main reporting tool in BW, it can be used to report some detailed data to the users, if needed. The goal for this section is to delineate some of the reporting needs of the DSO. This can affect how the DSO is set up and the various indices that might be needed.

Issues

Any open issues should be documented here. Any issues should also be entered into the central issues database maintained by the project.

Appendix

Any attachments or other design documents can be linked. Any supporting documents can also be linked or attached here.

Metadata Repositry Link

The Metadata Repository is a documentation tool in BW that is automatically updated with the latest BW configuration. Since the BW system is self-documenting and the Metadata Repository can be exported to HTML, this can be linked in the document to provide details on the specific InfoObjects and flow of data used in the BW system. This prevents all objects from being listed manually in this document.

C.3 InfoCube Document Template

The purpose of the InfoCube Document Template is to provide some guidelines for the documentation of the InfoCubes or InfoSets used in a data model. It helps record the business purpose of the structure, its design, and use. It should be completed and signed off prior to any configuration in the BW system. One document should be completed for each InfoCube or InfoSet used in the data model. This is an ideal document for transitioning a data model from the development team to the production support team.

Document Information

This section should list the name of the InfoCube, both technical and functional, and describe the BW team owner and the business SME owner. It should also describe, at a high level, the subject matter and intent of the InfoCube.

Related Documents

All related documents should be listed in this section. These include documentation on any other InfoProvider(s) (InfoCube, DSO) that is fed or feeds this InfoCube. It should also include the ETL document(s) that show this InfoCube as part of its flow. This section is useful to determine where this InfoCube fits in the entire data model.

Document History and Signoff

This section is used to track any versions of the document. Each edit to the document should be assigned versions and changes tracked using these versions. This shows who made edits to the document. This section is also reserved for the signoff. Projects differ on who signs off on this document. However, the signoff should at least include the BW data architect and the BW project manager. I recommend that a representative from business also signoff on this document. The signoff conveys that they have read and understand the structure and the data contained in this structure.

Business Functionality Description

This section is meant to show the business reason for the InfoCube in paragraph format. This describes why the InfoCube was created and some details about the data that is being stored.

Diagram and Data Flow

The diagram illustrates the flow of data, in a graphical format, from the DataSource through any other structures to this InfoCube. It should also show any other structures that feed or are fed to/from this InfoCube. This section helps to determine where the InfoCube falls into the data model as well as the downstream and upstream objects in the data flow affected by its use.

Business Content

If the InfoCube is activated or copied from business content, this section can show the original business content object that has been copied. This helps to clarify the origin of the structure. If the InfoCube is completely custom-created, this should be noted here as well.

Sources of Data

Understanding the sources of data used to fill the InfoCube is very important. It helps with understanding the purpose and use of the InfoCube. This section describes the DataSources used to fill the InfoCube. If the data is being filled by an ECC or R/3 DataSource, the DataSource name, description, and a brief summary of the extracted data should be documented. If the DataSource is related to an external source, this section should also describe the external source system and the data that is being fed from this system.

DataSource Profile

This is the most important section of the document. It describes each DataSource that feeds this InfoCube in detail. It shows each source, the type of data, frequency, and method of loading (flat file, DBConnect, SAP API). The goal of this section is to lay out the type(s) of data being loaded into the InfoCube.

Historical Data Profile

If historical data is being loaded into this InfoCube, this should be noted here. This section is useful if a new InfoCube is being created and legacy data needs to fill the InfoCube. This historical data should be documented in detail.

InfoCube Data Profile

This section describes the data that will be loaded into the InfoCube. This describes the various key performance indicators (KPIs) that will be loaded and/or used when reporting from this InfoCube. It also lists the most important characteristics and the granularity level of the InfoCube.

Partitioning

This section describes any partitioning needed in the InfoCube for faster query performance. Partitioning is only recommended if the volume of data is large. This section describes the InfoObject to be used for partitioning and the number of partitions made.

Reporting

The reporting needs of the InfoCube are very important to ensure that the design is sound. This section describes some of the analysis that is needed from the InfoCube and some mock-up reports, if possible. The more detailed understanding of the reporting requirements, the more useful this document becomes.

Issues

Any open issues should be documented here. Any issues should also be entered into the central issues database maintained by the project.

Appendix

Any attachments or other design documents can be linked. Any supporting documents can also be linked or attached here.

Metadata Repositry Link

As already discussed in Section C.2, the Metadata Repository is a documentation tool in BW that is automatically updated with the latest BW configuration. Since the BW system is self-documenting and the Metadata Repository can be exported to HTML, this can be linked in the document to provide details on the specific InfoObjects and flow of data used in the BW system. This prevents all objects from being listed manually in this document.

C.4 ETL (Extraction, Transformation, and Loading) Document Template

The purpose of the ETL Document Template is to provide some guidelines for the documentation of the BW data model as a whole. Documenting the model includes having one overall diagram of the entire landscape. However, it is also helpful to understand each process and the loads required for each separate function and how this data is loaded and transformed in the model. Without this document, it is very difficult to piece together the many DSO, InfoCube documents that make up the model and to understand how the data flows.

This document helps to record the technical flow of the design, and use. It should be completed and signed off prior to any configuration in the BW system. One ETL document should be completed for each subject area used in the data model. This is an ideal document for transitioning a data model from the development team to the production support team.

Document Information

This section should list the name of the subject area defined by the ETL flow Examples include: *Purchasing/Vendor Performance ETL Model* or *Sales Analysis ETL Model*. This section can also list the process team and the BW developer or steward responsible for the ETL flow from end to end.

Related Documents

All related documents should be listed here. These include documentation on all InfoProvider(s) (InfoCube, DSO) that are mentioned in this ETL document. It could also include any other related ETL document(s).

Document History and Signoff

This section is used to track any versions of the document. Each edit should be assigned a version. Changes can be tracked using these versions. This shows who made edits to the document. This section is also reserved for the signoff. Projects differ on who signs off on this document. However, the signoff should at least include the BW data architect and the BW project manager. It is also recommended that a representative from business also signs off. The signoff conveys that these individuals have read and understand the structure and data contained in this structure.

Business Functionality Description

This section is meant to show the business reason for the DSO in paragraph format. This describes why the DSO was created and gives some details about the data that is being stored in the structure.

ETL Diagram and Data Flow

The ETL diagram is the most important part of the ETL document. It shows the flow of data graphically, from the DataSource all the way to the InfoProvider. Typically the queries are not listed or mentioned in this document. However, any MultiProviders are related to the model should be shown along with all associated InfoProviders.

This section illustrates the the data from beginning to end. It should clearly show all related data model structures for the associated subject area and what downstream and upstream objects in the data flow are affected by its use. Typically these diagrams are done using MS Visio to allow as much detail as possible to be shown in one clear document.

Sources of Data

This section should clearly state each DataSource used to load the data and the source system that has the data. It should also detail the approximate volume that is loaded and if the load is a full or delta load.

Destinations of Data

This section lists the various destinations of data. Typically these are DSOs or InfoCubes.

Data Transformation

All custom transformations should be detailed in this section. The goal is to make sure that any custom transformation logic is clearly understood. Any custom start routines, end routines, expert routines, or transformation routines should be documented in detail. Each should show the source of data, the transformation logic used, the purpose, and who requested the transformation. The goal is not to show the actual ABAP code. The primary goal is to understand why, where, and how the transformation was done. This allows anyone troubleshooting the design to see where anything outside of standard mapping occurs.

This section can get long and involved depending on how complex the transformation is in the model. However, it allows one place to look for any custom logic and makes the handoff of the design much easier than looking through multiple documents.

Dependencies and Constraints

Typically in any model there are some dependencies. These are tasks and loads that have to take place before others can begin. Some of these are rather obvious, as shown in the ETL diagram. For example, an InfoCube may not be loaded before its source, the DSO.

These need not be listed here. The more important dependencies are external jobs that need to run before the data can be loaded. For example, an external invoice creation program needs to run before the legacy invoice data is loaded. There will also be similar constraints on the ECC or R/3 transactional systems to complete certain jobs before BW should load the data. This ensures that BW is getting the most current data. This helps to determine when the data loads should be scheduled and also points out potential issues that can occur if these dependencies do not run or fail.

Issues

Any open issues should be documented here. These issues should also be entered into the central issues database maintained by the project.

Appendix

Any attachments or other design documents can be linked. Any supporting documents can also be linked or attached here.

Metadata Repositry Links

As seen earlier, the Metadata Repository is a documentation tool in BW that is automatically updated with the latest BW configuration. Since the BW system is self-documenting and the Metadata Repository can be exported to HTML, this can be linked in the document to provide details on the specific InfoObjects and flow of data used in the BW system. This prevents all objects from being listed manually in this document. Typically there are multiple links associated with each ETL document.

D   Common Issues When Upgrading from BW Version 3.x to NW 2004s

Upgrading BW can be a very challenging task. When setting up a project plan for an upgrade project, it helps to know some of the common issues faced by others when developing your plan. This helps not only to estimate time for each activity, but also allows the team to be proactive in its overall planning so as to avoid or mitigate some of the common issues with the upgrade.

In most cases, the actual system time needed for the upgrade is approximately one week. This includes just the loading of the software, Java, etc. This time varies depending on the expertise of the team and the size of the database that needs to be upgraded. During the time the upgrade is loading, no activity can take place on the BW system. This can cause some issues with the end users. Therefore, some project organizations have opted to upgrade a shadow system and cutover from the shadow system to the production system when complete. This lessens the downtime for the upgrade. Other projects accept the downtime and communicate the need for it well in advance.

The NW 2004s system allows configuration running in the 3.x method of modeling (with InfoSources, transfer rules, and update rules). This means that any existing configuration in the 3.x system will continue to work in the NW 2004s system. For this reason, many project organizations opt for a technical upgrade, in which the configuration is moved to the new release, but the data model does not take advantage of the new loading methodology, Java functions, etc. This allows for a quicker and less risky upgrade because there are fewer changes to the application.

Listed in this appendix are some of the typical challenges in the 3.x-to-NW 2004s projects. The issues are broken down by project subject area. These include some of the issues that I, or some of my colleagues have experienced during upgrade projects. I hope it helps to highlight for you, some of the areas that are particularly challenging.

D | Common Issues When Upgrading from BW Version 3.x to NW 2004s

D.1 System, Basis-Related Issues

These challenges are related to the system and are examined below:

- **NW 2004s Involves Database Upgrade**
  The database administrator should be involved as early as possible during the upgrade process to plan and implement any database upgrade that is needed to support NW 2004s. The list of the compatible and recommended database versions can be found in the SAP Service MarketPlace at *www.service.sap.com/pam*.

- **Recommended Database Settings**
  SAP has provided notes in order to communicate the best database options and settings. These differ by database platform and have changed often. These settings need to be verified and checked. This is a task that often gets overlooked because the database administrator does not always get the list of recommended settings. A coordinated effort needs to be established to ensure that the database team knows about these settings.

- **Differing Database Settings**
  In some cases data settings differ from the ECC and R/3 to the BW system. These settings are a result of SAP suggestions. Expect that there could be some different database settings between the ECC and R/3 system and the BW system. Previously, many customers used identical or very similar settings between the two environments.

- **Tools Checked for Compatibility**
  There are several new tools in the NW 2004s environment. Each needs to be checked to ensure that all components on the server and desktop are compatible. Some common issues involve integration with Adobe, BEx Analyzer, and Visual Composer.

- **Additional Requirements for Upgrade**
  There are very specific system requirements in order to complete the upgrade. There are also other applications that run in conjunction or communicate directly on the BW base. Some popular components are XI, APO, CRM, etc. These should be checked to determine the necessary patch level before the upgrade is planned on their underlying BW system.

- **Larger Databases Take Longer**
  In some cases larger databases can take a very long time to complete the upgrade process. In order to reduce the time that is required, a database reorganization should be planned prior to the upgrade. This allows the database to be optimally organized to begin the upgrade process.

- **Upgrade Process Slows Periodically**
  The upgrade process changes the database tables rather dramatically. Periodically running the database statistics during the upgrade process on the tables and dictionary helps the database optimizer plan and execute tasks much more quickly.

- **Java Expertise Required.**
  There are many Java tuning parameters associated with the NW 2004s system. If there are plans to render the analysis using Java, this area needs to be tuned properly. Sub-optimal tuning slows performance and can even make the system unstable for the end user.
  It is recommended that SAP be involved in this tuning and stress testing be performed on the system. In one case, I worked with a customer that found multiple new issues with the environment after running a stress test. The system appeared to work fine with few users, once many users joined the system, performance issues surfaced.

D.2 BW Application-Related Issues

Let's look at BW application-related issues now related to the NW 2004s upgrade:

- **Large Number of SAP Notes**
  This release is a very extensive and complex release, and this leaves a potential for substantial software issues. SAP is releasing a large number of SAP Notes for each support stack. The team needs to keep the system updated as often as possible. Regression testing needs to be planned after each support-stack upgrade.

- **Java Analysis Queries Need Proper Planning**
  The Java analysis queries can sometimes gather huge volumes of data, depending on their design. In some cases this can monopolize the Java server, causing performance issues for everyone. This can be compensated for by good user training and intelligent query design. The query design element forces the user to utilize jump queries in order to get detailed data. This can keep the users from running very large queries and taking up a large share of the Java server.

- **Common Access Tools Issues**
  Those project organizations that use the 3.x BEx Browser and/or the web menu item will find these are not included in the current version of NW 2004s. This may mean that the upgrade requires a new way for the

users to launch queries to be developed. This can pose a rather difficult change-management issue.

- **Data Loading Issues**
Any ABAP transformation using update rules, transfer rules, start routines, etc. must be re-coded if the project wishes to implement the loading using the NW 2004s methodology of loading.
There are two main ways of loading data in the NW 2004s system. Data can be loaded using the 3.x methodology, using InfoSources, update rules and transfer rules. It can also be loaded using the NW 2004s methodology, using a mandatory persistent staging area (PSA) and transformation logic. If the 3.x configuration is switched to the NW 2004s methodology of loading, any ABAP code must be revisited. This is because the NW 2004s system using ABAP OO (object-oriented) coding to transform data. It is not mandatory to switch the configuration to the NW 2004s methodology, and SAP plans to continue to support the 3.x methodology of loading in the NW 2004s system.
If the model is to be upgraded to the new loading methodology, however, this code needs to be revisited and converted to the ABAP OO. No mass-conversion program from ABAP to ABAP OO currently exists.

- **Conversion of Queries**
Each query that is converted from the 3.x to the NW 2004s query processing method needs to be re-saved in the NW 2004s version. There is currently no mass-level program in order to provide this conversion. Depending on the number of queries, this effort can be substantial.

- **BI Accelerator Pricing Model**
The BI Accelerator is a tool designed to provide faster query performance. It is a hardware appliance used to supplement BW by providing faster indexes on the data. The current pricing model for the BI Accelerator makes it quite expensive for many projects. This should be investigated before planning on using the tool in any implementation.

D.3 Security-Related Issues

Now let's look at security related challenges in the NW 2004s upgrade:

- **3.x Method of Authorizations Not Supported**
It is highly recommended that quickly after the upgrade project teams migrate the authorization security to the NW 2004s Analysis Authorization security functionality. This can involve a rather large effort depend-

ing on the complexity the 3.x security model. In most cases, this should be managed as a separate project because of the effort involved.

- **Security Migration Tool**
  This tool does not always convert everything. SAP has provided a tool to convert existing 3.x security to the NW 2004s model. This program is RSEC_MIGRATION. It does not always convert all security; most customers report that it is converting about 80–85 % of security. This means some of the migration needs to be done manually. All security requires a regression test to ensure the migration was successful.

- **Regression Testing for Analysis Authorizations**
  This is really quite time consuming. The only way to really understand any issues that may result from the transition from the 3.x authorizations is to regression test fully. This is a rather labor-intensive process involving creating many user ids and manually testing the BW functionality to verify that the authorizations are set up correctly.

D.4 Portal-Related Issues

Now let's examine issues related to the portal:

- **Integration with Portal**
  This is much more vital in the NW 2004s release. There are many more touchpoints between the BW application team and the Portals team. The BW team needs to determine what strategy is to be used for publishing queries to the portal.
  The portal team needs to develop a clear strategy in conjunction with the BW and ECC or R/3 transactional teams to provide clear content to the end user. In the 3.x version, the SAP Enterprise Portal (EP) was not as tightly integrated with BW. In the NW 2004s version the integration is more dramatic.

- **Federated or BW Portal Strategy**
  This federated or BW portal strategy needs to be developed. If the project team plans to use the EP functionality to provide the end user access point for BW, several important decisions need to be made by the portal team. The portal can be run either from the BW system or from a centralized federated portal. There are advantages to each approach. There are several whitepapers that detail this decision on the SAP developer network site (SDN) at *www.sdn.sap.com*.
  This concludes our discussion about common issues when upgrading from 3.x to NW2004s.

E Sample BW Naming Standards Document

The purpose of the naming standards document is to ensure the project team is consistent in their approach to naming custom objects in BW. This document can serve as a template to create a BW naming standards document. This naming document should be established early in the project to keep naming consistent, allow for easy tracking of objects in BW and to allow a basis for authorizations, if needed. Let's take a look at some naming standards now:

- **InfoObject Catalogs**
  The InfoObject catalog is a structure used to group together the InfoObjects.
- **Standard: ZXXXXX_CHAR, ZXXXXX_KF**
  All custom InfoObject Catalogs should begin with Z, the XXXXX should describe the business area associated with the change. Since there is no need to separate out the InfoObjects into many separate catalogs, most projects simply have two custom InfoObject Catalogs, one for characteristics and one for key figures.
- **InfoObject**
  The InfoObject is a characteristic or key figure that are used as the building blocks (i.e. fields) for creating InfoCubes, DSO Structures, etc. Before any new InfoObject should be created all existing InfoObjects should be searched to ensure that there are no standard or existing InfoObjects to satisfy the requirement
- **Standard: ZXXXXXXXX**
  All custom InfoObjects should begin with the letter Z and should have a descriptive name. Standard abbreviations should be followed. Key figure values should end with a consistent value to denote the following: QT—Quantity, AT—Amount, CT—Count, PT—Percentage.
- **ODS/DSO**
  The ODS or DSO (Operational Data Store or Data Store Object) contains detailed typically transactional data. This data is typically the foundation for data being loaded into InfoCubes.

- **Standard: Zff_Onna**

  ff—Functional Name—FI for Finance, AM for Asset Management, etc.
  nn—Unique Number. A, B, C, etc. This is needed if there are several identical DSO/ODS structures, used for logically partitioning the DSO/ODS structures.

- **InfoCube**

  The InfoCube is used to store aggregated data for data analysis needs.

- **Standard: Z_ff_Cnna**

  ff—Functional Name—FI for Finance, AM for Asset Management, etc.
  nn—Unique Number. A, B, C, etc. This is needed if there are several identical InfoCubes, used for logically partitioning the InfoCube data.

- **MultiProvider**

  MultiProviders are used to union InfoProviders for data analysis needs.

- **Standard: Z_ff_Mnn**

  ff—Functional Name—FI for Finance, AM for Asset Management, etc.
  nn—Unique Number

- **Query**

  A query is an analysis object from an InfoProvider.

- **Standard: Z_ff_XXXXXXXXXXX, Y_ff_XXXXXXXXXXX, X_ff_XXXXXXXXXXX**

  Begin queries with Z if they have been transported from development. Begin queries with Y if they have been developed in production (if allowed). Begin X with queries that have been developed in production and are considered ad-hoc. XXXXXXX represents a description of the query. *ff*—Functional Name—FI for Finance, AM for Asset Management, etc.

- **Query View**

  A query view is a saved version of a query to preserve formatting.

- **Standard: Q_ff_XXXXXXXXXXX**

  XXXXXXX represents a description of the query view. *ff*—Functional Name—FI for Finance, AM for Asset Management, etc.

- **Web Template**

  Web templates are the HTML page(s) that are used to determine the structure of the web application analysis.

- **Standard—Z_tXXXXXXXXX**

  Web templates should begin with Z and end with a descriptor of the web template. *t*—Template or Query

- **Roles**
  Roles are used to group the BW analysis authorization objects to provide security in BW.
- **Standard: ZccT_ff_XXXXXXXXXXXXXXX**
  All custom roles should begin with Z and contain the following: cc—country code. t—Role Type (C—Composite, S—Single). XXXXXXXXXXXXX—Description of role
- **Restricted Key Figures**
  Restricted key figures are used to restrict values to certain characteristic values in a query.
- **Standard: RXXXX**
  Restricted key figures should begin with R and end with a descriptive value.
- **Calculated Key Figures**
  Calculated key figures are used to calculate one or more other key figure values in a query.
- **Standard: CXXXX**
  Calculated key figures should begin with C and end with a descriptive value.
- **Variables**
  Variables are used to pass parameter values to a query.
- **Standard: ZoXXXXX**
  Variables should begin with Z and end with a description of the variable. o—Optional or Mandatory
- **InfoPackages**
  InfoPackages are used to kick off and monitor the BW data loads.
- **Standard**
  The system creates the technical name for the InfoPackage, however the description should begin with PC_ if used in a process chain. It should end with _FULL if a full load and _DELTA if delta.
- **Application Components**
  Application components are used to group together common objects in BW.
- **Standard: ZXXXXXX**
  The application component should begin with Z and end with a clear description of the component.

- **Flat Files**

  Flat files are used to load. CSV (delimited) or ASCII format data files into BW.

- **Standard: SSSSSSS_DATE_TIME.CSV**

  The file name should have the source of the file along with the date and time that it was created. *SSSSSS* — Source System or description of file

F BW Integration Test Script

This document can be used as an integration test script for the BW data against the source data being loaded. It is important that all steps to load the data and run any analysis are clearly spelled out in the integration test script. It is typically a best practice that the author does not run his/her own test scripts. This ensures that the test script is written to a detailed level and that there are multiple sets of eyes on the data reconciliation.

The data must be reconciled against the source data. This typically means that the tester loads the BW data model, PSA, DSO and, InfoCube, etc. An associated query would then be run on this data model, which should be reconciled against a report or list within the ECC or R/3 system to verify that the data is consistent. It is vital that the test script not only reconcile data within the BW system. More importantly this data must be reconciled back to the source data to ensure data integrity.

BW Integration Test Script

The BW integration test script includes the following sections, which must be filled in with as much detail as possible:

- Test Case Title
- Author
- Date Created
- Team
- Executed By
- Execute Date
- Approved By
- Approval Date
- Test Case Description
- Prerequisites

Table F.1 describes the various steps you need to go through and also gives you the expected and actual results.

Step Description	Expected Results	Actual Results	Condition Tested
▶ Include step number, step description, and necessary input data. ▶ Create specific lists of steps required in order to load data and reconcile the data against the source. ▶ This should include specific loading, activation, rollup, etc., to get the data fully loaded. ▶ It may also include steps to start a process chain to load data. ▶ It should be very specific (including transaction codes, etc.) to show how data is reconciled to the source from the loaded data or from a specific query.	Describe verification steps	▶ Document actual results, document numberes, report that was executed, etc. ▶ Record issues in issue tracking database	▶ OK Or ▶ Issue

Table F.1 Description of Steps and Results

After the test script is run you can then proceed with the other requirements of the test script as described in the subsections that follow.

Comments

Any comments after running the test script should be placed here. Did the test script perform as designed? Were there any issues? If any issues occurred, these should be tracked separately in the issues database. All steps should have a screen print. These screen prints should be placed in this section with a clear link back to the test script and a clear explanation of the data being reconciled or collected. This will allow someone at a later time to see the full testing procedure and get proof that the data was reconciled properly.

Issues

All issues should be tracked in this section. These clearly show any issues that caused the test to fail. These should also be entered into the issue tracking database so they can be resolved separately.

Pass/Fail

Indicate if the test script passed or failed and if the test script should be rerun.

G   Bibliography

McDonald, K., Dixon D.C., Wilmsmeier A, and Inmon W.H. (2006): *Mastering the SAP Business Information Warehouse: Leveraging the Business Intelligence Capabilities of SAP NetWeaver (2nd edition)*. Wiley.

Egger, N., Fiechter, J., Rohlf J., Rose, J., and Schrüffer, O. (2006): *SAP BW Reporting And Analysis*. SAP PRESS.

TDWI's Data Quality Report—Data Quality and the Bottom Line: Achieving Business Success through a Commitment to High Quality Data (2002). The Data Warehousing Institute

Eckerson, E. (2004): *In Search of a Single Version of Truth: Drivers of Consolidating Analytic Consolidation*. The Data Warehousing Institute.

The Author

Highly regarded as an expert in his field, Gary Nolan is a SAP BW certified independent consultant specializing in implementation. He excels at evaluating customer requirements, configuring BW, and providing BW project management consulting in all areas of Business Intelligence. He also provides project expertise and consulting in BW performance management, data architecture, and data modeling.

A former Platinum Consultant with SAP America, Inc. he has over 10 years of SAP experience. He has worked with BW since version 1.2B. He has served as the lead consultant in many Fortune 500 company projects for the planning, system configuration, and testing phases, through go-live and post-implementation support. Gary has written over twenty articles for the *BWExpert* and *SCMExpert* newsletters and is also a technical advisor for these publications. He was a moderator on SAP's internal message board, and has spoken at Sapphire, ASUG, Managing SAP Projects conferences, SAP InfoDays, and the SAP BW & Portals conferences.

He can be reached at: gary.nolan@melvanconsulting.com.

Index

$TMP development package   72

A

ABAP   243
   Code   152, 236
   Developer   168
   Reports   227
Account receivable information   39
Advanced Planning and Optimization   199, 206
Aggregate rollup   318
Analysis goals   53
Analysis of data   30
Analytical system   34, 235
Application components   284
Application load monitoring   317
Archiving   98
ASCII fixed-length format   231
Authorization checks   269
Authorization strategy   93
Authorizations   269

B

Back-office system   114
Basis consultant   171
Basis group   78
Basis team   132, 152, 155
Batch window   98
BEx
   Analyzer   322
   Objects   281
   Queries   160
   Reporting   29
   Tool   138
   Variables   284
   Web queries   284
BI Accelerator   270, 348
Budget accountability   57
Business content   250
   Evaluating   215
   Review   208
Business expectations   274
Business modeling session   189
Business needs   195
Business processes   53
Business requirements   98
BusinessObjects   137
BW aggregates   182
BW applications developer   165
BW Basis developer   167
BW configuration documentation   275
BW content
   Activate   216
BW data architect   164, 223
BW Data Model Conceptual Review   355
BW Data Model Review   357
BW development team   223
BW implementation   26
   Challenges   147
BW key figure   204
BW landscape   66
BW landscape strategy   165
BW physical model   210
BW presentation developer   166
BW project manager   162
BW projects   147
   New   147
   Staffing   130, 169
   Upgrade   147
BW Query Development   353
BW requirements   195
   Analysis   187
BW structures   212
BW team members   211
BW timelines estimating   204

C

Cache   261, 262
   Main memory   262
   OLAP   262
   Settings   262
Center of Excellence   176, 307
   Goals   308
   Organization   308
Change control   142, 143
   Documentation   144
   Process   100

Index

Security   143
Change management   142, 146, 209
  Strategy   82
Characteristic values   259
Checklists   351
Cognos   137
Communication   107
  Issues   107, 131
  Plan   309
  Skills   49
Complexity factors   205
Control M   139
Core data   30
Critical success factors   98
Cronacle   139
Cross-reference table   201
Crystal Reports   137
CSV format   231
Custom tables   160
Customer number   115
Customer service   85
Cutover
  Final   286
  Mock   287
  Period   294
  Plan   106
  Planning   294
  Sample plan   294

D

Data   226
  Access   98
  Anomalies   112
  Completeness   112
  Consolidation layer   252
  Extraction   44, 134, 235
  Granularity   59, 124
  Harmonizing   147
  High volumes of   191
  Integrity   111
  Legacy   201
  Loading and transforming   237
  Master   226
  Modeling   251
  Quality   121
  Quality issues   110
  Realignment   119
  Timeliness   112

  Transactional   226
  Transformation   240
  Verification   315
Data analysis
  Large volume   43
Data architect   175, 211, 274
Data mart   38, 235
Data model   274
  Design review   274
  Signoff   221
Data object   69
Data quality   32
Data redundancy   28
Data warehouse   26, 37, 235
  Legacy   41
  Lifecycle   148
Database
  Indices   120
  Link   173
  Statistics   317
  Strategy   83
DataSources   199, 200, 212, 216, 223, 226, 230, 299
  Auditing   248
  Custom ABAP   228
  Extractors   213
  Generated   227
  Generic   227
  Testing   228
DataStore   160
DataStore Object   28, 180, 244, 276
DB2   83
DBConnect   233, 234
Decision paralysis   140
Dedicated upgrade landscape   151
Delta
  Failure   183
  Functionality   228
  Initialization process   183
  Process   183
  Queue   183, 301
Design lead   274
Design standards   273
Design, types
  Iterative   109
  Physical   208
  Realization   208
  Reviews   219
Destination system   73

Developing queries 89
Development environment 62
Development package 75
Development system 64, 67, 74, 154
Dirty data 32
Document template 367
   DSO 373
   ETL 379
   Functional Model 367
   InfoCube 376
Documentation
   Complete 274
   Scope 158
Documents
   BW development standards 161
   BW functional model 275
   Communication plan 159
   Communications 106
   Development Standards 105
   Disaster recovery 105
   ETL technical design 276
   Functional model 106, 195
   Functional model, sections of 198
   InfoCube technical design 276
   Landscape 105
   Naming standards 105, 159
   Signoff 109, 277
   Stakeholder 158
   System Copy –Refresh 106
   Technical design 276
   Transport strategy 105
Drill-down 126
DSO objects 284
DSO structure 69

E

EarlyWatch alerts 318
ECC environment 171
ECC jobs 300
ECC QA system 66
Efficient data analysis 26
Enduser requirements 189
Enterprise data warehouse 40, 84
   Global strategy 86
Enterprise portal 305
Escalation channels 54
External data 29
External team 57

Extracting, Transformation, and Loading 135, 235
Extractors 215

F

Files, types
   CSV 232
   Fixed-length 233
Final check 221
First customer ship 157
Flat files 316
   Generation 232
   Interface 234
   Interfaces 231
Flexible analysis 34
Front end support 92
Future rollouts 325
   Prepare for 326

G

Generic DataSource 227
Generic Extractor 227
Global BW project 175
Global enterprise data warehouse 40
Global views 215
Go-live 101, 273
   Checklist 106, 296
   Date 99
   Process 273
Governance 104
   Data of 113
   Of a project 104
   Standards 104

H

Harmonization of data 29
Help desk 311
Hotfix 92
Hybrid approach 125

I

Implementation strategy
   Resources 59
   Scope 59
InfoAreas 160, 284

InfoCube 28, 30, 31, 33, 56, 74, 125, 126, 144, 145, 264
InfoObjects 76, 112, 166, 212, 250, 278, 284
  Attitudes 268
  Standard 289
InfoPackage 78, 160
  In production 78
InfoProviders 215
Information assets 34
Information technology 85
InfoSets 284
InfoSources 160, 215, 246
Initial loads 298
Integration Test Script 393
Integration with other products 134
Intercompany sales 39
Interview process 179
Interview questions sample 180
Inventory management 85
Issues
  Resolution 255
  Tracking 255
  Tracking agreement 310
  Tracking lists 159
iView 191

J

Java connectors 234

K

Key figures 266
Key performance indicators 38
Keys, types of 116
Knowledge sharing 53
KPI Matrix 204, 210, 221
KPI values 204
  Mean Absolute Deviation 204
  Mean Absolute Percentage Error 204

L

Landscape strategy 70
Legacy databases 94
Legacy systems 90, 200
Lessons learned session 323
Loading Checks 352

Logistics Information System 227, 315

M

Master data 112, 114
  Alignment 115
  Governance 116
  Maintenance 116
  Object 69
  Requirements 99
  Time-dependent 267
  Values 201
Material codes 48
Material Master record 111
Material number 115
Materials Management 102
Measurement criteria 310
MetaData Repository 277, 279
Methodology 108
  Development 55
Microsoft Excel 29
Microstrategy 137
Milestones 99
Model Review
  Conceptual and Physical 220
  Functional 220
Models, types of
  Functional 100
  Physical 211
Multi-client systems 63
Multiple source systems 85
mySAP CRM 45

N

Naming standards 273, 274, 389
Naming structure 160
Navigational attribute 182
Net sales values 37
Non-SAP patches 322
  Database patches 322
  Kernel patches 322
  Operating system patches 322
NW 2004s 150, 237, 243, 244
NW 2004s Integrated Planning 46, 150, 237, 243, 244, 246

O

Obsolete queries 154
ODS structures 242
OLAP cache 261
OLAP cache settings 182
OLAP system 36
OLAP tools 137
On-the-fly data joining 43
Open Hub Service 236
Open Hub Transformation 236
Oracle 83
Organization chart 105
Outsourcing 177
Over-customization 133
Ownership issues 108

P

Partitioning 265
Performance goals 121, 122
Performance issues 121
Performance statistics InfoCubes 317
Performance sub team 123
Periodic jobs 317
Persistent Staging Area 243
Plug-in compatibility 91
Political issues 131, 133
Portal governance 304
   Goals 304
Portal objects 284
Portal strategy 304, 305
   Display 305
   Federated 305
Pre-aggregating of data 42
Preliminary Checks 351
Presentation of data 29
Presentation tools 98
Process chains 160, 299
Production environment 71, 221
   Upgrade 321
Production support 99
Production support changes 70
Production support environment 321
Production system 66, 152
Project manager 274
   Responsibilities 162
Project plan 105
   Integrated 159

Project Scope documentation 97
Project website 159
Proof of concept 170
Prototype demonstrations 50
Prototyping environment 62

Q

QA system 63, 64, 74
QA testing 69
Query 215
   Developers 126
   Housecleaning 154
   Monitor 261
   Performance 122, 125, 181
   Performance monitoring 318
   Strategy 86
Query bottlenecks 181
Query/Portal Checks 352

R

Ramp up process of BW software 157
Reasons for BW implementation 34
Reconciliation and validation process 313
Reconciliation strategy 313
Regression testing 320
Relational database structure 132
Relational database system 44
Relational database tables 35
Report Inventory 193
Report Painter 315
Report Writer tools 315
Reporting authorizations 94
Reporting requirements 215
Reporting strategy 90
Reporting, types
   Intra-day 190
   Real time 190
Reports, types
   Custom ABAP 315
   Legacy 193
   SAP Standard 315
Requestor 77
Requirements 202, 221
   Developing 221
   Gathering 189
   Presentation 202

Security 202
Resource issues 128
Review checklist 106
Rollout 209
   Scope 81
Rollout strategy 80
   Upgrade 82
Routines 245
   End 245
   Expert 245

S

Sales data 125
Sales information 39
Sandbox 61
   Basis BW 62
SAP APO 45
SAP BI front-end 92
SAP BW 25, 86
   Configuration 62
   Data security 94
   Data volume 28
   Database structure 36
   DataSources 25
   Developer 67
   Development environment 70
   New release 91
   Project manager 49
   Reporting 42
   Rollout 81
   Training 64
   Transport path 73
SAP data 187
SAP DBConnect 173
SAP ECC 60
   New implementation 199
SAP ECC system 190
SAP modules 121
SAP Notes 155, 320
SAP portal consultant 169
SAP Queries 315
SAP SCM 45
SAP SEM 45
SAP Service Marketplace 157
SAP UDConnect 173
SAS 137
Scope creep 99
Security 98, 209

Requirements 270, 274
Self-document 278
Service Level Agreement 122, 310
Service MarketPlace 255
Simple Application Object Protocol 235
Solution Manager 279
   Environment 280
Source systems 98, 112
Special Ledger 227
Spreadmarts 38
Stakeholders 98, 158, 189
Start routines 244
Status reports 107
Steward Process 76
Storage of data 31
Subject areas 175
Subject matter expert 163, 274
Supply chain 85
Support packages 62, 124, 320
   ABAP 320
   Basis 320
   BI content 320
   BI front-end 320
   Front-end 322
   Java 320
System orders 28
   ECC 28
   Legacy 28
System Review 220
System Validation Checklist 351

T

Team building 56
Technical issues 127
Technical upgrade 149
Templates 159
   Meeting minutes 159
   Position paper 159
   Status report 159
   Training plan 159
Test 203, 289
   Integration 203
   Scenarios 289
Test plan development 288
Test scripts 289
   Creation 82
Testing 60, 134, 208, 288
   Process 65, 101

Strategy 82
Tests 82, 288
   Executing 82
   Types of 288
Third-party scheduler 139
Third-party tools 29, 135
Third-party vendor 114
Third-party vendors 114
Total cost of ownership 311
Tracking Requirements 55
Training budget 293
Training requirements 184
Training system 292
Transactional data 48
Transactional data alignment 118
Transactional loads 300
Transactional system 26, 32, 81, 152, 235
Transactional team 103
Transfer Rules 242, 284
Transformation logic 246
Transformation rules 112
Transformations 245, 246
   Auditing 246
   Converting 246
   Implementing 245
Transport 72
   Approval process 75
   Strategy 73
Transport Management 280, 281
Transport Management System
   Tips 282
Transport number 77
Transport path 64, 281
Transport strategy 145
Transports 151, 209
   Coordination 165
   Troubleshooting 78
Tuning 208
Typical roles 162

U

UDConnect 234
Update Rules 241, 242
Upgrade cutover 154
Upgrade landscape 71
Upgrade strategy 60
Upgrade testing 153

Upgrades 62, 72
Upgrading from BW Version 3.x 383
User exit 230
User signoff 101

V

V3 jobs 301
ValiData 139
Validation 60, 114
Validation process 88
Validation tools 139
Variables 160
Virtual Characteristics 266
Visual Composer 90

W

Web reporting 29
Web templates 215, 284
Web tools 138
Web-reporting tools 138
Workbooks 215
Workflow 114

X

XML interfaces 235

Z

Zero Elimination 265

Complete and targeted overview of all new BI features and functionalities

Comprehensive information on SAP NetWeaver Visual Composer and BI Accelerator

Up-to-date for SAP NetWeaver 2004s BI

656 pp., 2007, 69,95 Euro / US$ 69,95
ISBN 978-1-59229-082-6

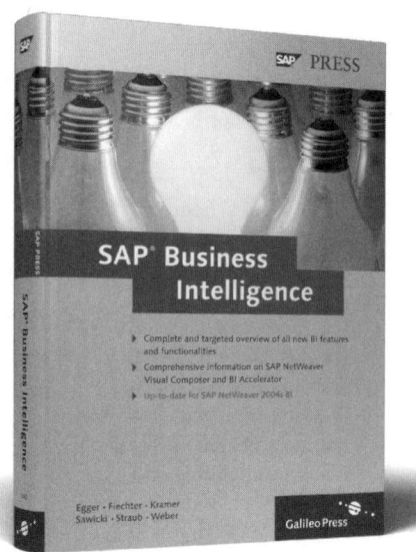

SAP Business Intelligence

www.sap-press.com

N. Egger, J.-M.R. Fiechter, S. Kramer, R.P. Sawicki, P. Straub, S. Weber

SAP Business Intelligence

Up-to-date for SAP NetWeaver 2004s BI

This book provides information on all the important new BI features of the SAP NetWeaver 2004s Release. Essential subjects like data modeling, ETL, web reporting, and planning are covered along with all of the newest functions making this book an unparalleled companion for your daily work. Real-life examples and numerous illustrations help you hit the ground running with the new release. Plus, useful step-by-step instructions enable the instant use of new features like Visual Composer, and many more.

Interested in reading more?

Please visit our Web site for all
new book releases from SAP PRESS.

www.sap-press.com